fine Cooking

VOLUME 3

A N N U A L

a year of great recipes, tips & techniques

Cooking

fine

VOLUME 3

A N N U A L

a year of great recipes, tips & techniques

From the Editors and
Contributors of *Fine Cooking*

The Taunton Press

The Taunton Press, Inc., 63 South Main Street, PO Box 5506, Newtown, CT 06470-5506
email: tp@taunton.com

EDITOR: Martha Holmberg
COPY EDITOR: Li Agen
INDEXER: Heidi Blough
JACKET/COVER DESIGN: Amy Russo
INTERIOR DESIGN: Alison Wilkes
LAYOUT: David Giammattei
PRINCIPAL PHOTOGRAPHER: Scott Phillips

LIBRARY OF CONGRESS CATALOGING-IN-PUBLICATION DATA

Fine Cooking Annual: a year of great recipes, tips & techniques from the
editors of Fine cooking / photography by Scott Phillips.
    p. cm.
 Includes bibliographical references and index.
 ISBN-13: 978-1-56158-916-6 (alk. paper) (vol. 1)
 ISBN-10: 1-56158-916-0 (alk. paper) (vol. 1)
 ISBN-13: 978-1-60085-005-9 (vol. 2)
 ISBN-13: 978-1-60085-043-1 (vol. 3)
 1. Cookery. I. Fine cooking.
 TX651.B4835 2006
 641.5--dc22

                    2006018123

Printed in China
10 9 8 7 6 5 4 3 2 1

The following manufacturer's/names appearing in *Fine Cooking Annual* are trademarks: Basil Hayden's®,
Bell's® seasoning, Blanton's®, Bûcheron®, Bundt®, Caffé Lolita®, Chavrie®, Deb El® Just Whites® egg whites,
Eagle Rare®, Eggology® egg whites, Grandma's® molasses, Grand Marnier®, Heaven Hill®, Jell-O®, Jim Beam®,
Kahlúa®, Knob Creek®, Lipton®, Maker's Mark®, Maytag® blue cheese, McCormick®, Noilly Prat®, Nutella®,
Old Amsterdam™, Old Crow®, Pernod®, Pomi® tomatoes, Pyrex®, Sambuca®, San Marzano® tomatoes,
Shake 'N Bake®, Tabasco®, The Spice Hunter®, Valbreso® feta cheese, Vya®, Wild Turkey®, Worcestershire®

The Taunton Press publishes *Fine Cooking*, the magazine for people who love to cook.

Contents

1
Starters
& Soups

p42

p13

Grilled Goat Cheese Crostini with a Tangle of Marinated Roasted Peppers (recipe on page 16)

Farmers' Market Crudités with Buttermilk Herb Dip

Serves twelve as an appetizer; yields 3 cups dip.

For the dip:

1 cup plain whole-milk yogurt

1 cup sour cream

1 cup freshly grated Parmigiano Reggiano

⅓ cup buttermilk

1 cup thinly sliced fresh chives

2 tablespoons chopped fresh dill

2 tablespoons chopped fresh thyme

1 small clove garlic, minced and mashed to a paste with a pinch of salt

1 tablespoon cider vinegar

¼ teaspoon Tabasco®; more to taste

1½ teaspoons kosher salt

1½ teaspoons coarsely ground black pepper

For the crudités:

1 pound pickling cucumbers (look for small French or Armenian types), cut into spears 3 to 4 inches long and ½ inch thick

1 pound sugar snap peas, strings and stem ends trimmed

1 pound small, slender carrots, peeled and cut into 3- to 4-inch lengths (halve or quarter them lengthwise if they're thick)

1 pint grape or cherry tomatoes

We've listed specific vegetables here to get you started, but you can choose whatever vegetables look good at the market. Try to create a variety of flavors, textures, and colors, or keep the colors to one or two, for a sophisticated, restrained palette. You can make the dip up to 1 day ahead.

In a large bowl, whisk all of the ingredients for the dip. Season with more Tabasco, salt, and pepper, to taste. Let sit for 15 minutes.

Arrange the vegetables on a large platter, with the dip in the center, or put each vegetable in its own bowl and arrange with the dip on a tray. Let guests help themselves. —*Tony Rosenfeld*

Prosciutto-Wrapped Melon with Mint & White Balsamic Vinegar

Serves eight as an appetizer.

1 ripe cantaloupe

2 tablespoons very thinly sliced fresh mint leaves

½ teaspoon freshly ground black pepper

2 to 3 teaspoons white balsamic vinegar

6 ounces very thinly sliced prosciutto, preferably imported

This riff on a classic Italian hors d'oeuvre is a great way to start a summer gathering. You can assemble it up to two hours ahead, if you like, but the mint will darken a bit.

With a sharp knife, trim the peel from the melon. Cut it in half lengthwise and scoop out the seeds. Slice one of the halves lengthwise into slender wedges, and then cut the wedges in half crosswise. (Wrap and save the other melon half for another use.)

Put the melon wedges in a medium bowl and toss them with the mint, pepper, and vinegar to taste—the sweeter the melon, the more vinegar you can use. Tear the prosciutto lengthwise into 1- to 2-inch-wide strips and wrap a strip or two around each piece of melon. Arrange the wrapped melon on a serving platter. If making ahead, cover with plastic and refrigerate until ready to serve. —*Jennifer Armentrout*

Look & listen for the ripest melons

At first glance, that mound of melons at the market all look the same. But we all know they don't taste the same. To find a ripe one:

Lift it. A melon should feel heavy for its size; compare a few.

Look at it. It's mainly what you don't see that counts: No blemishes, bruises, soft spots, wrinkles, or bumps.

Smell it. A fragrant aroma, especially near the stem end, is a good sign.

Thump it. Hold the melon to your ear and give it a few knocks. It should sound more cavernous and hollow than muffled.

Bacon-Wrapped Stuffed Apricots

Serves six to eight; yields 24.

24 dried Turkish apricots (about 7 ounces)

3 ounces plain Havarti, cut into ½- to ¾-inch squares ¼ inch thick

24 almonds (about 1 ounce)

12 strips bacon (about 12 ounces), cut in half crosswise

24 toothpicks, soaked in water

Freshly ground black pepper

Apricot sizes can vary; if yours are on the smaller side, just trim the cheese a bit and squish it in. The apricots can be assembled up to 1 day ahead and refrigerated; grill them just before serving.

Heat a gas grill to high or prepare a hot charcoal fire.

Pry open the apricots and put a piece of cheese and an almond into each one. Wrap a piece of bacon around each apricot, trimming as necessary so it overlaps by ½ inch, and secure it with a toothpick. Season the apricots all over with pepper.

Reduce the grill heat to medium (scatter the coals a bit or raise the grate if using charcoal). Use tongs to grill the apricots on all sides with the grill open, propping them between the bars to hold them up on the narrow sides. Move the apricots around often to avoid flare-ups. Cook until the bacon is crisp all over, about 6 minutes total. Serve immediately and remind guests to remove the toothpicks. —*Allison Ehri Kreitler*

Pancetta & Pineapple Skewers with Smoked Paprika Vinaigrette

To make things easier at party time, make the vinaigrette up to 2 days ahead, assemble the skewers up to 1 day ahead and actually marinate them up to 4 hours ahead and refrigerate.

Chop the garlic, sprinkle it with the salt, and mash it into a paste with the side of a chef's knife (or use a mortar and pestle). In a medium bowl, mix the garlic paste, oil, lemon juice, vinegar, pimentón, and pepper.

Put the pancetta in a small pot, cover it with cold water, and bring to a boil. As soon as the water boils, drain the pancetta in a colander and let it cool slightly.

Heat a gas grill to medium high or prepare a medium-hot charcoal fire. Thread two pancetta cubes and two pineapple cubes onto each skewer, alternating the pancetta and the pineapple. Put the skewers in a large Pyrex® baking dish (or other large nonreactive container) and pour the paprika vinaigrette over the skewers, turning to coat them completely. Grill the skewers (covered on a gas grill, uncovered on a charcoal grill), checking for flare-ups and turning and flipping the skewers as necessary to cook on all sides until the pancetta is crisp, about 6 minutes total. *—Allison Ehri Kreitler*

Serves six; yields 12 skewers.

- 1 large clove garlic
- Generous ½ teaspoon kosher salt
- ¼ cup extra-virgin olive oil
- 1½ tablespoons fresh lemon juice
- 1 tablespoon sherry vinegar
- 1 teaspoon sweet (dulce) smoked paprika (pimentón)
- ½ teaspoon freshly ground black pepper
- 4 ounces pancetta, cut into twenty-four ½- to ¾-inch cubes
- 6 ounces fresh pineapple (about ½ small pineapple), peeled and cut into twenty-four ½- to ¾-inch cubes
- Twelve 8-inch bamboo skewers, soaked in water

Smoky Eggplant & White Bean Dip with Pita Crisps

Yields 1½ cups dip; serves four to six.

5 tablespoons extra-virgin olive oil; more for the pan

1½ pounds small eggplant (2 to 3 small), trimmed and cut in half lengthwise

¾ teaspoon plus a generous pinch kosher salt

¼ teaspoon freshly ground black pepper

2 anchovy fillets (optional)

1 small clove garlic

1 cup canned cannellini beans, drained and rinsed

3 pitas (preferably pocketless), each cut into eight wedges

2 tablespoons fresh lemon juice; more to taste

1 tablespoon chopped fresh mint, plus 1 tablespoon small leaves for garnish

2 teaspoons chopped fresh oregano

2 tablespoons pine nuts, toasted

The pita crisps are addictively delicious, but this dip is also great with crudités, especially bell peppers and fennel.

Position a rack 4 inches from the broiler element and heat the broiler to high. Line a rimmed baking sheet with foil and grease lightly with oil. Rub the eggplant all over with 2 tablespoons of the oil and sprinkle the flesh side with ½ teaspoon of the salt and the ¼ teaspoon pepper. Arrange the eggplant, flesh side down, on the baking sheet and broil until the skin is charred and the eggplant flesh is very tender, 20 to 30 minutes.

Meanwhile, if using anchovies, mash them into a paste with the side of a chef's knife. Roughly chop the garlic, sprinkle it with a generous pinch of kosher salt, and mash it into a paste with the side of a chef's knife. Transfer the anchovy and garlic pastes to a food processor and add the beans, 2 tablespoons of the oil, and 1 tablespoon water. Purée until smooth.

When the eggplant is done, set it aside to cool briefly. Meanwhile, in a medium bowl, toss the pita wedges with the remaining 1 tablespoon oil and ¼ teaspoon salt. Arrange in a single layer on a baking sheet. Lower the rack so it's 6 inches from the broiler. Broil the pita wedges until golden brown on both sides, 1 to 2 minutes per side.

Scrape the eggplant flesh from the skin and add the flesh to the puréed beans in the food processor, along with the lemon juice, chopped mint, and oregano. Pulse briefly to form a chunky dip. Adjust the seasoning with more salt, pepper, or lemon juice to taste. Serve sprinkled with the pine nuts and mint leaves, with the toasted pita crisps on the side for dipping.

—Allison Ehri Kreitler

Wild Mushroom Toasts

Serves six.

1 pound fresh wild mushrooms, such as chanterelles, maitakes, hedgehogs, or morels

2 tablespoons unsalted butter

2 tablespoons extra-virgin olive oil; more as needed

Kosher salt

2 medium shallots, finely chopped (about ¼ cup)

2 teaspoons chopped fresh thyme

½ cup crème fraîche (about 4 ounces)

1 tablespoon chopped fresh flat-leaf parsley

Freshly ground black pepper

18 slices baguette (cut ¼ to ½ inch thick)

¼ cup freshly grated Parmigiano-Reggiano

The mushroom topping can be made several hours ahead and refrigerated, but hold back about half of the crème fraîche. When you're ready to serve, reheat the mushrooms over low heat and add the rest of the crème fraîche (don't overheat or the cream will break). These toasts are best slightly warm, so hold off on toasting the bread itself until just before serving. You can use cremini mushrooms if you can't find the exotic varieties listed at left.

Gently clean the mushrooms with a damp cloth or a paring knife to remove any dirt or dark spots. Cut off any tough stems. If the mushrooms appear muddy, quickly dip them into a large basin of water and drain. Leave small, bite-size mushrooms whole; quarter or halve larger mushrooms.

Melt 1 tablespoon of the butter together with 1 tablespoon of the oil in a 10-inch straight-sided sauté pan over medium-high heat. Add the mushrooms and a generous pinch of salt and cook, stirring frequently, until any liquid has evaporated and the mushrooms are nicely browned, 5 to 8 minutes. (If the mushrooms are dry and the pan begins to scorch, add a drizzle of olive oil.) Remove the pan from the heat and transfer the mushrooms to a cutting board. Let them cool slightly and chop them coarsely.

Return the pan to the stovetop over medium heat and add the remaining 1 tablespoon butter and 1 tablespoon oil. When the butter has melted, add the shallots, thyme, and a pinch of salt. Cook, stirring, until the shallots are tender and lightly golden, about 3 minutes. Return the mushrooms to the pan, stir in the crème fraîche (if you're making this ahead, see the note above), and cook, stirring, to coat the mushrooms with the crème fraîche. Stir in the parsley and season with several grinds of pepper. Season with more salt and pepper to taste. Remove from the heat and hold in a warm spot.

Shortly before serving, position an oven rack about 6 inches from the broiler element and heat the broiler to high. Arrange the bread slices on a baking sheet and brush them with olive oil. Broil until the bread is golden, 1 to 2 minutes. Flip and toast the other side, about 1 minute. Spread the warm mushroom mixture on the toasts, sprinkle some of the Parmigiano-Reggiano on top, and serve. —*Tasha DeSerio*

Grilled Goat Cheese Crostini with a Tangle of Marinated Roasted Peppers

Serves eight as an appetizer.

3 medium bell peppers (1 red, 1 orange, and 1 yellow)

3 tablespoons balsamic vinegar

2 tablespoons extra-virgin olive oil

1½ teaspoons fresh thyme

¼ teaspoon kosher salt

Freshly ground black pepper

1 recipe Grilled Garlic Bread (see recipe on facing page)

One 4½- to 5½-ounce container of soft, spreadable goat cheese (such as Chavrie®), at room temperature

Goat cheese speckled with fresh thyme is the perfect creamy counterpoint to the sweet, tangy roasted peppers in this recipe. Serve these crostini as an appetizer or paired with a simple green salad for a light lunch.

Prepare a medium-hot grill fire. Grill the bell peppers, turning occasionally, until the skin chars all over, 15 to 20 minutes. Put the charred peppers in a heatproof bowl, cover with plastic wrap, and let sit until cool enough to handle, about 30 minutes.

Meanwhile, in a large bowl, combine the balsamic vinegar, olive oil, ½ teaspoon of the thyme, the salt, and about 5 grinds of pepper. Mix well.

Remove the pepper skins and seeds and cut the peppers into thin strips. Add the peppers to the vinegar mixture and let them marinate for at least 1 hour and up to 3 days. (Refrigerate if making more than a few hours ahead and return to room temperature before assembling the crostini.)

Spread each slice of the grilled garlic bread with a generous layer of goat cheese, sprinkle with some of the remaining thyme, and top with a tangle of the peppers and a small grind of black pepper. Serve immediately.

—Elizabeth Karmel

Grilled Garlic Bread

Prepare a medium-low charcoal or gas grill fire. Brush both sides of the bread with the oil and grill, covered, turning once, until golden and marked on both sides, 1 to 3 minutes per side. Take off the heat but while the bread is still hot, lightly rub one side of each bread slice with the cut sides of the garlic—heat and friction from the bread will cause the garlic to *"melt"* into the bread. Sprinkle with salt and top with grilled peppers. *—Elizabeth Karmel*

Serves eight.

Eight ¾- to 1-inch-thick slices crusty, artisan-style bread, like ciabatta

¼ cup extra-virgin olive oil for brushing

1 to 2 large cloves garlic, peeled and halved

Sea salt or kosher salt

Getting grilled bread just right

- **Choose artisan or rustic** country breads; ciabatta is a good choice, but you can also try sourdough or a French boule.

- **Slice the bread** ¾ to 1 inch thick.

- **Clean the grill grates** and heat thoroughly.

- **Grill the bread, covered,** over direct medium-low heat.

- **Have a pair of tongs** handy to turn the bread and remove it from the grill.

- **Patience is the key** to great grilled bread. Don't be tempted to use higher heat, or the bread will burn.

Grilled Bruschetta with Rosemary-White Bean Purée & Heirloom Tomatoes

Serves ten to twelve.

¾ cup extra-virgin olive oil; more as needed

4 cloves garlic, smashed and peeled

Two 3- to 4-inch sprigs plus 1 teaspoon chopped fresh rosemary

2 large ripe heirloom tomatoes (about 1¼ pounds), cut into ½-inch dice (about 3 cups)

2 tablespoons chopped fresh mint

1½ teaspoons kosher salt; more as needed

One 15-ounce can cannellini beans, rinsed well and drained

⅓ cup freshly grated Parmigiano-Reggiano

1 to 2 tablespoons fresh lemon juice

½ teaspoon freshly ground black pepper; more as needed

1 pound baguette, cut into ½-inch-thick slices

If good heirloom tomatoes aren't in season, you can make a delicious version of this recipe using ripe cherry or grape tomatoes, which are pretty decent even in winter months.

Heat the oil, garlic, and rosemary sprigs in a small saucepan over medium heat until they start to sizzle steadily and become fragrant, 2 to 3 minutes. Let the oil cool to room temperature. Strain the oil into a measuring cup. (If making ahead, store in the refrigerator and use within 3 days.)

Put the tomatoes in a medium bowl and toss with 3 tablespoons of the garlic oil, the mint, and 1 teaspoon of the salt.

Put the beans in a food processor and add about 6 tablespoons of the garlic oil, the Parmigiano, 1 tablespoon of the lemon juice, the chopped rosemary, the remaining ½ teaspoon salt, and the black pepper and purée until smooth. Season to taste with more salt, pepper, and lemon juice.

Heat a gas grill to medium high or prepare a medium-hot charcoal fire. Brush both sides of the bread with the remaining garlic oil. (If you run out, use plain olive oil to finish.) Sprinkle lightly with salt. Grill the bread until crisp, with nice grill marks on both sides, 1 to 2 minutes per side.

Spread the grilled bread with the bean purée, top with a generous spoonful of the tomatoes and their juices, sprinkle lightly with pepper, and set out on a large platter so your guests can help themselves. —*Tony Rosenfeld*

Feta & Dill Galette
with Lemony Spinach Salad

This can be a lovely starter for a big meal or a light meal on its own. Thaw the puff pastry in the refrigerator overnight or all day while you're at work, or thaw it at room temperature for at least 45 minutes (less if your kitchen is quite warm).

Position a rack in the center of the oven and heat the oven to 450°F. In a medium bowl, whisk the eggs, crème fraîche or cream, chopped dill, lemon zest, salt, and about 10 grinds of pepper.

On a lightly floured surface, gently roll out the puff pastry until it measures about 11x13 inches. Line a rimmed baking sheet with parchment or a silicone baking mat. Lay the pastry on the baking sheet, wet the edges with water, and fold over a ³/₄-inch border, mitering the corners for neatness. Distribute the feta evenly within the border, and then carefully pour the egg mixture over the cheese, taking care that it doesn't slosh onto the border. Carefully transfer the baking sheet to the oven and bake until the pastry is puffed and brown on the border and the underside, and the filling is golden brown, 18 to 20 minutes.

Slide the galette off the pan and onto a rack to cool until still warm but not hot. Move the galette to a cutting board and cut into four rectangles, so that each piece gets some border. Put the four pieces on plates.

In a large bowl, toss the spinach and dill sprigs (if using) with the olive oil and lemon juice until evenly coated. Sprinkle with salt, pepper, and more lemon juice to taste. Arrange a handful of salad on each piece of galette and serve immediately. —*Martha Holmberg*

Serves four.

2 large eggs

¹/₃ cup crème fraîche or heavy cream

2 tablespoons chopped fresh dill, plus ¹/₂ cup loosely packed dill sprigs for the salad (optional)

1 teaspoon lightly packed, finely grated lemon zest

¹/₂ teaspoon kosher salt; more for the salad

Freshly ground black pepper

1 sheet frozen puff pastry, thawed

1 cup crumbled feta (about 4 ounces)

4 small handfuls baby spinach (about 3 ounces), washed and dried, large stems removed

3 tablespoons extra-virgin olive oil

1 tablespoon fresh lemon juice; more to taste

Leek Tart with Bacon & Gruyère

Serves six as a main course, twelve as an appetizer.

For the tart shell:

9 ounces (2 cups) unbleached all-purpose flour

1 tablespoon chopped fresh thyme

¼ teaspoon table salt

¼ teaspoon freshly ground black pepper

5½ ounces (11 tablespoons) cold unsalted butter, cut into ½-inch cubes

5 to 6 tablespoons ice-cold water

For the filling:

3 thick slices bacon, cut into small dice

1 ounce (2 tablespoons) unsalted butter

3 large leeks (white and light green parts only), cleaned and sliced crosswise ¼ inch thick, to yield about 4 cups

1 tablespoon unbleached all-purpose flour

2 large eggs

⅓ cup heavy cream

⅓ cup whole milk

¾ teaspoon kosher salt

⅛ teaspoon freshly grated nutmeg

Freshly ground black pepper

⅔ cup grated Gruyère (or Emmenthaler)

Paired with a green salad and a glass of crisp white wine, this tart is perfect for lunch or a light dinner. Cut into thin wedges and served along with ápéritifs, it's a filling yet sophisticated appetizer. The tart is delicious warm or at room temperature.

Make the tart shell: In a food processor, pulse the flour, thyme, salt, and pepper to blend thoroughly. Add the butter and pulse until the butter pieces are about the size of rice grains (about eight 1-second pulses). Add the ice water 1 tablespoon at a time through the feed tube while pulsing in short bursts until the dough starts coming together. It may still look crumbly, but if you press it with your fingers, it should become compact. (Don't add more water than absolutely necessary to get the dough to cling together.) Turn the dough out onto a clean work surface and, using your hands, gather and press the dough into a rough ball, blotting up the stray crumbs. Transfer the dough to a piece of waxed paper, shape it gently into a disk, and wrap it tightly to keep it from drying out. Refrigerate for at least 45 minutes. (The dough can be made up to 2 days ahead.)

Position a rack in the center of the oven and heat the oven to 450°F.

Unwrap the dough, set it on a lightly floured surface, and if necessary, let sit until pliable. Roll the dough out to a 14-inch circle about ⅛ inch thick.

Transfer the dough to an 11-inch fluted tart pan with a removable bottom and press it carefully into the corners and up the sides of the pan. Let the edges of the dough hang over the rim of the pan and then roll the rolling pin over the top of the pan to cut away the excess dough. Prick the surface of the dough all over with a fork, line it with parchment, and fill it with pie weights or dried beans. Put the pan on a rimmed baking sheet and bake until the edges of the tart shell are dry and flaky (but not browned), about 10 minutes. Remove the weights and parchment; the center should still be moist and raw. Prick the bottom again and return the shell to the oven. Bake until the bottom surface is completely dry, 5 to 7 minutes more. Remove from the oven and let cool. Lower the oven temperature to 375°F.

Make the filling: In a 12-inch skillet, cook the bacon over medium heat until it's crisp and golden brown, about 5 minutes. With a slotted spoon, transfer the bacon to a dish and set aside. Discard all but about 2 teaspoons of the bacon fat. Set the skillet over medium-low heat, add the butter, let it melt, and then add the leeks. Stir to coat them with the fat, cover, and cook, stirring occasionally, until soft, 8 to 10 minutes. Stir the flour into the leeks and cook uncovered, stirring, for about 2 minutes to cook off the raw-flour flavor. Set aside and let cool slightly.

In a medium bowl, lightly whisk the eggs. Add the cream, milk, salt, nutmeg, and several grinds of pepper and whisk until blended. Add the bacon and leeks to the mixture and stir to combine.

To assemble the tart, scatter ⅓ cup of the cheese over the cooled tart shell and pour in the egg mixture. Spread the leeks evenly. Scatter the remaining ⅓ cup cheese evenly over the top. Bake until the custard is set and the top is light golden brown, about 35 minutes. Let cool on a rack for at least 30 minutes before serving.

Store leftovers in the refrigerator, covered. Reheat for 10 to 15 minutes at 350°F. —*Ruth Lively*

Clean leeks carefully

Since leeks are grown with soil piled all around them, there is plenty of opportunity for dirt and grit to settle between their onion-like layers. The easiest way to clean a leek is to trim the root end and the dark green tops and cut it in half lengthwise (or, if you want to retain the appearance of whole leeks in your dish, just cut about two-thirds of the way through the stalk, as shown at left). Hold the leek root end up under cold running water and riffle the layers as if they were a deck of cards. Do this on both sides a couple of times until all the dirt has been washed out.

Egg Salad Canapés with Smoked Salmon, Capers & Dill

Serves eight as an appetizer; four as a main course.

6 large eggs

6 ounces cold-smoked salmon, cut into small dice (1 scant cup)

6 tablespoons extra-virgin olive oil

½ small red onion, cut into small dice (about ⅔ cup)

⅓ cup capers, drained

2 tablespoons minced fresh dill

1 tablespoon fresh lemon juice

1 teaspoon finely grated lemon zest

Kosher salt and freshly ground black pepper

This classic salad may feel slightly surprising as an appetizer, but it will be more than welcome, especially with this update of smoked salmon, capers, and fresh herbs. Serve on toasted pita triangles or other toast points, or tucked into a spear of endive.

Put the eggs in a medium saucepan with enough water to cover. Cover the pan and bring the water to a simmer over medium-high heat. As soon as the water simmers briskly, remove the pan from the heat and let stand, covered, until the eggs are hard-cooked, 10 minutes. Put the eggs in ice water to cool.

Peel the eggs, chop finely, and put them in a medium bowl. Add the salmon, oil, onion, capers, dill, and lemon juice and zest. Season with salt and pepper to taste. Toss gently but well and serve on a bed of lettuce or on toasted sandwich bread as a main course; spoon it onto toasted pita triangles for an hors d'oeuvre. —*Pam Anderson*

Boiling an egg may not be rocket science, but timing is important. Here are some guidelines.

Getting started

Put the eggs in a saucepan and add enough cold water to cover them by about 1 inch. Set the pan over medium-high heat and as soon as the water reaches a brisk simmer, start timing. As the eggs cook, adjust the heat as needed to maintain a brisk simmer. (Though we talk about hard-boiled eggs—and we're using that term here—the fact is that cooking eggs in boiling water cracks the shell and makes the eggs tough and rubbery. A simmer works much better.)

Peeling eggs

When the eggs are cooked, carefully pour out most of the hot water, leaving the eggs in the pan. Set the pan in the sink under cool running water for a few minutes until the eggs are barely warm. If the shells are stubborn, try peeling them under running water. The fresher the egg, the more attached the shell, so for boiling, older eggs are preferable.

Soft boiled: 2 minutes

The white is solid, but the yolk is still runny. Serve in an egg cup for breakfast. Use the side of a small spoon to crack and remove the pointed end of the egg, making a hole in the shell large enough to fit the spoon. Or use egg scissors, if you have them.

Medium boiled: 4½ minutes

The yolk is solid but still dark orange-yellow, moist, and dense in the middle. Beautiful and delicious quartered on a salad.

Hard boiled: 8 minutes

The yolk is completely solid, light yellow, and crumbly, with no sign of the telltale green or gray ring around the yolk that's caused by overcooking. Perfect for egg salad or deviled eggs.

The boil-and-walk-away method

This is a great way to hard-boil eggs when you're multitasking and can't pay careful attention to the eggs. Begin as directed, with the eggs in cold water, but once the water reaches a brisk simmer, turn off the heat and let the eggs sit uncovered in the hot water for at least 10 minutes and up to 30 minutes—the water cools gradually, preventing the eggs from overcooking.

Quesadillas with Roasted Poblanos & Onions (Rajas)

Serves four as a main course, six to eight as an appetizer.

2 small fresh poblanos

1 tablespoon plus 2 teaspoons vegetable oil

½ large white onion, thinly sliced lengthwise (about 1½ cups)

Kosher salt and freshly ground black pepper

Four 8-inch flour tortillas

2 cups grated Monterey Jack cheese (about 8 ounces)

½ cup loosely packed fresh cilantro

½ cup sour cream

Strips of roasted and peeled poblanos have their own special name: rajas (pronounced RAH has), and they're a wonderful ingredient to have on hand, to pair with mild cheese as in this punchy quesadilla, or simply to toss into scrambled eggs, a frittata, pasta, rice pilaf—anywhere you'd enjoy the grassy-sweet flavor of a poblano.

Roast and peel the poblanos following the directions below. Slice them into ¼-inch-wide strips and put them in a small bowl.

Put a baking sheet in the oven and heat the oven to 150°F (or its lowest setting).

Make the rajas: Heat 1 tablespoon of the oil in a 10- or 12-inch nonstick skillet over medium-high heat. Add the onion and cook, stirring frequently, until soft and lightly browned, 3 to 5 minutes. Add the poblano strips, season with a generous pinch of salt and a few grinds of pepper, and cook, stirring occasionally, until the peppers are heated through, 1 to 2 minutes more. Transfer to a plate and wipe the skillet clean.

Make the quesadillas: Heat ½ teaspoon of the oil in the skillet over medium-high heat until hot. Add one tortilla and scatter over it a quarter of the cheese, a quarter of the poblano mixture, and a quarter of the cilantro. When the tortilla smells toasty and the bottom is browned in spots, in 1 or 2 minutes, fold it in half, pressing it with a spatula to flatten it. Transfer to the baking sheet in the oven to keep warm. Repeat with the remaining ingredients to make three more quesadillas. Cut each quesadilla into wedges and serve with the sour cream on the side. —*Ruth Lively*

How to roast poblanos

You can roast poblanos on a gas burner, a hot grill, or under a broiler. Whatever method you choose, your goal is to blister and char the skin all over.

Blacken the peppers. Turn a burner to high and char the poblanos directly over the flame, turning them with tongs as soon as each side becomes fully blackened. It will take 6 to 8 minutes per pepper.

If you don't have a gas stove, you can char poblanos similarly over a hot grill fire or lay them on a foil-lined baking sheet and char them under a hot broiler, turning them with tongs.

Steam and peel. Immediately after roasting, put the poblanos in a bowl, cover, and set aside to steam and loosen the skins. When cool enough to handle, peel the charred skin off with your hands or a small paring knife. Pull out and discard the stems and seed clusters.

In our experience, most supermarkets do a decent job of stocking a variety of fresh hot chiles, but identifying them is another thing. They're often mislabeled, and sometimes they're just in an anonymous jumble. On these pages are some of the varieties that commonly appear in markets.

All fresh chiles should be smooth, firm, and glossy. Some jalapeños may have "scar cracks" at their stem ends, but other varieties should be blemish-free. And know that the heat level of chiles can vary even within the same variety, so always taste as you add when cooking with chiles.

Serrano

Very hot. Sold green (unripe) or red (ripe). Tangy, herbal, vegetal flavor. Use raw in hot salsa or cooked in curries and chili.

Jalapeño

Medium hot. Usually sold green, but occasionally sweeter, ripe red jalapeños appear in markets. Vegetal flavor. An all-purpose hot chile often used raw in salsas and guacamole.

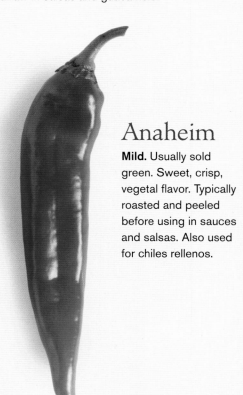

Poblano

Mild to medium hot. Dark green and large. Sweet vegetal flavor, reminiscent of green bell pepper but hot. Usually roasted for use in sauces and enchiladas, or stuffed, batter-dipped, and fried to make chiles rellenos.

Anaheim

Mild. Usually sold green. Sweet, crisp, vegetal flavor. Typically roasted and peeled before using in sauces and salsas. Also used for chiles rellenos.

Fresno

Mild to medium hot. Almost always sold red; often mistaken for a red jalapeño. Spicy, sweet flavor, like that of a red bell pepper but hot. Try raw in slaws and dips or cooked in soups.

Banana wax

Mild. Yellow-green, long, and tapered. Sweet, slightly fruity flavor. Add raw to mild salsas or roast and use in tacos or as a pizza topping.

Thai bird

Very hot. Either red (most common), green, orange, or yellow. Peppery, nutty flavor. Use in Southeast Asian stir-fries, curries, soups, and salads.

Habanero

Very, very hot. Either orange (most common), red, yellow, or green. Incendiary, fruity flavor. Use in fruit salsas, hot sauces, and marinades.

Farmers' Market Quesadillas

Yields 4 quesadillas.

5 tablespoons vegetable oil

1 cup small-diced fresh, mild chiles, such as Anaheim or poblano (from about 2 large chiles)

1½ cups small-diced summer squash (from about 2 small zucchini, yellow squash, or yellow crookneck)

Kosher salt and freshly ground black pepper

1 cup fresh corn kernels (from 2 medium ears)

⅛ teaspoon chipotle chile powder

1 cup diced tomato (from 2 small tomatoes)

¼ cup chopped fresh cilantro

1 tablespoon fresh lime juice

Four 9-inch flour tortillas

2 cups grated sharp Cheddar (8 ounces)

Sour cream for serving (optional)

Chipotles are dried smoked jalapeños, and in any form they add an intriguing depth to dishes. McCormick® makes ground chipotle, and The Spice Hunter® sells a crushed chipotle, which would be a fine substitute in this recipe; just add a bit more than you would of the ground.

Heat the oven to 200°F. Fit a cooling rack over a baking sheet and put in the oven.

Heat 1 tablespoon of the oil in a 12-inch skillet over medium-high heat until hot. Add the chiles and cook, stirring, until soft, 3 to 4 minutes. Add the squash, season with salt and pepper, and cook, stirring, until the squash softens and starts to brown, 3 to 4 minutes. Stir in the corn and chipotle powder and cook 2 minutes more. Spoon into a bowl, let cool for a few minutes, and then fold in the tomato, cilantro, and lime juice. Season to taste with salt and pepper. Set aside ¾ cup of the mixture.

Lay several layers of paper towel on a work surface. Wipe out the skillet, put it over medium-high heat, and add 1 tablespoon of the oil. When it's hot, put one tortilla in the pan. Quickly distribute ½ cup of the cheese evenly over the tortilla and about a quarter of the remaining vegetable mixture over half the tortilla. When the underside of the tortilla is browned, use tongs to fold the cheese-only side over the vegetable side. Lay the quesadilla on the paper towels, blot for a few seconds, and then move it to the rack in the oven to keep warm while you repeat with the remaining oil and tortillas. Cut the quesadillas into wedges and serve immediately with the reserved vegetable mixture and sour cream. —*Martha Holmberg*

Tomato & Olive Pizzettas with Fennel Seeds & Aged Goat Cheese

You can find pizza dough in the grocery store, or try your favorite pizzeria—most will sell their dough. Sambuca® or Pernod® makes a nice sweet contrast with the salty cheese, and it brings out the flavor of the fennel. The pizzetta toppings can be prepared up to 1 day ahead and refrigerated. The dough can be rolled and cut up to 1 hour ahead and refrigerated, covered.

Heat a gas grill to medium high or prepare a medium-hot charcoal fire with the coals banked to one side to provide a cooler area on the grill.

On a well-floured surface, roll out the pizza dough with a rolling pin until it's ⅛ inch thick. If the dough is very elastic and resists rolling, cover it with plastic and let it rest for about 5 minutes. (Repeat this step as needed until the dough is relaxed and willing to roll.) Using a 3-inch ring cutter, cut the dough into 18 rounds. Discard the excess dough. Brush the top of the rounds with oil and sprinkle with salt, pepper, and fennel seeds, pressing gently so they adhere. Transfer the rounds to a baking sheet, fennel side up.

Working with half of the pizzettas at a time, grill them fennel side down (covered on a gas grill, uncovered on a charcoal grill) for 1 minute. If they puff up, flatten them with a metal spatula. Brush the floured sides (which are facing up) with oil. Grill until the bottom is nicely browned and crisp, about 1 more minute. Loosen with a metal spatula, if necessary, and return the pizzettas, grilled side up, to the baking sheet. (If using a gas grill, turn the heat down to medium.)

Working quickly, top each with 2 wedges of Bûcheron, 3 olive pieces, 3 tomato slices, and a pinch of red pepper flakes. Use a small spoon to sprinkle each pizzetta with a few drops of Sambuca or Pernod.

Return the pizzettas to the medium-hot gas grill or to the cooler side of a charcoal grill. Continue grilling, covered, until the pizzettas are crisp and the cheese is melted, about 2 minutes. Transfer to a platter and serve while you repeat with the remaining dough rounds.
—Allison Ehri Kreitler

Serves six to eight; yields 18 mini pizzas.

Flour for the work surface

1 pound pizza dough

Extra-virgin olive oil for brushing

Kosher salt and freshly ground black pepper

2 teaspoons fennel seeds, coarsely chopped

One 1-inch-thick slice Bûcheron® (about 6 ounces), cut into 36 thin wedges (if the cheese crumbles, let it warm to room temperature) or a log of fresh goat cheese, cut into thin rounds

14 pitted Kalamata olives, quartered

18 cherry or grape tomatoes, sliced into ¼-inch rounds, ends discarded

Crushed red pepper flakes

1½ teaspoons Sambuca or Pernod

Seeded Crackers

Yields about 3½ dozen
2x4-inch crackers.

For the topping:

1 tablespoon sesame seeds

2 teaspoons poppy seeds

2 teaspoons fennel or caraway seeds

¾ teaspoon kosher salt

For the dough:

6¾ ounces (1½ cups) unbleached all-purpose flour; more for rolling

2 ounces (scant ½ cup) whole-wheat flour

1 teaspoon table salt

3 tablespoons extra-virgin olive oil

Unfussy and quick to make, even for the most pastry-challenged, these crackers bake beautifully into crisp, light flatbread-style snacks, perfect with wine and cheese at a cocktail party or with crocks of soup at an after-ski gathering. The dough can be refrigerated for 2 days or frozen for up to a month, and then thawed for 2 hours at room temperature.

Position a rack in the lower third of the oven and heat the oven to 450°F.

Make the topping: In a small bowl, stir the sesame seeds, poppy seeds, and fennel or caraway seeds. Fill another small bowl with water and set it aside along with a pastry brush and the kosher salt.

Make the dough: In a large bowl, whisk the all-purpose flour, whole-wheat flour, and table salt. Add the olive oil and ½ cup water to the flour; stir with a rubber spatula until it collects into a soft, crumbly ball of dough. Use the spatula or your hands to press the dough against the sides of the bowl to gather all the stray flour.

Set the dough on a lightly floured work surface and portion it into thirds. Pat each portion into a square. Set two squares aside and cover with a clean towel. Roll the remaining dough into a rectangle about ¹⁄₁₆ inch thick and 7 or 8 inches wide by 14 or 15 inches long. Whenever you feel resistance, lift up one edge of the dough and sprinkle more flour underneath before you continue rolling.

With a pastry brush, brush the dough lightly with water and sprinkle about a third of the seed mix evenly over the surface. Sprinkle with ¼ teaspoon of the kosher salt. With a dough scraper, pizza cutter, ravioli cutter, or sharp knife, cut the dough in half lengthwise and then cut across to make rectangles roughly 2x4 inches. Don't bother trimming the edges; rustic edges add character. Transfer to an unlined baking sheet. Bake until nicely browned, about 10 minutes. Let cool on a wire rack.

While each batch is baking, clean your work surface as needed and repeat the rolling and cutting with the remaining portions of dough. Store the cooled crackers in a zip-top plastic bag. They'll keep for up to a week.

—*Lynne Sampson*

Making them thin and crisp

Roll the dough into a very thin rectangle; the thinner the dough, the snappier the crackers.

Cut the dough into smaller rectangles and don't worry about trimming the outer edges.

Velvety Carrot Soup with Ginger

Yields about 8½ cups;
serves eight.

For the broth:

¼ cup medium-diced peeled carrots

½ cup medium-diced dark green leek tops (from 1 to 2 leeks; rinse thoroughly after dicing; save the white and pale green parts for the soup)

½ medium onion, cut into medium dice (about ¾ cup)

¼ fennel bulb, cut into medium dice (about ½ cup)

¼ celery rib, cut into medium dice (about 2 tablespoons)

1 small clove garlic, smashed and peeled

1 small bay leaf

1 sprig fresh thyme

1 sprig fresh parsley

For the soup:

3 tablespoons extra-virgin olive oil

5 medium shallots, thinly sliced (about 1 cup)

¾ cup thinly sliced leeks, white and pale green parts only (from 1 to 2 leeks; rinse thoroughly after slicing)

2 small cloves garlic, smashed and peeled

Kosher or sea salt

3¾ cups medium-diced peeled carrots (about 1½ pounds)

2 tablespoons granulated sugar

2 cups carrot juice, either homemade or store-bought

1 tablespoon peeled and finely grated fresh ginger

Freshly ground black pepper

3 to 4 teaspoons fresh lemon juice

1 small Fuji apple

This recipe looks long, but half of the ingredients are used to make a quick vegetable broth. Look for carrot juice in the produce section of your supermarket.

Make the broth: Put the carrots, leek tops, onion, fennel, celery, garlic, bay leaf, thyme, and parsley in a 4-quart (or larger) saucepan. Add 10 cups cold water and bring to a simmer over medium-high heat. Reduce the heat to medium low and simmer for 1 hour. Strain the broth into a heatproof bowl and discard the solids. Measure out 5 cups of broth for use in the soup; save the remaining broth for another use. Rinse and dry the saucepan and return it to the stove.

Finish the soup: In the saucepan, heat the olive oil over medium-low heat. Add the shallots, leeks, garlic, and a generous pinch of salt. Cook, stirring occasionally, until the vegetables are softened but not browned, about 5 minutes. Stir in the carrots and sugar. Cover, reduce the heat to low, and cook, stirring occasionally, until the carrots are soft, 15 to 20 minutes.

Add the 5 cups broth and the carrot juice. Bring to a simmer, uncovered, over medium-high heat. Reduce the heat to low and simmer gently for 10 minutes.

Wrap the ginger in a small square of cheesecloth and use the cloth to squeeze the ginger juice into the soup (discard the squeezed-dry ginger). Remove the pan from the heat.

Working in batches, purée the soup in a blender until smooth. Pour each batch of the puréed soup into a medium-mesh sieve set over a clean heatproof container. Use a rubber spatula to help the soup pass through, but don't press on the solids yet. Once the last batch has drained through the sieve, press lightly on the solids (but don't mash them through the sieve) to extract the remaining liquid. Discard the solids. Season to taste with salt, pepper, and 1 to 2 teaspoons of the lemon juice.

When ready to serve, peel and core the apple and cut it into medium dice. In a small bowl, toss the apple with 2 teaspoons of the remaining lemon juice. Reheat the soup, if necessary, and ladle it into individual serving bowls or cups. Serve immediately, garnishing each bowl with a small spoonful of the diced apple. —*Dan Barber*

Green Gazpacho

*Yields a scant 6 cups;
serves six.*

1½ pounds cucumbers (4 to 5
  picklers or 2½ large slicers),
  peeled, seeded, and cut into
  1-inch pieces (to yield 3 cups)

1 tablespoons kosher salt; more
  to taste

1 large yellow pepper

1 medium ripe avocado

1 medium sweet onion, cut into
  1-inch pieces (2 cups)

¼ teaspoon freshly ground
  black pepper; more to taste

3 ounces fresh crustless Italian
  country-style bread, cut into
  1-inch cubes (2 cups)

1 teaspoon chopped garlic

¼ cup coarsely chopped fresh
  flat-leaf parsley

3 tablespoons coarsely chopped
  fresh cilantro

1 tablespoon coarsely chopped
  fresh basil or mint

⅔ cup extra-virgin olive oil;
  more for garnish

2 tablespoons red-wine vinegar

You don't always need to seed a cucumber, especially if you're using it in a salad and the seeds are small, but the texture of this puréed soup will be nicer if you do. To seed a cucumber, cut it in half lengthwise and scoop out the seeds with a spoon or a melon baller. You can dress up this cold soup by serving it with lumps of cooked lobster, crab, or shrimp.

Put the cucumbers in a colander over a bowl or in the sink and toss with 1½ teaspoons of the salt. Let them sit for 30 minutes to draw out the juices and remove any trace of bitterness. Meanwhile, core and seed the pepper and cut three-quarters of it into 1-inch pieces. Wrap the remaining quarter and refrigerate; you'll need it later. Cut the avocado in half, peel one half, and cut it into 1-inch chunks. Lightly coat the cut surface of the remaining half with oil, wrap it in plastic, and refrigerate for later.

Rinse and drain the cucumber. Put the cucumber, pepper, avocado, onion, the remaining 1½ teaspoons salt, and the pepper in a food processor and purée. Transfer the purée to a large bowl and reassemble the processor. Process the bread, garlic, and herbs until the bread is reduced to crumbs and the herbs are fully chopped. Add the oil and vinegar to the mixture and process briefly to thoroughly combine. Add the bread mixture and 1 cup water to the cucumber purée and stir until well blended. Cover and refrigerate for at least 2 hours or overnight. Let come to a cool room temperature before serving.

When ready to serve, peel the reserved avocado half and cut it into ½-inch dice. Cut the reserved pepper into ¼-inch dice. Stir the soup and assess its consistency. If it seems too thick, add water until it's thinned to your liking. Season to taste with salt and pepper. Divide the soup among shallow bowls and garnish with the avocado and pepper. Drizzle about 1 teaspoon of olive oil over each bowl and serve. —*Ruth Lively*

A world of cucumbers

There are dozens of cucumber varieties, all of which can be used pretty much interchangeably. Here are some of the most common types available:

Picklers

Picklers are short and blocky, with blunt ends and bumpy skins. Their firm texture makes them perfect for pickling, but you can use them raw as well.

Slicers

Slicers are your basic, all-purpose cucumbers. They're about 8 inches long with round ends and smooth to slightly knobby dark-green skin. The ones you buy at the supermarket are often waxed to protect them during shipping and to extend their shelf life. Scrub them well or peel before using.

English

Also known as greenhouse, European, or seedless cucumbers, English cucumbers are 10 to 12 inches long and slender and are usually sold in plastic sleeves. With their thin skins, undeveloped seeds, and uniform shape, they are ideal for slicing into salads and garnishing appetizers.

Tomatillo Gazpacho

Yields about 5 cups; serves four to six as a first course.

One 14-ounce can low-salt chicken broth

1 pound tomatillos (8 to 12 medium), husked, rinsed, and cut into medium dice (3 cups)

1 medium clove garlic, minced

2 tablespoons extra-virgin olive oil

2 medium avocados, cut into small dice (1½ cups)

½ seedless English cucumber, cut into small dice (2 cups)

½ large red bell pepper, cut into small dice (½ cup)

¼ small red onion, finely diced (¼ cup)

2 tablespoons chopped fresh cilantro

1 tablespoon fresh lime juice; more as needed

Kosher salt and freshly ground black pepper

Tortilla chips, for serving (optional)

Tomatillos make a nice change-up from the typical tomato gazpacho. They're usually covered with a papery husk that peels away easily, though not every fruit will have a husk. The surface of a tomatillo is often sticky, so rinse well before dicing. This recipe is quick to prepare but needs to chill for at least an hour for the flavors to develop.

Heat the broth in a 3-quart saucepan over medium-high heat. Add the tomatillos and garlic, bring to a boil, reduce the heat, and let simmer until the tomatillos are cooked through but still hold their shape, about 1 minute. Let cool slightly, about 5 minutes, and then carefully purée the mixture in a blender along with the olive oil. Pour the purée into a nonreactive 9x13-inch pan and refrigerate to cool quickly.

When the purée has cooled, remove the pan from the refrigerator and stir in the avocado, cucumber, bell pepper, onion, cilantro, and lime juice. Season to taste with salt and pepper. Refrigerate for at least 1 hour and up to 4 hours. Before serving, taste and adjust the seasoning with more lime juice, salt, and pepper as needed. Spoon the gazpacho into individual serving bowls or mugs. Serve with tortilla chips, if you like. —*Pam Anderson*

Summer Bouillabaisse with Smoky Rouille

This vibrant soup is marvelously adaptable. At its simplest, it's a savory but quick weeknight meal, but it's also easy to dress up for entertaining: add ½ pound peeled medium or large shrimp and ½ pound Manila clams or mussels. Wash the shellfish well before adding and use only those with tightly closed shells. Simmer until the shells open. For convenience, you can make the soup ahead except for adding the seafood, which you should do at the last minute.

In a 5- to 6-quart soup pot or Dutch oven, heat the oil over medium heat. Add the 1½ tablespoons chopped garlic and cook until fragrant, about 30 seconds. Add the tomatoes and wine, increase the heat to medium high (if necessary), and simmer vigorously until the tomatoes are broken down and the mixture is slightly soupy, about 15 minutes.

While the tomatoes are cooking, whisk the ½ teaspoon grated garlic, paprika, and mayonnaise in a small bowl. Whisk in a little olive oil and enough cool water to make a creamy, pourable sauce. Taste and add salt if you like.

Add the broth and saffron to the tomato mixture and simmer to slightly reduce the broth and concentrate the flavors, 5 minutes. Add the fish and simmer until it's opaque throughout, 3 to 5 minutes more. Stir in the corn. Season to taste with salt and black pepper. Serve in large bowls with a big drizzle of the sauce on top and a generous sprinkle of parsley, if using.

—Martha Holmberg

Serves four.

3 tablespoons extra-virgin olive oil; more for the sauce

1½ tablespoons chopped garlic, plus ½ teaspoon finely grated or minced garlic

2 pounds ripe tomatoes, cored and large diced (about 4½ cups)

1 cup dry white wine

1 teaspoon sweet smoked paprika (Spanish pimentón)

¼ cup mayonnaise

Kosher salt

One 14-ounce can low-salt chicken broth (1¾ cups)

1 large pinch of saffron

1 pound halibut, cod, or other firm white fish, cut into 1-inch chunks

2 cups fresh corn kernels (from 4 medium ears)

Freshly ground black pepper

1 to 2 tablespoons chopped fresh flat-leaf parsley, for garnish (optional)

Summer Corn Chowder with Scallions, Bacon & Potatoes

Yields about 5¹/₂ cups; serves six as a first course.

5 ears fresh corn

7 ounces scallions (about 20 medium)

3 slices bacon, cut into ¹/₂-inch pieces

1 tablespoon unsalted butter

1 jalapeño, cored, seeded, and finely diced

1 teaspoon kosher salt; more to taste

Freshly ground black pepper

3¹/₂ cups low-salt chicken broth

1 large Yukon Gold potato (8 to 9 ounces), peeled and cut into ¹/₂-inch dice (about 1¹/₂ cups)

1¹/₂ teaspoons chopped fresh thyme

2 tablespoons heavy cream

This is summer in a bowl and a wonderful destination for some sweet, end-of-season corn. Unlike many corn chowders, there's very little cream in this recipe; puréeing part of the soup creates a full texture and an added feeling of richness.

Husk the corn and cut off the kernels. Reserve two of the corn cobs and discard the others. Trim and thinly slice the scallions, keeping the dark-green parts separate from the white and light-green parts.

Cook the bacon in a 3- or 4-quart saucepan over medium heat until browned and crisp, about 5 minutes. With a slotted spoon, transfer the bacon to a paper-towel-lined plate. Pour off and discard all but about 1 tablespoon of the bacon fat. Return the pan to medium heat and add the butter. When the butter is melted, add the white and light-green scallions and the jalapeño, salt, and a few grinds of black pepper. Cook, stirring, until the scallions are very soft, about 3 minutes.

Add the broth, corn, corn cobs, potatoes, and thyme and bring to a boil over medium-high heat. Reduce the heat to medium low and simmer until the potatoes are completely tender, about 15 minutes. Discard the corn cobs.

Transfer 1 cup of the broth and vegetables to a blender and purée. Return the purée to the pot and stir in the cream and all but ¹/₃ cup of the scallion greens. Simmer, stirring occasionally, for a couple of minutes to wilt the scallions and blend the flavors. Season to taste with salt and pepper and serve sprinkled with the bacon and reserved scallions. —*Tony Rosenfeld*

White or green: What part of the scallion to use?

Scallions' dark-green ends have a light, crisp texture and a delicate sharpness reminiscent of chives, but they wilt and discolor when cooked too long. The white parts have an oniony punch, and because their texture is more substantial, they withstand longer cooking times. In general, scallions cook pretty quickly when sautéed, grilled, roasted, or even braised, so you can use both the white and green parts. But when cooking them for a longer time (as an aromatic base for soups or stews, for example), it's best to use only the white and light-green parts.

You can use scallions instead of leeks to add depth and sweetness to a creamy potato soup. Or use scallions to start a braise of chicken thighs in a spicy Szechuan sauce or as a base for a simple Italian seafood stew with sausage, tomatoes, and clams.

Ginger Chicken Soup

Serves four as a light main course.

One 1-inch piece fresh ginger

2 medium cloves garlic, unpeeled

10 to 12 ounces boneless, skinless chicken thighs, trimmed of excess fat (about 3 medium)

2 cups low-salt chicken broth

1 tablespoon soy sauce

2 teaspoons fresh lemon juice

¼ teaspoon Asian chile paste, like sambal oelek

¼ cup packed fresh cilantro

2 tablespoons thinly sliced scallion (green tops only)

Kosher salt

1 tablespoon mild vegetable oil, like canola or safflower oil

1 cup packed baby spinach (about 2 ounces)

This quick soup gets part of its personality from a dollop of cilantro paste that you make with a mortar and pestle. If you don't have a mortar and pestle, mince the scallions and cilantro, transfer to a small bowl to combine with the oil, and scrape the mixture back onto a cutting board. Position the blade of a chef's knife at a 30-degree angle to the board and repeatedly drag the blade over the cilantro mixture, using a bit of pressure to mash it.

Peel the ginger and slice it into four ¼-inch coins. Using the flat side of a chef's knife or a meat pounder, smash the coins. Smash the garlic and remove the skin.

In a medium saucepan, combine the ginger, garlic, chicken, broth, soy sauce, lemon juice, chile paste, and 1 cup water. Bring to a boil over medium-high heat. Reduce the heat to low and gently simmer until the chicken is cooked through, about 10 minutes. Using a pair of tongs, transfer the chicken to a plate. Use a slotted spoon to remove the ginger and garlic and discard. Keep the broth warm.

Finely chop the cilantro and scallion. Put them in a mortar, add a pinch of salt and 2 teaspoons of the oil, and pound and mash with the pestle. Once the mixture begins to blend, add the remaining 1 teaspoon oil. Continue to grind the pestle into the cilantro mixture until it is aromatic and has the consistency of a paste.

Once the chicken is cool, slice it thinly and portion it into four soup bowls. Return the broth to a simmer and season with salt to taste. Add the spinach to the broth and continue to simmer until it's wilted, 1 to 2 minutes more. Ladle the broth and spinach evenly over each portion of chicken and then top each with a dollop of the cilantro paste.

—Maryellen Driscoll

Curried Lentil Soup

Take a moment to pick over the lentils because every once in a while, an errant pebble will sneak in, which would be a highly unwelcome surprise in anyone's soup bowl. Garnish this warming soup with a dollop of plain whole-milk yogurt and chopped fresh mint or cilantro, or both.

Pulse the garlic and ginger in a food processor until chopped. Add the fennel or celery, carrot, parsnip, and shallot and pulse until coarsely chopped.

Melt 2 tablespoons of the butter in a 4-quart saucepan over medium-high heat. Add the chopped vegetables and cook, stirring, until softened, about 3 minutes. Add the curry powder and cook, stirring, until the curry powder is fragrant, about 30 seconds. Add the lentils, broth, salt, and pepper. Bring the soup to a boil over high heat, reduce the heat to maintain a brisk simmer, cover, and cook until the lentils are tender, 25 to 30 minutes.

Transfer 1½ cups of the soup to a blender or a food processor and purée until smooth. Stir the purée back into the soup, along with the remaining 1 tablespoon butter. Season to taste with salt and pepper, and adjust the consistency with water, if you like. —Allison Ehri Kreitler

Yields about 1 quart; serves four.

1 large clove garlic

1 piece (⅓ inch long) peeled fresh ginger

½ small bulb fennel, cored and cut into large chunks, or 1 small rib celery, cut into large chunks

1 small carrot, peeled and cut into large chunks

1 small parsnip, peeled and cut into large chunks

1 large shallot, cut in half

3 tablespoons unsalted butter

2 teaspoons curry powder

1 cup brown lentils, picked over and rinsed

1 quart homemade or low-salt canned chicken or vegetable broth

¼ teaspoon kosher salt; more as needed

¼ teaspoon freshly ground black pepper; more as needed

Tuscan Peasant Soup with Rosemary & Pancetta

Yields 3½ quarts; serves six to eight.

5 tablespoons extra-virgin olive oil

1¼ cups small-diced pancetta (about 6 ounces or 6 thick slices)

4 cups large-diced Savoy cabbage (about ½ small head)

2 cups medium-diced onion (10 to 12 ounces or 2 small)

1½ cups medium-diced carrot (about 4 medium carrots)

½ teaspoon kosher salt; more as needed

2 tablespoons minced garlic

1 tablespoons plus 1 teaspoon minced fresh rosemary

1 teaspoon ground coriander

One 28-ounce can diced tomatoes, drained

7 cups homemade or low-salt canned chicken broth

Two 15½-ounce cans small white beans, rinsed and drained (about 2½ cups, drained)

1 to 2 teaspoons fresh lemon juice

Freshly ground black pepper

1 cup fresh breadcrumbs, toasted

1 cup grated Parmigiano-Reggiano

This is indeed a peasant-style soup, made from beans, leftover bread, and humble winter vegetables, yet when you use good ingredients, this soup is as luxurious as they come. Pancetta, which is an unsmoked bacon, adds depth, and real imported Parmigiano is a must.

Heat 2 tablespoons of the olive oil in a 4- to 5-quart Dutch oven over medium heat. When hot, add the pancetta and cook, stirring frequently, until quite shrunken, golden brown, and crisp (the oil will also be golden brown), about 6 minutes. Remove the pan from the heat and with a slotted spoon or strainer carefully transfer the pancetta to a paper-towel-lined plate. Pour off and discard all but 2 tablespoons of the fat from the pan.

Return the pan to medium-high heat and add the cabbage. Cook the cabbage, stirring occasionally, until limp and browned around the edges, about 3 minutes. Remove the pan from the heat again and transfer the cabbage to another plate.

Put the pot back over medium heat and add 2 tablespoons more of the olive oil. When the oil is hot, add the onions, carrots, and salt. Cook, stirring occasionally, until the onions are softened and the vegetables are browned around the edges and beginning to stick to the bottom of the pan, 8 to 9 minutes. Add the last 1 tablespoon olive oil, the garlic, 1 tablespoon of the fresh rosemary, and the ground coriander and cook, stirring, until the garlic is fragrant, about 1 minute. Add the tomatoes, stir together, and cook the mixture 2 to 3 more minutes.

Return the cabbage to the pan and add the chicken broth. Stir well, bring to a boil, and reduce to a simmer. Cook for 10 to 15 minutes to infuse the broth with the flavor of the vegetables. Add the beans, bring back to a simmer, and cook for a minute or two. Remove the pan from the heat, stir in the remaining 1 teaspoon fresh rosemary, and let rest for a few minutes.

Taste the soup and add lemon juice to brighten it—you'll want at least 1 teaspoon. Season with more salt if necessary and a few grinds of fresh pepper. Serve the soup hot, garnished with the reserved pancetta crisps, the toasted breadcrumbs, and the grated Parmigiano. —*Susie Middleton*

2 Salads

p64

p72

**Mixed Green Salad with
Red-Wine & Dijon Vinaigrette
(recipe on page 46)**

Mixed Green Salad with Red-Wine & Dijon Vinaigrette

See photo on page 45.

Serves six to eight.

1 tablespoon red-wine vinegar

¾ teaspoon Dijon mustard

¼ teaspoon minced garlic

3 tablespoons extra-virgin olive oil

Kosher salt and freshly ground black pepper

1 head red or green romaine (¾ to 1 pound), trimmed, washed, dried, and torn into bite-size pieces (about 5 cups)

1 cup mâche, trimmed, washed, and dried (1 to 2 ounces)

1 cup oak leaf lettuce, trimmed, washed, and dried (1 to 2 ounces)

1 cup mizuna or baby spinach leaves, trimmed, washed, and dried (1 to 2 ounces)

Leaves from 1 head celery

½ cup basil leaves (green or purple), torn into small pieces

½ cup chervil sprigs

¼ cup chopped chives

Consider this a guide to building a mixed green salad and use whichever leaves are available at the grocery store or farmers' market. The addition of fresh herbs and celery leaves provides for an extra flavor boost.

Combine the vinegar with the mustard and garlic in a small bowl and whisk in the olive oil. Season with salt and pepper to taste.

Just before serving, toss the romaine, mâche, oak leaf lettuce, mizuna or spinach, celery leaves, and herbs in a large bowl with just enough of the vinaigrette to lightly coat them (you may not need all of the vinaigrette). Season with salt and pepper to taste and serve. —*Annie Wayte*

How to wash salad greens

To minimize bruising, wash greens in a large bowl of cold water rather than under running water. Gently swirl the leaves in the water to encourage the soil and grit to disperse. Then lift the leaves out, drain the water in the bowl, and repeat until the leaves are thoroughly clean. Finally, spin the leaves in small batches in a salad spinner until thoroughly dry. The salad spinner should be only half full. If you overload it, the greens won't dry well.

Arugula & Fennel Salad with Orange & Fennel Seed Dressing & Toasted Hazelnuts

Orange and fennel seeds add a lovely aromatic note to peppery arugula, while thin slices of fennel and chopped hazelnuts provide a nice crunch.

Toast the fennel seeds lightly in a small dry skillet over medium heat for about 2 minutes. Transfer to a cutting board and let the seeds cool. Chop them coarsely.

Combine the orange juice, lemon juice, shallot, orange zest, and garlic in a small bowl. Let sit for 20 minutes and then stir in the fennel seeds and Dijon mustard. Whisk in the olive oil and hazelnut oil and season to taste with salt and pepper.

Cut off the top and bottom of the fennel bulb. Cut it in half lengthwise. Lay one half flat on its cut surface and slice crosswise as thinly as possible. Stop slicing when you hit the core (a little core is all right, but you don't want wide areas of core in your slices). Repeat with the second half. You should have about 1½ cups sliced fennel.

Put the sliced fennel in a large bowl with the arugula and toasted hazelnuts. Toss with enough of the dressing to lightly coat the leaves (you may not need all of the dressing). Season with salt and pepper to taste and serve.

—*Annie Wayte*

Serves four.

½ teaspoon fennel seeds

¼ cup fresh orange juice

1 tablespoon fresh lemon juice

1 tablespoon minced shallot

2 teaspoons finely grated orange zest

Scant ¼ teaspoon minced garlic

¼ teaspoon Dijon mustard

1½ tablespoons extra-virgin olive oil

1½ tablespoons hazelnut oil

Kosher salt and freshly ground black pepper

1 small fennel bulb

5 ounces arugula, trimmed, washed, and dried (about 5 cups)

¼ cup hazelnuts, toasted and coarsely chopped

Butter Lettuce with Poppy Seed & Tarragon Crème Fraîche Dressing

Serves six.

1 tablespoon poppy seeds

¼ cup crème fraîche

2 tablespoons plain yogurt

2 tablespoons coarsely chopped fresh tarragon plus 2 tablespoons whole tarragon leaves

2 teaspoons fresh lemon juice

¼ teaspoon minced garlic

Pinch cayenne

Kosher salt

2 or 3 heads butter lettuce (about 12 ounces total), trimmed, washed, dried, and torn by hand into bite-size pieces (about 10 cups)

Freshly ground black pepper

Crème fraîche gives this salad a mild tanginess that marries beautifully with butter lettuce's delicate flavor. Toasting the poppy seeds further enhances their flavor and adds another layer of depth to this dressing.

Toast the poppy seeds lightly in a small skillet over medium heat for 1 to 2 minutes. Transfer to a cool plate.

In a small bowl, combine the crème fraîche, yogurt, chopped tarragon, lemon juice, garlic, and poppy seeds. Stir in 1 or 2 tablespoons water to thin the mixture to a creamy salad-dressing consistency. Season with cayenne and salt to taste.

Just before serving, toss the butter lettuce in a large bowl with just enough of the dressing to lightly coat the leaves. Season with salt and pepper to taste. Arrange the salad on individual serving plates, scatter the whole tarragon leaves on the top, and serve. —*Annie Wayte*

In summertime, grocery stores and farmers'
markets abound with a variety of salad greens,
ranging from sweet to spicy to bitter, with textures
that can be silky, crunchy, or even bristly. Here are
some wonderful varieties to look for.

Watercress

has a spicy kick and is very versatile.
It's often used in sandwiches and
soups, but it will be the star of a
salad. Trim the base of the stalks and
keep the bouquet of leaves intact.

Mâche

is also known as lamb's lettuce. It has dainty,
velvety-textured leaves with a mild yet tangy
flavor. It's usually sold in small rosettes with
the root attached. Use it alone or tossed into
a mixed green salad.

Butter lettuce

(including bibb and Boston) has a subtle,
buttery flavor that marries well with citrus
and dairy-based vinaigrettes. The silken
leaves require very gentle handling.

Red & green leaf lettuces

(such as the frilly Lollo Rossa and the smooth Red Oak Leaf) have leaves that grow from a single stalk in a loose bunch rather than forming a tight head. They have a sweet, delicate flavor that's delicious both on its own and mixed with other greens.

Mizuna

looks pretty and has a mild, earthy flavor, which makes it a great salad green on its own, although it also blends well with other leaves. Keep the leaves whole.

Romaine

has a sweet, gentle flavor and a crisp bite, and it's versatile: It partners well with most greens and a variety of dressings. For milder flavor and softer texture, remove the outer leaves or buy hearts of romaine.

Garden Lettuces with Garlic Chapons

Serves six.

¾ **pound crusty, country-style bread (such as an Italian bâtard or levain)**

6 **tablespoons extra-virgin olive oil; more for brushing on the bread**

Kosher salt

1 **clove garlic, peeled and halved**

2 **medium shallots, minced (about ¼ cup)**

3 **tablespoons sherry vinegar or red-wine vinegar**

6 **large handfuls mixed baby lettuce (about ½ pound), washed and spun dry**

Freshly ground black pepper

Chapons are large, rustic croutons that are made from the crust of bread rather than the crumb and then rubbed with garlic. They add a nice hint of garlic to a simple tossed green salad.

Position a rack in the center of the oven and heat the oven to 400°F.

Using a serrated knife, carve the crust off the bread into rustic, curved slabs that are about ¼ inch thick. Save the rest of the bread for another use (such as making breadcrumbs). Brush the crusts on both sides with olive oil and season lightly with salt. Put the crusts on a baking sheet and bake until crisp and golden brown, 6 to 8 minutes. When cool enough to handle, rub the crusts lightly with the cut sides of the garlic clove. Snap the crusts into bite-size pieces. Discard the garlic.

In a small bowl, combine the shallots and vinegar with a pinch of salt and let sit for at least 10 minutes and up to 2 hours.

When ready to serve, put the chapons and lettuce in a large mixing bowl and season with a generous pinch of salt and a few grinds of pepper. Drizzle the lettuce with the 6 tablespoons olive oil. Scoop the shallots out of the vinegar and sprinkle them on the lettuce. Gently toss the salad, making sure that all of the lettuce is evenly dressed. Taste and adjust the seasoning with more olive oil, the remaining vinegar in the bowl (or more if necessary), salt, and pepper. Serve immediately on a chilled platter or individual plates, with the chapons tucked in among the lettuces. —*Tasha DeSerio*

Mâche with Spicy Melon & Pink-Peppercorn Dressing

Serves four.

1 teaspoon pink peppercorns

3 tablespoons unsalted sunflower seeds

1 medium ripe melon (cantaloupe, Crenshaw, Charentais, or Galia), peeled, cut into thirds, and seeded

1 tablespoon white balsamic vinegar; more to taste

2 teaspoons fresh lime juice; more to taste

¼ teaspoon chopped fresh hot chile (such as serrano, jalapeño, or Thai bird)

¼ teaspoon minced garlic

1 tablespoon extra-virgin olive oil

1 teaspoon coarsely chopped mint leaves, plus 12 large mint leaves, torn into small pieces

Kosher salt

3 ounces mâche, trimmed, washed, and dried (about 3½ cups)

Mâche, a tender lettuce, has been popular in Europe but has just recently made the jump to American markets. It has a mild flavor and often comes in tiny clusters. Puréed melon adds a hint of sweetness to the dressing, while pink peppercorns impart a perfumy note to this pretty salad.

Toast the pink peppercorns lightly in a small dry skillet over medium heat for 1 to 2 minutes. Lightly crush them with a mortar and pestle or on a cutting board with the bottom of another small skillet. Set aside. In the same skillet you used to toast the peppercorns, lightly toast the sunflower seeds over medium heat for 1 to 2 minutes. Remove from the pan and set aside.

Coarsely chop approximately one-third of the melon and purée it in a blender until smooth, about 45 seconds. You should have 1 scant cup melon purée. Pour it into a medium bowl and add the vinegar, lime juice, chile, garlic, and half the crushed peppercorns. Slowly whisk in the olive oil. Stir in the chopped mint leaves and salt to taste. If the dressing is too sweet, add a little more vinegar or lime juice.

Just before serving, cut the remaining melon lengthwise into 8 long, elegant slices, each about 1 inch thick. In a large bowl, toss the mâche and torn mint leaves with just enough of the dressing to lightly coat the leaves. Season with salt to taste. Arrange the mâche on serving plates with two slices of melon per plate. Scatter the toasted sunflower seeds and remaining pink peppercorns on the top. Serve the remaining melon dressing on the side. —*Annie Wayte*

The best way to store salad greens

The way in which you store delicate salad greens makes a big difference in how long they stay fresh. Greens can remain fresh for as long as two weeks using this method from food scientist Shirley Corriher.

Discard any leaves that have brown spots. Soak the greens in very cold water for 15 to 30 minutes to replenish water lost since harvesting, and then spin them dry. Wrap them loosely in dry paper towels, and put them in a zip-top plastic bag. The towels absorb excess moisture, so the greens stay moist enough that they don't wilt but not so moist that they get soggy and rot.

Partially seal the bag, gently squeeze out as much air as possible without crushing the greens, and then finish sealing the bag. This step limits the greens' exposure to air and slows down their breathing—that's right, they breathe—which in turn slows deterioration. Store the greens in your refrigerator's produce bin.

Spinach Salad with Apples, Dried Apricots & Pappadam Croutons

Serves six as a first course, four as a main course.

For the vinaigrette:

¼ cup extra-virgin olive oil

½ teaspoon curry powder

¼ teaspoon ground cumin

1 medium clove garlic, minced (about 1 teaspoon)

2½ tablespoons fresh lemon juice (from 1 large lemon)

Kosher salt and freshly ground black pepper

For the salad:

½ cup whole almonds (about 3 ounces)

Four 7-inch round plain, cumin-seed, or black-peppercorn pappadams

10 cups loosely packed baby spinach leaves, washed and dried (about 10 ounces)

1 small red apple (preferably Gala, Cortland, or McIntosh), cored and thinly sliced

1 small tart green apple (preferably Granny Smith or Pippin), cored and thinly sliced

¾ cup dried apricots (about 5 ounces), thinly sliced

Pappadam is a traditional Indian flatbread often made from lentil flour. It has a light and crisp quality. It is the perfect foil for the tart apples and sweet dried apricots in this salad. Toasting spices is also another distinctive characteristic of Indian cooking. Here the spices are heated in olive oil, further infusing it with their essential oils.

Position a rack in the center of the oven and heat the oven to 375°F.

Make the vinaigrette: In a small saucepan or skillet, heat the olive oil, curry powder, cumin, and garlic over medium-low heat until sizzling and very fragrant, 1 to 2 minutes. Set aside until cool. Whisk in the lemon juice and season to taste with salt and pepper.

Make the salad: Scatter the almonds on a baking sheet and bake in the oven until lightly browned and fragrant, 8 to 12 minutes. Remove from the oven and let cool. Chop coarsely.

Turn off the oven, position a rack 6 inches from the broiler element and heat the broiler on high. Arrange the pappadams in a single layer on a baking sheet and broil until they bubble and crisp on one side, 15 to 30 seconds. Don't let them take on more than a light golden color. Turn the pappadams over and continue to broil until bubbly and crisp on the other side, about 5 seconds. Remove from the oven and let cool—they will continue to crisp. Break each pappadam into several pieces.

In a large bowl, toss the spinach, apples, apricots, and almonds with enough of the dressing to coat lightly. Divide the salad among four or six plates, garnish with the pappadam pieces, and serve immediately.

—Joanne Weir

Garlic Crostini with Spinach, Mushroom & Parmigiano Salad

Serves six as a first course, four as a main course.

For the vinaigrette:

2 tablespoons extra-virgin olive oil

1 tablespoon fresh lemon juice (from about half a lemon)

1 teaspoon finely grated lemon zest (from about half a lemon)

1 small shallot, minced (1½ tablespoons)

1 medium clove garlic, minced

Kosher salt and freshly ground black pepper

For the salad and crostini:

Six ½-inch-thick slices coarse-textured Tuscan-style bread

2 cloves garlic, cut in half lengthwise

Kosher salt

2 tablespoons extra-virgin olive oil; more for drizzling

10 ounces small fresh button mushrooms, stems discarded, caps halved (about 2½ cups)

Freshly ground black pepper

6 cups loosely packed baby spinach leaves, washed and dried (about 6 ounces)

Parmigiano-Reggiano for shaving

The color contrast between the dark green spinach leaves and white mushrooms is both striking and elegant. The simple vinaigrette allows all of the flavors to really shine. And the crostini provide a satisfying crunch.

Make the vinaigrette: In a small bowl, whisk together the vinaigrette ingredients, seasoning to taste with the salt and pepper.

Make the salad: Position a rack 6 inches from the broiler element and heat the broiler on high. Arrange the bread slices on a baking sheet and broil until crispy and light golden on top, 1 to 2 minutes. Flip and broil the other sides until golden, about 1 minute. Rub one side of the toasted bread with the cut sides of the garlic. Sprinkle each slice with a small pinch of salt and set aside.

Heat the oil in a 10-inch skillet over medium-high heat. When the oil is shimmering, add the mushrooms and stir to coat in the oil. Let the mushrooms cook undisturbed until the liquid they release evaporates and they're deep golden brown, 5 to 7 minutes. Sprinkle with ½ teaspoon salt, stir, and continue cooking, stirring occasionally, until most sides are nicely browned, 3 to 5 minutes more. Season to taste with more salt and pepper. Remove from the heat and let cool slightly.

Toss the spinach and vinaigrette in a large bowl. Put the bread slices on four or six plates and drizzle each slice with a little olive oil. Divide the spinach among the plates, arranging it on the top of the bread but leaving part of the bread exposed. Top with the mushrooms. Using a cheese shaver or vegetable peeler, shave a few thin slivers of Parmigiano over the top. Serve immediately.

—Joanne Weir

Arugula Salad with Pears, Prosciutto & Aged Gouda

Serves four.

2 tablespoons white-wine vinegar

½ teaspoon Dijon mustard

¼ teaspoon kosher salt

⅛ teaspoon freshly ground black pepper

¼ cup extra-virgin olive oil

5 to 6 ounces arugula, any large stems removed, leaves washed and dried (6 loosely packed cups)

2 medium ripe pears, peeled if you like, cored, and cut into 1-inch chunks

4 thin slices prosciutto, cut crosswise into ½-inch-wide ribbons

3 ounces aged Gouda, cut into 2-inch-long sticks (1 cup)

1 ounce walnuts, toasted and coarsely chopped (¼ cup)

Gouda that's been aged for a couple of years takes on a rich, almost toffee-like character; the older it is, the drier and more intense the flavor becomes. (Don't worry if it falls apart when you cut it.) If you can't find aged Gouda, try Comté, Gruyère, or Parmigiano-Reggiano.

In a small bowl, whisk the vinegar, mustard, salt, and pepper. Slowly whisk in the oil.

In a large salad or mixing bowl, toss the arugula and the pears with half of the dressing. Divide among four plates, scatter the prosciutto and cheese on top of each salad, and drizzle with a little of the remaining dressing. Sprinkle on the nuts and serve immediately. —*Martha Holmberg*

Five tips for a perfectly dressed salad

Thoroughly dry the leaves before adding the dressing. Droplets of water will dilute your dressing and prevent it from clinging to the leaves.

Dress your salad just before you serve it. Tossing the greens with the dressing any earlier will cause them to become limp and soggy.

Use just enough dressing to lightly coat the greens. Pick up and taste a leaf as a test. If it needs a little more moisture, add a few additional drops of dressing. But keep checking the leaves to make sure they don't become too wet.

Toss with your hands. Tossing a salad with clean hands rather than utensils is easier on the leaves. You can also get a feel for whether the leaves have enough dressing.

Scatter a few toppings on the salad for excitement—just be sure to use a light hand. Chopped or whole fresh herbs such as basil, mint, parsley, chives, cilantro, chervil, tarragon, dill, and celery leaves contribute a bright, aromatic note. Thinly sliced raw vegetables like fennel, zucchini, radishes, and mushrooms add flavor and texture. Toasted whole sunflower, poppy, or sesame seeds are good for crunch. And toasted and chopped nuts add both crunch and richness.

Carrot Salad with Walnut Oil & Honey

Serves six.

1½ pounds carrots, peeled and grated on the medium holes of a box grater

1 cup walnuts, toasted and chopped

½ cup dried currants

1 orange, juiced (about ½ cup)

3 tablespoons apple-cider vinegar

1 tablespoon honey

3 tablespoons untoasted walnut oil

Kosher or sea salt

Freshly ground black pepper

2½ tablespoons finely chopped fresh chives

You might be surprised how well the toasty flavors of the walnuts and walnut oil complement the freshly grated carrot. This salad would be a delicious accompaniment to roast pork or chicken.

Combine the grated carrots, walnuts, and currants in a medium serving bowl.

In a small bowl, whisk together the orange juice, cider vinegar, and honey. Slowly whisk in the walnut oil. Season with salt and pepper to taste.

Toss the carrot mixture with the vinaigrette and 2 tablespoons of the chives. Adjust the seasoning to taste. You can serve the salad immediately, but it will taste even better if you let it sit at room temperature for 15 to 20 minutes. Sprinkle with the remaining ½ tablespoon chives right before serving.

—Dan Barber

Chopped Tomato & Cucumber Salad with Mint & Feta

This salad is a great addition to a large summer buffet, though it also makes a fine lunch or light dinner accompanied by some warm pita. If you are serving it as a main course, toss in some diced grilled chicken breasts for more substance.

In a medium bowl, toss the tomatoes with ¼ cup of the mint, ½ tablespoon of the thyme, the salt, and ½ teaspoon of the pepper. In another medium bowl, toss the feta with the lemon zest, the remaining ½ teaspoon pepper, ¼ cup mint, and ½ tablespoon thyme. Let both sit for at least 15 minutes and up to 1 hour at room temperature.

In a large bowl, toss the cucumber, scallions, and olives with the tomatoes and feta. Combine up to 1 hour ahead; let sit at room temperature. Just before serving, add the olive oil and half of the lemon juice and toss well. Season with pepper and more lemon juice if needed, and serve. —*Tony Rosenfeld*

Serves ten to twelve.

- 2 pints ripe grape or cherry tomatoes, halved lengthwise
- ½ cup lightly chopped fresh mint
- 1 tablespoon chopped fresh thyme
- 2 teaspoons kosher salt
- 1 teaspoon freshly ground black pepper; more as needed
- ½ pound feta cheese, coarsely crumbled (2 cups)
- 1 lemon, zest finely grated (1 tablespoon) and juiced (¼ cup)
- 1 English (seedless) cucumber, cut into ½ -inch dice (4 cups)
- 4 scallions (both white and green parts), trimmed and thinly sliced (½ cup)
- 2 cups pitted Kalamata or Gaeta olives, halved
- ⅓ cup extra-virgin olive oil

Warm Spinach Salad with Eggs, Bacon & Croutons

Serves six as a first course, four as a main course.

2 large eggs

Kosher salt

4½ tablespoons extra-virgin olive oil

2 cloves garlic, crushed and peeled

3 to 4 ounces rustic, coarse-textured bread, crust removed, cut into ¾-inch cubes (to yield 3 cups)

3 tablespoons sherry vinegar

1 tablespoon Dijon mustard

Freshly ground black pepper

3 slices bacon, cut into ¾-inch squares

1 small shallot, minced (1½ tablespoons)

10 cups loosely packed baby spinach leaves, washed and dried (about 10 ounces)

When buying spinach, look for leaves that are uniformly green and crisp. Avoid those that are wilted, excessively wet, or yellowed. Fresh spinach can be quite gritty, especially the larger bundled leaves, so wash it very carefully.

Put the eggs in a small saucepan of water and bring to a boil over medium-high heat. Boil for 4 minutes. Turn off the heat and let cool in the water. When the eggs are cool, crack and peel them. Chop the eggs, season to taste with salt, and reserve.

Position a rack in the center of the oven and heat the oven to 375°F. Heat 1½ tablespoons of the olive oil in a small saucepan over medium-high heat. Add the garlic and cook, stirring occasionally, until it starts to turn gold, about 1 minute. Discard the garlic.

Arrange the bread in a single layer on a baking sheet. Drizzle with the garlic-infused oil, sprinkle with a little salt, and toss. Bake, shaking the bread cubes once, until golden and crispy, 8 to 10 minutes. Remove from the oven and let cool.

In a small bowl, whisk together the remaining 3 tablespoons olive oil, the sherry vinegar, and the mustard. Season with salt and pepper to taste.

In a 10-inch skillet, cook the bacon over medium-high heat, stirring frequently, until golden brown and crisp, 3 to 5 minutes. With a slotted spoon, transfer the bacon to a plate lined with paper towels. Add the shallot to the pan and cook, stirring, until softened, about 1 minute. Let the pan cool slightly and add the vinaigrette to the pan, whisking well to blend the ingredients.

Toss the warm vinaigrette and the spinach together in a large bowl. Transfer to a platter and garnish with the chopped eggs, bacon, and croutons. Serve immediately. —*Joanne Weir*

Grilled Southwestern Potato Salad

Serves ten to twelve.

2 large red onions, cut into ½-inch disks and threaded onto metal skewers

4 red bell peppers, halved, cored, and seeded

¾ cup extra-virgin olive oil

2 teaspoons plus 2 tablespoons kosher salt; more as needed

1 teaspoon freshly ground black pepper; more as needed

1½ cups cooked fresh corn kernels (from 2 ears)

½ pound bacon (8 to 9 slices), cooked until crisp, drained, and crumbled

¾ cup chopped fresh cilantro

1 teaspoon chili powder

3 pounds red potatoes, cut into 1½-inch pieces

3 tablespoons cider vinegar; more as needed

This potato salad is filled with favorite flavorings of the Southwest—corn, chiles, red onions, peppers, and crisp bacon. To add a bit of Southwestern fire, substitute a poblano chile for one of the bell peppers.

Heat a gas grill to medium or prepare a charcoal fire with medium- and low-heat areas. Put the onions and peppers on a rimmed baking sheet and sprinkle with 2 tablespoons of the oil, 2 teaspoons of the salt, and the pepper. Turn and rub the vegetables to coat all over with the oil and seasonings.

Grill the vegetables, covered, until they have good grill marks, about 5 minutes. Flip, cover, and continue to grill until the peppers are softened and nicely browned, about 5 more minutes. As they finish cooking, transfer the peppers to the baking sheet. Reduce the heat on the gas grill to medium low or transfer the onions to the cooler part of the fire and continue cooking until they are just tender and browned (it's fine if they're charred in places), about 8 more minutes. Move to a cutting board and let cool. Scrape the skins off the peppers if you like. Coarsely chop the peppers and onions and toss in a large serving bowl along with the corn, bacon, cilantro, and chili powder.

Put the potatoes in a large pot, cover with cold water by a couple of inches, stir in the remaining 2 tablespoons salt, and bring to a boil. Reduce to a simmer, cover, and cook until the potatoes are just tender, 12 to 15 minutes. Drain and toss with the grilled vegetables, the remaining ½ cup plus 2 tablespoons oil, and the vinegar. Season with salt, pepper, and more vinegar to taste. Let sit at least 30 minutes and up to 2 hours at room temperature before serving.
—*Tony Rosenfeld*

Grilled Corn, Shrimp & Chorizo Salad

Serves eight.

For the vinaigrette:

⅔ cup extra-virgin olive oil; more for drizzling

4 to 5 large cloves garlic, peeled and grated on the small holes of a box grater to yield about 2 tablespoons

Kosher salt

1 teaspoon sweet smoked paprika (Spanish pimentón)

⅓ cup sherry vinegar

Freshly ground black pepper

For the salad:

8 large ears fresh corn, husked

Extra-virgin olive oil

Kosher salt

1 cup thinly sliced scallions, both white and green parts (about 1 large bunch)

24 easy-peel shrimp in the shell (16 to 20 per pound)

4 Spanish chorizo sausages (about 14 ounces total), split lengthwise

1 pint cherry or grape tomatoes, cut in half

Freshly ground black pepper

1 recipe Grilled Garlic Bread, (see recipe on page 17)

This one-dish meal marries the best flavors from summer shore dinners—seafood and corn—with the smokiness of Spanish paprika and chorizo.

Make the vinaigrette: Combine the olive oil and the grated garlic in a small saucepan. Cook over low heat until the garlic begins to brown slightly, about 10 minutes. Add a pinch of salt and stir to dissolve. Remove from the heat and let sit until the oil cools a bit, about 3 minutes. Add the paprika and let it infuse the oil for about 12 minutes more. Strain the oil through a fine sieve and discard the garlic. (If making in advance, store in the refrigerator for up to 2 days.)

Put the vinegar in a small bowl. Add a pinch of salt and a couple of grinds of black pepper and whisk to combine. Slowly drizzle in the garlic-paprika oil, whisking constantly until well incorporated. Taste and adjust the seasonings if necessary.

Make the salad: Prepare a medium-hot charcoal or gas grill fire. Brush the corn all over with olive oil and season with salt. Grill, covered, turning occasionally until all sides are charred and deeply blistered in places, 6 to 10 minutes. Remove from the grill, cut the kernels off the cobs while still warm, and put the kernels in a large bowl. Add half the vinaigrette and toss to coat the kernels. Stir in the scallions and set aside.

Reduce the grill temperature to medium, or if using charcoal, let the coals die down a bit. Grill the shrimp and the sausages, turning once halfway through the cooking time, until the shrimp are pink, curled, and cooked through, 4 to 6 minutes, and the sausages are plump and well browned, 5 to 8 minutes. Transfer the shrimp and sausages to separate platters and cover with foil to keep warm.

While still warm, peel the shrimp and gently fold into the salad, along with the rest of the vinaigrette. Slice the sausages into ⅓-inch-thick half-moons and mix into the salad. Add the tomatoes and mix gently. Taste and season with pepper and more salt if necessary. Serve the salad warm or at room temperature spooned over slices of the grilled garlic bread. —*Elizabeth Karmel*

Lemony Chicken Caesar Salad with Garlic-Parmesan Toasts

Serves four to six as a main course.

For the vinaigrette:

1 lemon

¼ cup freshly grated Parmigiano-Reggiano

2 tablespoons mascarpone (or cream cheese)

2 teaspoons Dijon mustard

1 small clove garlic, chopped, sprinkled with a pinch of kosher salt, and mashed to a paste

¼ teaspoon Worcestershire® sauce

½ cup extra-virgin olive oil

1 teaspoon chopped fresh thyme

Couple dashes of Tabasco

Kosher salt and freshly ground black pepper

For the salad:

2 tablespoons extra-virgin olive oil

1 small clove garlic, chopped, sprinkled with a pinch of kosher salt, and mashed to a paste

⅛ teaspoon crushed red pepper flakes

½ baguette, cut into eight ½-inch-thick slices on an extreme diagonal so they're about 6 inches long

¾ cup freshly grated Parmigiano-Reggiano

2 cups thinly sliced leftover roast chicken

1 pound romaine hearts (about 2 medium), cored, washed, spun dry, and cut into 2-inch pieces

This take on Caesar salad is lighter and brighter than most. Lemon juice and zest punch up the vinaigrette, while a little mascarpone, instead of the traditional raw egg yolks, creates richness. If you're not roasting your own chicken, use a rotisserie bird.

Make the vinaigrette: Finely grate about 1 tablespoon zest from the lemon. Squeeze the lemon to get 2 tablespoons juice. In a blender or mini chopper, purée (as much as possible) the lemon juice, Parmigiano, mascarpone, mustard, garlic, and Worcestershire sauce, scraping the sides as needed. While puréeing, drizzle in the oil, slowly at first and then in a more steady stream as the mixture thickens and emulsifies. Thin the vinaigrette with water if needed. Add the lemon zest, thyme, and Tabasco and purée. Taste and season generously with salt and pepper (about 1 teaspoon of each) and more lemon juice if you like.

Prepare the salad: Heat the oven to 425°F. In a small bowl, mix the oil, garlic, and red pepper flakes. Set the baguette slices on a baking sheet and brush them with the oil mixture. Sprinkle with ¼ cup of the Parmigiano. Bake until browned, 10 to 12 minutes.

In a small bowl, toss the chicken with about ¼ cup of the vinaigrette. In a large bowl, toss the romaine and ¼ cup of the Parmigiano with enough of the vinaigrette to coat lightly (you might not need it all). Add salt and pepper to taste.

Put the dressed greens on plates and top with the chicken and a drizzle of dressing, if any remains. Sprinkle with the remaining ¼ cup Parmigiano and some black pepper and serve immediately with the toasts. —*Tony Rosenfeld*

Thai Seafood Salad (*Yum Talay*)

Serves four as a light main course or six as an appetizer.

6 tablespoons fresh lime juice (from 2 limes)

4½ tablespoons fish sauce

1½ tablespoons granulated sugar

2 teaspoons finely chopped unseeded fresh hot green chiles (like serrano or jalapeño)

2 teaspoons finely chopped garlic (2 medium cloves)

3 tablespoons thinly sliced shallot (1 large)

⅓ cup thinly sliced scallions (4 to 5, white and green parts)

¼ cup coarsely chopped fresh cilantro

¼ cup coarsely chopped fresh mint

2 cups bite-size pieces of Boston lettuce, rinsed and spun dry (1 large head)

4 cups cooked seafood (see instructions on page 74)

½ cup sliced English cucumber (halve cucumber lengthwise and slice into ¼-inch-thick half-moons)

½ cup halved cherry or grape tomatoes

This dish is easy to pull together, but it does require a little organization and prep. First cook the seafood, then make the dressing, and finally mix the dressing and seafood right before serving—this is the key to keeping the vibrant flavors of this signature Thai dish distinct.

Make the dressing: In a medium-large bowl, combine the lime juice, fish sauce, sugar, chiles, and garlic. Stir to dissolve the sugar and combine everything well. Set aside, along with the shallots, scallions, cilantro, and mint for mixing just before serving.

Assemble the salad: Arrange the lettuce on a large serving platter or on individual serving plates as a bed for the seafood.

Transfer the cooked seafood to the bowl containing the lime-juice dressing. Add the shallots and use your hands or a wooden spoon to gently toss everything well. Add the scallions, cilantro, and mint and mix well again. Scoop the seafood onto the platter or serving plates with a slotted spoon. Toss the cucumber and tomato in the dressing remaining in the bowl and scatter around the seafood. Drizzle any remaining dressing from the bowl over the salad, especially over any lettuce not covered by the seafood. Serve immediately. —*Nancie McDermott*

What's the best way to prep the herbs?

In some Thai dishes, like soups and curries, herb sprigs and leaves are often left whole. But for a *yum*, the herbs are chopped coarsely at the last minute, so their flavor won't have time to fade.

Whole mint

Whole cilantro

Coarsely chopped herbs

Cooked Seafood for Thai Salad

You can find frozen cleaned squid in 1-pound packages in the freezer section. Some markets have thawed cleaned squid on ice at the seafood counter. When you buy fresh mussels they still have *beards*. Beards are a hair-like tail attached to the side of the mussel shells that must be removed prior to cooking.

Yields about 4 cups.

24 small mussels

1 tablespoon table salt

¾ pound medium (51 to 60 per pound) fresh shrimp, peeled and deveined

½ pound cleaned squid, bodies sliced crosswise into ¼-inch rings and tentacles cut in half if large

½ pound sea scallops or bay scallops

¼ pound fresh or pasteurized jumbo lump crabmeat

Scrub the mussels well under running water and gently pull off any beards. Discard any mussels that don't close tightly when tapped on the counter. Put closed mussels in a medium saucepan. Add about ½ cup water, just enough to cover the bottom of the pan by about ¼ inch. Cover and set over high heat. Bring to a rolling boil and cook until the shells have opened, 1 to 2 minutes. Remove from the heat, transfer to a plate, and let stand until cool enough to handle. Discard any unopened mussels. Remove the cooked mussels from their shells and put in a medium bowl; discard the shells and cooking liquid.

To cook the remaining seafood, bring a 3-quart saucepan of water to a rolling boil over high heat. Add the salt and let the water return to a boil. Pour the shrimp into the boiling water and cook until the largest one is pink on the outside, opaque on the inside, and just cooked through, about 2 minutes. The water may not return to the boil before they are done. Scoop them out with a slotted spoon and drop into the bowl with the mussels.

After the water returns to a rolling boil, add the squid and cook just until they become firm and the rings turn bright white, about 1 minute. Scoop them out and drop them into the bowl along with the shrimp and mussels.

When the water returns to a rolling boil, cook the scallops until just cooked through and no longer translucent inside, 1 to 2 minutes for bay scallops, 2 to 3 minutes for sea scallops. Scoop them out and drop into the bowl as well (if using sea scallops, you may want to halve or quarter them first).

Add the lump crabmeat chunks to the bowl of seafood. Set the seafood aside on the counter while you prepare the dressing and other ingredients for the salad. Or, if making more than 30 minutes ahead, cover and refrigerate for up to 4 hours. Let sit at room temperature for 20 to 30 minutes before dressing.

—*Nancie McDermott*

Colossal Shrimp with Watercress & Tomato Salad

Colossal shrimp are often called prawns in the United States, even though prawns are technically a different creature. For this recipe, look for shrimp that weighs about 2 ounces each, which means each diner gets plenty to eat with just two shrimp. To help the shrimp cook evenly, arrange them on the broiler pan in a line that will be directly under the broiler element.

Peel and chop the garlic clove. Sprinkle with ¼ teaspoon of the salt and, using the side of a chef's knife, mash and scrape the garlic into a paste. Transfer to a medium bowl and whisk in half the onion, 2 tablespoons of the olive oil, 2 tablespoons of the parsley, 1 tablespoon of the lemon juice, 1 teaspoon of the zest, and a generous ⅛ teaspoon pepper. Add the shrimp and marinate, stirring occasionally, for 20 minutes.

Meanwhile, in another bowl, stir together the tomatoes, ¾ teaspoon salt, the remaining onion, and the remaining ¼ cup olive oil, ¼ cup parsley, 2 tablespoons lemon juice, 2 teaspoons zest, and ¼ teaspoon pepper. Stir from time to time.

Position an oven rack 3 to 4 inches from the broiler element and heat the broiler to high. Line the bottom of a broiler pan with foil and replace the perforated top part of the pan. Arrange the shrimp on the broiler pan. Broil until the shrimp are beginning to turn bright pink and are firm to the touch on top, about 3 minutes. Turn the shrimp over, rotate the broiler pan from back to front, and broil until the shrimp are just opaque throughout (cut into a piece to check), 1 to 2 minutes longer.

To serve, arrange the watercress on four plates, top with the tomatoes and their sauce, and arrange two shrimp on top. *—Lori Longbotham*

Serves four.

- 1 clove garlic
- 1 teaspoon kosher salt
- 1 small red onion, finely diced (about ¾ cup)
- 6 tablespoons extra-virgin olive oil
- 6 tablespoons coarsely chopped fresh flat-leaf parsley
- 3 tablespoons fresh lemon juice
- 3 teaspoons finely grated lemon zest (from 1 lemon)
- ⅜ teaspoon freshly ground black pepper
- 8 colossal shrimp (6 to 8 count; about 1 pound), peeled and deveined
- 2 pints red or yellow grape or cherry tomatoes, or a combination, halved
- 8 cups watercress sprigs, washed and dried (from about 8 ounces untrimmed watercress)

Chinese Chicken Salad

Serves four as a main course.

For the salad:

2 bone-in, skin-on split chicken breasts (about 2¼ pounds)

Kosher salt and freshly ground black pepper

8 square wonton wrappers

Vegetable oil cooking spray

⅔ cup sliced almonds

2 ounces snow peas, trimmed and cut on the diagonal into thirds (½ cup)

1 tablespoon white sesame seeds

½ small head Napa cabbage, trimmed and cut crosswise into ½-inch-wide strips (3 to 3½ cups)

½ romaine heart, cut crosswise into ½-inch-wide strips (1½ to 2 cups)

3 large scallions (white and green parts), thinly sliced on the diagonal (½ cup)

For the dressing:

¼ cup rice vinegar

1½ tablespoons tamari or soy sauce

1 tablespoon sweet Asian chile sauce

2 medium cloves garlic, finely chopped (2 teaspoons)

2 teaspoons minced fresh ginger

½ teaspoon kosher salt

½ teaspoon hot Asian chile sauce

¼ teaspoon freshly ground black pepper

¼ cup peanut oil

1 tablespoon Asian sesame oil

The bright dressing in this fresh take on the popular restaurant salad gets its sweet and hot flavors from two types of Asian chile sauces, tamari, garlic, and fresh ginger, all balanced by the cool acidity of rice vinegar. Most supermarkets carry sweet and hot chile sauces, but if you have trouble finding them, try an Asian market.

Prepare the salad ingredients: Heat the oven to 425°F. Season the chicken breasts with salt and pepper. Roast on a rack set in a rimmed baking sheet or roasting pan until an instant-read thermometer inserted in the thickest part of a breast registers 165°F, 40 to 45 minutes. Let cool.

Remove and discard the skin and then shred the meat. Reduce the oven temperature to 375°F.

Stack the wonton wrappers on a cutting board and cut them into ½-inch-wide strips. Line a baking sheet with foil and spray lightly with cooking spray. Separate the strips, lay them on the baking sheet, and mist them lightly with the cooking spray. Sprinkle lightly with salt. Scrunch each strip to give it a wavy shape, if you like. Bake at 375°F until golden, 7 to 9 minutes. Reduce the oven heat to 350°F.

Spread the sliced almonds on a baking sheet and toast in the oven until golden, 6 to 8 minutes.

Bring a medium saucepan of salted water to a boil. Have a bowl of ice water ready. Boil the snow peas just until bright green but still crisp, about 20 seconds. Drain and transfer to the ice water to stop the cooking. Drain.

Put the sesame seeds in a dry skillet and shake or stir over medium heat until light golden brown, 3 to 4 minutes. Remove them from the hot pan to prevent overcooking.

Make the dressing and assemble the salad: In a medium bowl, combine the vinegar, tamari, sweet chile sauce, garlic, ginger, salt, hot chile sauce, and pepper. Gradually whisk in the peanut and sesame oils.

In a large bowl, toss the cabbage, romaine, and snow peas. In another bowl, toss the chicken and scallions with ¼ cup of the dressing. Add the chicken to the greens, and then add the sesame seeds and almonds. Toss with enough of the remaining dressing to coat well. Garnish each serving with the baked wonton strips. —*Barbara Lauterbach*

Three ways to add crunch

Blanch the snow peas to set their color and retain their crispness.

Cut the Napa cabbage and romaine crosswise for juicy strips.

Bake—don't fry—the wonton wrapper strips and scrunch them for maximum crunch and eye appeal.

Steak, Egg & Blue Cheese Salad

Serves four.

1 small clove garlic

Kosher salt

3 tablespoons red-wine vinegar

1½ teaspoons Dijon mustard

½ cup plus 1 tablespoon extra-virgin olive oil

Freshly ground black pepper

1 pound beef sirloin steak tips

2 heads Boston lettuce, washed, spun dry, and torn into bite-size pieces (about 6 cups loosely packed)

4 hard-cooked eggs, peeled and quartered lengthwise

¾ cup crumbled blue cheese (about 4 ounces)

1 medium carrot, peeled and very thinly sliced crosswise

6 medium red radishes, thinly sliced

¼ cup 1-inch-long sliced fresh chives

While part of the appeal of this salad is the contrast between warm, juicy steak and cool vegetables, you can also make it with leftover cold steak or roast beef. If you have a mandoline, use it to cut the carrots and radishes into very thin slices.

Roughly chop the garlic, sprinkle it with the generous pinch of salt, and mash it into a paste with the side of a chef's knife. Transfer the garlic to a small bowl and whisk in the vinegar and mustard. Whisk in the ½ cup oil in a thin, steady stream. Season the vinaigrette to taste with salt and pepper. Drizzle the sirloin tips with 2 tablespoons of the vinaigrette and let sit while preparing the other salad ingredients. Reserve the remaining vinaigrette for dressing the salad.

Season the meat all over with 1 teaspoon salt and ½ teaspoon pepper. Heat the remaining 1 tablespoon oil in a 10-inch skillet (preferably cast iron), over high heat. When the oil is shimmering hot, add the meat and sear on both sides until cooked to your liking, about 3 minutes per side for medium rare. Let the meat rest briefly on a cutting board while assembling the salad.

Put the lettuce in a large serving bowl. Whisk the vinaigrette and toss the lettuce with just enough of the vinaigrette to coat. Slice the sirloin tips on the diagonal into ½-inch-thick medallions. Scatter the meat (and any accumulated juices), eggs, cheese, carrot, radishes, and chives on top of the lettuce. Drizzle the toppings with some of the remaining vinaigrette to taste (you may not need it all) and toss gently at the table. Serve any remaining vinaigrette on the side. —*Allison Ehri Kreitler*

Warm French Lentil Salad with Smoked Sausage

Serves four to six.

1½ cups du Puy lentils (about 10 ounces)

3 sprigs fresh thyme

2 bay leaves

3 garlic cloves, smashed

¼ teaspoon black peppercorns

1 small onion, peeled

1 small carrot, peeled and split lengthwise

8 ounces smoked sausage, such as kielbasa

1 cup dry white wine or dry white vermouth

2½ tablespoons red-wine vinegar; more as needed

2 teaspoon Dijon mustard

Kosher salt

3 tablespoons extra-virgin olive oil

3 tablespoons walnut oil

¼ cup chopped fresh flat-leaf parsley

¼ cup finely chopped scallions (3 to 4 scallions)

Freshly ground black pepper

The very small, dark greenish-brown du Puy lentils (also called French lentils) are firmer than brown lentils and hold their shape better during cooking. In France, the sausage would be saucisson à l'ail, a semi-cooked, smoked garlic sausage. Kielbasa makes a fine substitute.

Pick over and rinse the lentils, and put them in a 3- to 4-quart saucepan. Pile the thyme, bay leaves, garlic, and peppercorns on a 5-inch square of double-layer cheesecloth. Gather up the edges and tie into a little pouch with kitchen twine. Add the pouch to the pan along with the onion and carrot. Fill the pan with cold water to cover the lentils by about 2 inches, and bring to a boil over medium-high heat. Immediately lower to a gentle simmer—boiling can break the lentils—and simmer, uncovered, until just tender, 30 to 40 minutes. (If the water level drops below the surface of the lentils as they simmer, add a little more water.)

Meanwhile, put the sausage in a small saucepan or deep skillet. Add the wine and enough water to cover by about ½ inch. Bring to a simmer. Reduce the heat as needed to cook at a bare simmer (bubbles should only occasionally break the surface), uncovered, until a metal skewer or fork inserted into the center comes out feeling hot to the touch, 15 to 20 minutes.

While the lentils and sausage cook, make the vinaigrette: In a medium bowl, whisk 1½ tablespoons of the vinegar with the mustard and a pinch of salt. In a steady stream, whisk in the olive and walnut oils. Season to taste with salt.

Drain the lentils, discarding the herb pouch, carrot, and onion. Transfer to a large bowl and add 1 teaspoon salt and the remaining 1 tablespoon vinegar, tossing to coat. Drain the sausage, and, if necessary, peel off the casing (bite into a piece first—many sausage casings are thin enough to leave on). Slice into ¼-inch rounds. Add the sausage and vinaigrette to the lentils, tossing to coat. Stir in the parsley and scallions, and season with a generous amount of black pepper, plus more salt and vinegar to taste. *—Molly Stevens*

Season while hot for superior flavor

Toss the lentils with a little vinegar and salt immediately after draining, and you'll see a big boost in the flavor of the salad. Like potatoes, lentils firm up as they cool, which slows their ability to absorb seasonings.

3 Pasta & Grains

p106

p119

Spaghetti with Spicy Shrimp,
Cherry Tomatoes & Herbed Breadcrumbs
(recipe on page 88)

Cavatappi with No-Cook Tomato Sauce

Serves four to six.

- **2 pounds ripe tomatoes (about 3 large or 4 medium), cored and cut into ½-inch dice (about 4 cups)**
- **½ cup good-quality extra-virgin olive oil**
- **⅓ cup roughly chopped fresh flat-leaf parsley or basil or both**
- **1 tablespoon coarsely chopped fresh thyme**
- **1 teaspoon minced garlic (1 medium clove)**
- **1 teaspoon kosher salt; more to taste**
- **¼ teaspoon freshly ground black pepper; more to taste**
- **Pinch of crushed red pepper flakes (optional)**
- **1 pound dried cavatappi, penne or other pasta shape**

It goes without saying that ripe, in-season tomatoes are a must, but how you cut the tomatoes is important, too. A half-inch dice is perfect, because it will give you a juicy sauce while maintaining the integrity of the tomatoes. And don't be afraid to use a good amount of olive oil—it combines with the juices drawn by the salt to make the sauce, as well as adds its rich flavor to the dish, giving it lots of body and depth. Finally, toss the sauce with hot pasta; the heat helps release the flavors in the tomatoes and creates a better integrated dish than if you mixed the sauce with cold pasta.

Combine all the ingredients except the pasta in a nonreactive bowl large enough to hold the tomatoes and the cooked pasta; mix well. Let the sauce sit at room temperature for at least 30 minutes and up to 3 hours.

Bring a large pot of well salted water to a boil over high heat. Add the pasta and cook until done, according to package directions. Drain well.

Toss the sauce with just-cooked pasta. Adjust the seasoning to taste with salt and pepper and serve immediately. *—Evan Kleiman*

While salsa cruda is delicious on its own, you can choose one of these tasty additions for a little variety.

Cheese

Stir the cheese (see choices below) into the No-Cook Tomato Sauce after it has sat at room temperature and just before adding the pasta. In addition to the 1 cup Parmigiano, choose ¼ to ½ pound of another cheese, depending on how strong or sharp it is.

1 cup grated Parmigiano-Reggiano

¼ to ½ pound of one cheese:

Feta, crumbled

Asiago, grated

Maytag blue, chopped

Gorgonzola, chopped

Fresh mozzarella, diced

Fresh goat cheese, crumbled

Basil Pesto

Stir the basil pesto into the No-Cook Tomato Sauce after it has sat at room temperature and just before adding the pasta.

Yields about 1¼ cups.

2 cups firmly packed fresh basil (preferably Italian Genovese)

1 large clove garlic

1 teaspoon kosher salt

Freshly ground black pepper

½ cup extra-virgin olive oil

½ cup freshly grated Parmigiano-Reggiano

½ cup pine nuts or walnuts

Put the basil, garlic, salt, and 2 or 3 grinds of pepper in a food processor and process until the basil and garlic are finely chopped, about 15 seconds. With the machine running, pour ¼ cup of the olive oil down the feed tube in a slow, steady stream. Turn off the processor and add the Parmigiano. Process until the cheese is incorporated, about 20 seconds. With the machine running, slowly add the remaining ¼ cup oil. Add the nuts and pulse until they're coarsely chopped.

Tapenade

Mix half the tapenade into the No-Cook Tomato Sauce before it sits at room temperature. Garnish each serving of pasta with some of the remaining tapenade.

Yields about ¾ cup.

½ cup pitted Kalamata olives

¼ cup pitted green olives

¼ cup pitted oil-cured black olives

3 tablespoons extra-virgin olive oil

1 teaspoon finely grated lemon zest

1 teaspoon minced fresh rosemary (from 1 medium sprig)

Put all of the ingredients in a food processor and pulse until very roughly chopped, about 13 pulses.

Linguine with Clam Sauce

Serves two to three.

24 littleneck clams

6 tablespoons extra-virgin
olive oil

½ teaspoon crushed red pepper
flakes

⅓ cup dry white wine

5 tablespoons finely chopped
fresh flat-leaf parsley, plus a
few whole leaves for garnish

3 large cloves garlic, minced

Kosher salt

8 ounces linguine or spaghettini

Freshly ground black pepper

Linguine with clam sauce should be packed with flavor—nicely garlicky and a little spicy—with firm (but not chewy) pasta. Most of all, it should taste of fresh, delicious clams with the unmistakable tang of the sea. The pasta water is very flavorful, so be sure to save some before draining the pasta. If you find yourself with too little clam juice, add about ½ cup of this reserved cooking water to the broth. To ensure heat in every bite, the olive oil is infused with crushed red pepper flakes—don't skip this simple, fast step, as it creates a subtle spiciness throughout the dish.

Scrub the clams under cold water and set aside. In a heavy 3-quart saucepan, heat 3 tablespoons of the oil over medium heat. Add the pepper flakes and cook briefly to infuse the oil, about 20 seconds. Immediately add the wine, 2 tablespoons of the chopped parsley, and half of the minced garlic. Cook for 20 seconds and add the clams.

Cover and cook over medium-high heat, checking every 2 minutes and removing each clam as it opens. It will take 5 to 6 minutes total for all the clams to open. Transfer the clams to a cutting board and reserve the broth. Remove the clams from the shells and cut them in half, or quarters if they're large. Return the clams to the broth. Discard the shells.

Bring a large pot of well-salted water to a boil over high heat. Add the pasta and cook until it's almost al dente, 6 to 9 minutes. Don't overcook.

While the pasta is cooking, heat the remaining 3 tablespoons olive oil in a 10- or 12-inch skillet over medium heat. Add the remaining 3 tablespoons chopped parsley and the rest of the garlic and cook until the garlic is just soft, about 1 minute. Set the skillet aside.

When the pasta is done, reserve about ¼ cup of the pasta cooking water and then drain the pasta. Add the pasta, the clams, and the broth the clams were cooked in to the skillet. Return to low heat, toss the pasta in the sauce, and simmer for another minute to finish cooking it, adding a little of the pasta water if you prefer a wetter dish.

Taste for salt and add a large grind of black pepper. Serve immediately, garnished with the parsley leaves. *—Perla Meyers*

Tips for buying and storing clams

When shopping for clams, you'll want to head for a market with rapid turnover. Since clams are such an important part of this dish, it'll be worth the extra time it takes to get to a good seafood market.

Look for intact, tightly closed (or just slightly gaping) shells, and a sea-like smell. Clams are sold alive, so don't store them in plastic or they'll suffocate. As soon as you get home, put them in a bowl, cover with a wet towel, and refrigerate. Just before cooking, look for any shellfish that are open and tap them on the counter. If they don't close, discard them. Also discard any clams that remain closed after cooking.

If you are not preparing this dish the day you buy the clams, it's smart to wash and cook them in the wine and herb broth, remove them from their shells, and refrigerate; they will keep for two or three days.

Spaghetti with Spicy Shrimp, Cherry Tomatoes & Herbed Breadcrumbs

Serves four.

⅓ cup plus 4 tablespoons extra-virgin olive oil

1 tablespoon plus 2 teaspoons chopped fresh flat-leaf parsley

2 teaspoons chopped fresh chives

Heaping ¼ teaspoon crushed red pepper flakes

Pinch of cayenne

½ teaspoon kosher salt; more as needed

1 pound raw shrimp (21 to 25 per pound) peeled, deveined, and cut crosswise into quarters

¼ cup coarse fresh breadcrumbs (made from a baguette or other artisan bread)

1 tablespoon chopped fresh mint

Freshly ground black pepper

2 medium shallots, finely chopped

1 pound dried thin spaghetti

4 cups cherry or grape tomatoes (2 pints), halved

Marinating the shrimp in oil, herbs, and two forms of hot pepper gives this dish a zippy warmth. Because the marinade doesn't contain acid, you don't need to worry about the shrimp getting mushy. Fresh mint added to the breadcrumbs contributes a bright, unexpected twist.

In a large bowl, combine 2 tablespoons of the olive oil, 2 teaspoons of the parsley, the chives, red pepper flakes, cayenne, and salt. Add the shrimp and stir to coat evenly. Cover the bowl with plastic and marinate in the refrigerator for about 20 minutes.

Bring a large pot of well-salted water to a boil over high heat.

In a small sauté pan, heat 2 tablespoons of the olive oil over medium heat. Add the breadcrumbs and cook, stirring frequently, until lightly browned, 1 to 3 minutes. Transfer to a small bowl and let cool. Mix the remaining 1 tablespoon parsley, the mint, a grinding of pepper, and a pinch of salt into the breadcrumbs.

Heat the remaining ⅓ cup olive oil in a 12-inch skillet over medium heat. When the oil is hot, add the shallots and cook, stirring occasionally, until lightly browned, 2 to 4 minutes.

Put the spaghetti in the boiling water and cook until just shy of al dente, about 5 minutes.

While the spaghetti cooks, add the shrimp and halved tomatoes to the skillet. Season with salt and pepper and cook, stirring frequently, until the tomatoes start to soften and the shrimp is nearly cooked through, about 5 minutes.

Reserve ½ cup of the pasta-cooking water and drain the spaghetti. Return the pasta and 2 tablespoons of the reserved water to the pot. Add the shrimp mixture and toss over medium heat until the shrimp is cooked through and the spaghetti is perfectly al dente, 1 to 2 minutes more. Add more of the pasta water as necessary to keep the dish moist. Season to taste with salt and pepper, transfer to warm shallow bowls, and top each serving with the breadcrumbs. *—Scott Conant*

Coarsely vs. finely chopped herbs

When it comes to chopped herbs, one size doesn't fit all.

Coarsely chopped herbs are good for garnishing and mixing into salsas and cold salads. The leaves are chopped just enough to break them into smaller pieces and release their flavor but still large enough that some pieces have intact edges, so they're identifiable by sight rather than being anonymous chopped green bits.

Finely chopped herbs are usually best for mixing into dishes in which the flavor of the herb is more important than its appearance.

Though by no means a firm rule, fresh herbs are generally added near the end of cooking, giving them enough time to infuse a dish but not so long as to overcook and muddy their flavor nuances.

Linguine with Shrimp & Chorizo

Serves four to six.

Kosher salt

2 tablespoons extra-virgin olive oil; more as needed

6 ounces chorizo, sliced ⅛ inch thick (1⅓ cups)

1 pound large shrimp (31 to 40 per pound), peeled and deveined

1 small onion, finely diced

4 medium cloves garlic, thinly sliced

One 26-ounce box Pomi® brand chopped tomatoes (or two 14-ounce cans petite-cut diced tomatoes)

¼ to ½ teaspoon crushed red pepper flakes

1 pound dried thin linguine

¼ cup roughly chopped fresh flat-leaf parsley

Smoky chorizo and shrimp is a wonderful combination that, along with the garlic, onion, and tomato, gives this dish a Spanish feel. Spanish chorizo comes fully cooked and can be mild or spicy, so choose the heat level you enjoy most.

Bring a pot of generously salted water to a boil. Heat the olive oil in a 12-inch skillet over medium-high heat. Cook the chorizo, stirring occasionally, until browned, 2 to 3 minutes. Add the shrimp and cook, stirring occasionally, until it curls up and just begins to turn pink, about 2 minutes; don't cook it through. Off the heat, use a slotted spoon to transfer the chorizo and shrimp to a bowl.

Pour off all but 2 tablespoons of the fat from the skillet (or add more oil so you have 2 tablespoons fat in the pan) and set the skillet over medium heat. Add the onion and garlic and cook until softened, about 3 minutes. Stir in the tomatoes with their juices and the pepper flakes, scraping the bottom of the pan, and simmer briskly for 5 minutes to blend the flavors.

Meanwhile, cook the linguine in the boiling water until barely al dente, 4 to 6 minutes. Reserve ½ cup of the pasta water and drain the pasta in a colander.

Add the shrimp and chorizo to the sauce and simmer until the shrimp is just cooked through, another 1 to 2 minutes. Season the sauce to taste with salt. Toss the pasta, sauce, and parsley in the pasta pot over medium-low heat for 2 minutes. The sauce should just coat the pasta; add some of the pasta water to moisten if necessary. Drizzle each serving with a little oil.

—Allison Ehri Kreitler

Rigatoni with Summer Squash, Spicy Sausage & Goat Cheese

Serves four to six.

Kosher salt

1 pound dried rigatoni

3 tablespoons extra-virgin olive oil

¾ pound bulk hot Italian sausage (or links, casings removed)

⅓ cup finely chopped shallots (about 3 medium)

2 cups ¾-inch-diced yellow and green summer squash

3 ounces fresh goat cheese, crumbled (about ¾ cup)

2 teaspoons finely chopped fresh flat-leaf parsley

Freshly ground black pepper

¼ cup grated Parmigiano-Reggiano (optional)

Goat cheese brings the flavors of this pasta together while adding its own rich nuance. Use whatever type of summer squash looks firmest and freshest. Be sure to scrub the skin gently, but don't peel it.

Bring a large pot of well-salted water to a boil over high heat. Put the rigatoni in the boiling water and cook until just shy of al dente, about 10 minutes.

While the pasta cooks, heat ½ tablespoon of the oil in a 12-inch skillet over medium-high heat. Add the sausage and cook, breaking it into pieces with a spatula or spoon, until it's almost cooked through, 3 to 5 minutes. Using a slotted spoon, transfer the sausage to a bowl. Pour the fat out of the skillet but do not wipe it clean. Heat the remaining 2½ tablespoons oil in the skillet over medium heat and cook the shallots until they begin to soften, about 1 minute. Raise the heat to medium high and add the squash. Cook, stirring frequently, until the squash is barely tender, 3 to 5 minutes.

Reserve ½ cup of the pasta cooking water and drain the rigatoni. Return the rigatoni to its cooking pot and add the sausage, the squash mixture, and 2 tablespoons of the reserved pasta water. Toss over medium heat until the sausage is cooked through and the rigatoni is perfectly al dente, about 3 minutes. Add more of the pasta water as necessary to keep the dish moist.

Remove from the heat, add the goat cheese and parsley, and toss until the cheese melts and coats the pasta. Season to taste with salt and pepper, transfer to warm shallow bowls, and top each serving with some of the grated Parmigiano, if using. *—Scott Conant*

Pasta water: the secret ingredient

To moisten the dish and help the flavors come together, follow these steps:

Reserve about ½ cup of the pasta cooking water. The water contains starches released by the pasta, which will help enrich the overall dish and create a more saucy consistency.

Drain the pasta when it's just shy of al dente. You'll briefly cook the pasta with the rest of the ingredients and the pasta water; if the pasta is slightly underdone when everything is combined, it won't overcook.

Add the reserved pasta water to the pasta and sauce and toss. The starches in the water help the sauce cling to the pasta, which in turn acts like a sponge, absorbing the flavors.

Angel Hair Pasta with Sautéed Cherry Tomatoes, Lemon & Tuna

Serves three to four.

Kosher salt

2 tablespoons extra-virgin olive oil

4 cups cherry or grape tomatoes (about 1½ pounds; a mix of colors, if possible)

1 large clove garlic, minced

One 6-ounce can light tuna in oil, drained and separated into chunks

2 tablespoons minced jarred pepperoncini (about 4 medium peppers, stemmed and seeded)

1 tablespoon lightly chopped capers

1 teaspoon fresh lemon juice

1 teaspoon cold unsalted butter

½ teaspoon packed, finely grated lemon zest

8 ounces dried angel hair pasta

3 tablespoons coarsely chopped fresh flat-leaf parsley

For a real treat, try one of the imported Spanish tunas (Ortiz brand, in particular), which are fairly expensive but very delicious. The pepperoncini are pickled, medium-spicy peppers that add both warmth and tang to this easy dish.

Bring a large pot of generously salted water to a boil over high heat. Meanwhile, in an 11- to 12-inch skillet, heat the oil over medium-high heat until very hot. Add the tomatoes (be careful because the oil and juice can spatter) and cook until they begin to collapse and their juices run and start to thicken, 6 to 10 minutes. (If you have big, stubborn tomatoes, you may need to crush them a bit with a spatula or pierce them with a knife.) Add the garlic and cook for 30 seconds.

Remove the pan from the heat and stir in the tuna, pepperoncini, capers, lemon juice, butter, and lemon zest. Season the sauce to taste with salt and keep it warm while you cook the pasta.

Cook the pasta in the boiling water according to package directions. Drain well, arrange in individual pasta bowls, and top with the sauce and the parsley.
—*Martha Holmberg*

Penne with Asparagus, Olives & Parmigiano Breadcrumbs

To save time, you can fry the breadcrumbs ahead and store them in a sealed container. Also, you can just snap rather than cut the asparagus into 2-inch pieces. Take care not to overcook it, otherwise you'll lose its sweetness and pretty green color.

Bring a large pot of well-salted water to a boil.

In a 12-inch skillet, heat 3 tablespoons of the oil over medium heat. Add the breadcrumbs and cook, stirring occasionally, until they're crispy and golden brown, about 5 minutes. Transfer to a medium bowl and stir in the Parmigiano and a pinch of salt. Wipe the skillet clean with a paper towel.

Cook the pasta in the boiling water until al dente. Reserve a few tablespoons of the cooking water and drain the pasta.

Heat 1 tablespoon of the oil over medium-high heat in the skillet. Add the asparagus and cook, stirring frequently, until crisp-tender, about 4 minutes. Lower the heat to medium low and push the asparagus to the side. Add the remaining 1 tablespoon oil and the garlic and cook, gently mashing with the tip of a wooden spoon or spatula until fragrant, about 30 seconds. Toss the garlic with the asparagus. Remove from the heat.

Stir in the olives and lemon zest, and season with salt and pepper to taste. Add the pasta to the skillet, stirring to blend. Add enough of the reserved cooking water to slightly moisten, as needed, and drizzle with olive oil to enrich. Serve garnished with the breadcrumbs. *–Maryellen Driscoll*

Serves four.

Kosher salt

5 tablespoons extra-virgin olive oil; more for drizzling

1 cup coarse fresh white breadcrumbs (from about 4 slices of bread, crusts removed)

¼ cup finely grated Parmigiano-Reggiano

½ pound dried penne rigate

1 pound medium asparagus, woody ends snapped off, cut diagonally into 2-inch pieces

1 medium clove garlic, minced

½ cup coarsely chopped pitted Kalamata olives (about 20)

Finely grated zest of 1 medium lemon (about 1½ tablespoons loosely packed)

Freshly ground black pepper

Orecchiette with Caramelized Onions, Green Beans, Fresh Corn & Jalapeño

Serves four.

Kosher salt

⅓ cup extra-virgin olive oil

2 cups thinly sliced sweet onion (from 1 large onion)

1 pound dried orecchiette

½ pound fresh green beans, washed, trimmed, and sliced on the diagonal into 1-inch lengths

1 cup fresh corn kernels (from about 2 ears)

1 jalapeño, stemmed, halved lengthwise, seeded, and thinly sliced crosswise

Freshly ground black pepper

¼ cup grated Pecorino Romano

1 tablespoon chopped fresh flat-leaf parsley

The flavors in this pasta build with each bite. Try it once, and it will become a summertime staple. Be sure to check the cooking time on the package of orecchiette because often this shape takes longer to cook than other pasta shapes, especially if you're using an artisan brand. If you can't find orecchiette, you can use farfalle instead.

Bring a large pot of well-salted water to a boil over high heat.

Heat the olive oil in a 12-inch skillet over medium-high heat. When the oil is hot, add the onion and a large pinch of salt and cook, stirring frequently, until the onion is beginning to soften and brown, about 5 minutes. Lower the heat to medium and continue cooking, stirring frequently, until the onion is very soft and a light golden brown, about 15 more minutes (if the onion begins to look like it's burning, add 2 tablespoons warm water and lower the heat).

Put the orecchiette in the boiling water and cook until just shy of al dente, about 9 minutes. Add the green beans to the pasta water in the last minute of cooking.

While the pasta cooks, add the corn, jalapeño, and a pinch of salt to the onions and cook, stirring occasionally, until the corn kernels begin to soften, 3 to 5 minutes. Remove from the heat.

Reserve ½ cup of the pasta and green bean cooking water and drain the pasta and green beans together in a colander.

Return the orecchiette, green beans, and 2 tablespoons of the reserved water to the pot. Add the onion mixture and toss over medium heat until the green beans are crisp-tender and the orecchiette is perfectly al dente, 1 to 2 minutes. Add more of the pasta water as necessary to keep the dish moist. Season to taste with salt and pepper, transfer to warm shallow bowls, and top each serving with the Pecorino and parsley. —*Scott Conant*

Pan-Fried Gnocchi with Bacon, Onions, & Peas

Serves three.

Kosher salt

1 pound frozen gnocchi

3 ounces thick-cut bacon (about 3 slices), cut into ½-inch-wide pieces

4 tablespoons extra-virgin olive oil

2 medium-small yellow onions, thinly sliced (about 2 cups)

½ cup frozen peas

1 teaspoon minced fresh thyme

Freshly ground black pepper

2 tablespoons grated Parmigiano-Reggiano; more for serving

Gnocchi are Italian dumplings usually made with potatoes, flour, and eggs. Homemade gnocchi aren't difficult, but ready-made gnocchi are a delicious solution to getting dinner on the table fast. Look for them in the frozen foods section of the supermarket.

Bring a large saucepan of salted water to a boil. Cook the gnocchi according to package directions. Reserve ½ cup of the cooking water, and drain.

Meanwhile, in a large (preferably 12-inch) nonstick skillet, cook the bacon over medium heat until crispy on both sides, about 5 minutes. Transfer to a plate lined with paper towels and set aside. Pour off any fat from the skillet.

In the same skillet, heat 2 tablespoons of the oil over medium-high heat. Add the onions and cook until they begin to brown, 3 to 5 minutes. Reduce the heat to medium and continue to cook, stirring occasionally, until the onions are limp and golden brown, 10 minutes more. Stir in the peas and thyme, season with salt and pepper to taste, and transfer to a small bowl.

Wipe the skillet clean with a paper towel, and heat the remaining 2 tablespoons oil over medium-high heat. Add the gnocchi and cook, tossing occasionally, until they're lightly brown, about 5 minutes. Gently stir in the onion mixture, bacon, and Parmigiano, along with enough of the reserved cooking water to moisten and coat the gnocchi, about 4 tablespoons. Serve immediately, sprinkled with additional Parmigiano. *—Maryellen Driscoll*

Cavatappi with Roasted Peppers, Capocollo & Ricotta

Capocollo is a lightly aged cured pork usually flavored with white wine and nutmeg. If you can't find it, an excellent substitute is prosciutto di Parma.

Bring a large pot of salted water to a boil. Lightly coat a large shallow baking dish with olive oil.

Roast the peppers by turning them over the flames of a gas burner until the skins are charred or by putting them under a broiler, turning until all sides are well blistered. When they're cool enough to handle, peel off the skins, core and seed the peppers, and cut the flesh into thin strips.

Heat the oven to 425°F. In a large skillet, heat about 3 tablespoons of olive oil over medium heat. Add the onion and cook, stirring occasionally, until it begins to soften. Add the peppers, season with salt and pepper, and sauté until soft and fragrant, about 5 minutes. Add the tomatoes and cook another 5 minutes. Turn off the heat and add the capocollo and thyme. Mix and set aside.

In a medium bowl, combine the ricotta, cream, orange zest, and nutmeg. Season with salt and pepper and whisk until smooth (you can do this in a food processor if you like).

Cook the cavatappi in the boiling water until al dente. Meanwhile, in a small bowl, toss the Pecorino with the breadcrumbs. Season with salt and pepper and add a drizzle of olive oil. Mix well.

Drain the pasta well and return it to the pot. Add the pepper mixture and toss. Add the ricotta mixture, toss again, and taste for seasoning.

Pour the pasta into the baking dish. Top with an even coating of the breadcrumb mixture and a drizzle of olive oil. Bake uncovered until browned and bubbling, 15 to 20 minutes. Serve right away. *—Erica DeMane*

Serves four.

Olive oil

5 medium red bell peppers

1 large onion, thinly sliced

Kosher salt and freshly ground black pepper

5 plum tomatoes, seeded and chopped (or one 14½-ounce can diced tomatoes, drained)

⅓ pound very thinly sliced capocollo, chopped

A few large sprigs fresh thyme, leaves chopped

1½ cups fresh ricotta

1½ cups heavy cream, preferably not ultrapasteurized

1 to 2 teaspoons finely grated orange zest

Pinch of nutmeg, preferably freshly grated

1 pound dried cavatappi (or fusilli or penne)

¼ cup freshly grated Pecorino Romano

⅓ cup coarse fresh breadcrumbs

Spaghetti with Portabellas, Sage & Walnuts

Serves four.

Kosher salt

¾ **pound spaghetti**

3 tablespoons extra-virgin olive oil

½ **cup unsalted butter**

3 large portabella mushroom caps, gills scraped out and discarded, caps thinly sliced and cut into 2-inch pieces

Freshly ground black pepper

⅔ **cup loosely packed fresh sage leaves**

⅓ **cup toasted walnuts, coarsely chopped**

½ **cup freshly grated Parmigiano-Reggiano**

Sage and mushrooms are one of those perfect culinary combinations. Another plus for this recipe is that the portabellas make it feel substantially "meaty," although the dish itself is meatless. Scraping out the gills of the portabellas keeps them from turning the pasta a grayish color.

Bring a large pot of salted water to a boil. Add the spaghetti and cook until al dente, about 9 minutes. Reserve 1 cup of the pasta cooking water and then drain the pasta and set aside.

Meanwhile, heat the olive oil and 2 tablespoons of the butter in a 12-inch skillet over medium-high heat until the butter is melted. Add the mushrooms, season with salt and pepper, and cook, stirring occasionally, until they're brown and tender, 4 to 5 minutes. Transfer the mushrooms to a bowl and set aside.

In the same skillet, melt the remaining 6 tablespoons butter over medium heat. Add the sage leaves and cook, stirring occasionally, until they darken and crisp and the flecks of milk solids in the butter are golden brown, 3 to 5 minutes. Return the mushrooms to the pan and pile in the walnuts, the cooked pasta, and ½ cup of the pasta water. Toss the pasta continuously with tongs to coat well, adding more water as needed so the pasta is moist, 1 to 2 minutes. (If your skillet isn't big enough, you can toss everything together in the pasta pot.) Season with salt and pepper, mound into bowls, and sprinkle generously with the Parmigiano. Serve immediately. —*Arlene Jacobs*

Oil & pasta water don't mix

If you're in the habit of adding a little oil to the cooking water to keep the pasta from sticking, here's a good reason to stop: Pasta that's cooked in oily water becomes oily itself, and as a result, the sauce slides off, doesn't get absorbed, and you have less flavorful pasta. You can avoid sticking by stirring the pasta often at the start of cooking.

And while adding oil may keep the pasta water from boiling over, you can also prevent this problem by making sure you use a large pot and by reducing the heat a little (but still maintaining a boil).

Baked Fettuccine with Asparagus, Lemon, Pine Nuts & Mascarpone

Serves four.

2 tablespoons olive oil; more for the baking dish

2 pounds medium-thick asparagus, ends trimmed, cut into 1-inch pieces on an angle

8 scallions, whites and tender greens cut into thin rounds

Finely grated zest from 2 lemons

Juice from 1 lemon (about 4 tablespoons)

A few sprigs fresh thyme or savory, leaves chopped

Kosher salt and freshly ground black pepper

1 tablespoon unsalted butter

1 tablespoon all-purpose flour

1 cup whole milk

1 cup mascarpone

1 cup freshly grated Grana Padano

Small pinch of cayenne

Generous pinch of ground allspice

¾ cup coarse fresh breadcrumbs

1 pound fresh fettuccine

½ cup pine nuts, lightly toasted

Mascarpone is a rich Italian cream cheese. It usually comes in a plastic tub and is available at most supermarkets. Grana Padano is a hard Italian grating cheese similar to Parmigiano but with a milder flavor and a lower price.

Heat the oven to 450°F. Lightly coat a large shallow baking dish with olive oil. Bring a large pot of salted water to a boil. Add the asparagus pieces and blanch until crisp-tender, about 2 minutes. With a large slotted spoon, transfer them to a colander, and run under cold water to preserve their green color. Drain well. Keep the water boiling for the pasta.

In a large skillet, heat the olive oil over medium heat. Add the scallions and sauté for 1 minute to soften. Add the asparagus and sauté briefly, about 1 minute. Take the skillet off the heat and add half of the zest, the lemon juice, and the thyme or savory. Season with salt and pepper, mix well, and reserve.

In a medium saucepan, heat the butter and flour over medium heat, whisking until smooth. Cook for 1 minute, whisking constantly, to cook away the raw taste of the flour. Add the milk and cook, whisking all the while, until it comes to a boil. Lower the heat a bit and cook until smooth and slightly thickened (to about the consistency of heavy cream), 3 to 4 minutes.

Turn off the heat and add the remaining lemon zest, the mascarpone, and ½ cup of the Grana Padano, whisking until the mixture is fairly smooth (there will be a slight grainy texture from the cheese). Season with the cayenne, the allspice, and more salt and pepper.

In a small bowl, combine the breadcrumbs and the remaining Grana Padano. Season with salt and pepper and add a drizzle of olive oil. Mix well.

Return the cooking water to a full boil and cook the fettuccine, leaving it slightly underdone. Drain well. Return the fettuccine to the cooking pot. Add the pine nuts, the mascarpone sauce, and the asparagus mixture. Toss and taste for seasoning.

Pour into the baking dish and sprinkle the breadcrumb mixture evenly over the top. Bake uncovered until bubbling and golden, 15 to 20 minutes. Serve right away. *—Erica DeMane*

Baked Ziti with Tomato, Mozzarella & Sausage

Using freshly made ricotta and mozzarella, as well as imported San Marzano tomatoes, takes this dish from a typical baked pasta to a rustic dish full of clear flavors and appealing textures.

Heat the oven to 375°F. Lightly oil a large, shallow baking dish. Bring a large pot of salted water to a boil.

In a large skillet, heat about 2 tablespoons of olive oil over medium heat. Add the onion and sauté until soft, about 5 minutes. Add the crumbled sausage and garlic and sauté until the sausage starts to brown. Season with salt and pepper. If the sausage gives off a lot of fat, pour off most of it, but leave a little to add flavor to the sauce. Add the red wine and let it boil until it's almost gone. Add the tomatoes with all of their juice and cook, uncovered, at a lively simmer for about 10 minutes. The sauce will thicken slightly. Add the marjoram or oregano and taste for seasoning.

In a large bowl, mix the ricotta, about half the Pecorino, the parsley, and the nutmeg. Season with salt and pepper.

Meanwhile, cook the ziti in the boiling water until al dente. Drain well and toss it with the ricotta mixture until well coated. Add the sausage sauce and mix again. Add the mozzarella and toss gently. Pour everything into the baking dish and sprinkle the remaining Pecorino on top. Bake uncovered until lightly browned and bubbling, about 20 minutes. Serve right away. —*Erica DeMane*

Serves four.

Olive oil

1 large onion, cut into small dice

¾ pound sweet Italian pork sausage, removed from its casing and crumbled

2 cloves garlic, minced

Kosher salt and freshly ground black pepper

¼ cup dry red wine

One 35-ounce can whole plum tomatoes, chopped, with their juice

¼ cup chopped fresh marjoram or oregano (from about 6 large sprigs)

1 cup fresh ricotta

1 cup freshly grated mild Pecorino Romano

⅓ cup chopped fresh flat-leaf parsley

Pinch of nutmeg, preferably freshly grated

1 pound dried ziti

½ pound mozzarella, preferably fresh, cut into small cubes

Baked Rigatoni with Cauliflower in a Spicy Pink Sauce

Serves six to eight.

Kosher salt

3 tablespoons olive oil

Two 28-ounces cans whole tomatoes

1 pound yellow onions, halved and thinly sliced (about 3 medium)

2 cloves garlic, minced

½ cup heavy cream

¼ cup chopped fresh flat-leaf parsley

½ teaspoon crushed red pepper flakes

1 pound dried rigatoni

1 pound 1- to 1½-inch cauliflower florets (about 4 cups)

10 ounces shredded Fontina (about 2½ cups)

2 ounces freshly grated Parmigiano-Reggiano (about ¾ cup)

The duo of Fontina and Parmigiano-Reggiano is what makes this dish so delicious, with creamy richness from the Fontina and a nutty savory character from the Parmigiano.

Position a rack in the center of the oven and heat the oven to 450°F. Fill a large pot with a pasta insert with water, salt it well, and bring to a boil. Grease a 9x13-inch baking dish with 1 tablespoon olive oil.

Pour off 1 cup of juice from one of the cans of tomatoes and discard it. In a blender or food processor, purée both cans of tomatoes with their remaining juice and set aside.

Heat the remaining 2 tablespoons olive oil in a 6- to 8-quart Dutch oven or heavy-based pot over medium-high heat. When the oil is shimmering, about 1 minute, add the onions and ¼ teaspoon salt and cook, stirring occasionally, until nicely browned, 5 to 10 minutes. Push the onions to the side of the Dutch oven with a wooden spoon and add the garlic. Cook until it just starts to sizzle and becomes fragrant, about 10 seconds.

Add the puréed tomatoes and cream (be careful; it will splatter), plus 1 teaspoon salt. Bring to a boil over medium-high heat, reduce to a gentle simmer, and cook for 10 minutes, stirring occasionally, so that the sauce thickens slightly. Add the parsley and the red pepper flakes, and cook until the flavors are melded, about 5 minutes more. Taste for salt and pepper and remove from the heat.

Meanwhile, when the salted water comes to a boil, cook the rigatoni until it's al dente, about 10 minutes. Drain the pasta by lifting out the insert and leaving the water in the pot. Add the pasta to the sauce. Return the water to a boil (with the pasta insert in the pot) and cook the cauliflower until barely tender, about 2 minutes. Drain and add it to the sauce.

Add 1½ cups of the shredded Fontina to the pasta mixture and toss well. Transfer to the prepared baking dish and spread evenly. Top the pasta with the remaining 1 cup Fontina and then the Parmigiano-Reggiano.

Bake uncovered until the cheese is golden brown, about 15 minutes. Let the pasta rest for 10 minutes before serving. *—Tony Rosenfeld*

Classic Macaroni & Cheese

This dish will taste best if you assemble it ahead of baking time so the pasta can soak up the sauce. But sprinkle on the crumb topping just before baking. The recipe calls for a 9x13-inch baking dish, but it's also nice to use individual ramekins.

Heat the oven to 375°F and butter a 9x13-inch baking dish. Bring a large pot of salted water to a boil and add the macaroni; cook according to package directions until just tender and drain well.

Melt 12 tablespoons of the butter in a heavy-based medium saucepan over medium heat. Add the flour, onion, bay leaf, thyme, and peppercorns; reduce the heat to medium low and cook for 2 to 3 minutes, stirring constantly, to make a roux. Slowly whisk the milk into the roux until smooth and blended. Raise the heat to medium high; whisk constantly until the mixture boils. Cook for 3 to 4 minutes, stirring constantly, until thickened. Lower the heat and continue simmering for about 10 minutes, stirring constantly.

Strain the sauce into a large bowl, removing the onion, herbs, and peppercorns. Add the salt, pepper, nutmeg, and Cheddar, stirring until the cheese is just melted. Toss the pasta with the cheese sauce and pour the mixture into the baking dish.

Melt the last 2 tablespoons butter and toss with the breadcrumbs. Spread the buttered crumbs over the casserole. Bake until sizzling and lightly browned, about 40 minutes, less time for individual dishes (cover with foil if the top browns too quickly). *—Mary Pult & Rebecca Fasten*

Serves six to eight.

1 pound macaroni

14 tablespoons (7 ounces) unsalted butter

6 tablespoons all-purpose flour

½ medium onion, thinly sliced

1 bay leaf

1 sprig fresh thyme

9 black peppercorns (optional)

4½ cups whole milk

2 teaspoons table salt

1 teaspoon freshly ground black pepper

Pinch nutmeg

6 cups (1 pound) finely grated sharp Cheddar

1¼ cups coarse fresh breadcrumbs

Don't skimp on the salt

When you bring a pot of water to a boil to cook pasta, be sure to add a generous amount of salt. Well-salted water seasons the pasta internally as it absorbs liquid and swells. If the pasta is sufficiently salted during boiling, the pasta dish may even require less salt overall.

For one pound of pasta, use 4 quarts of water and 2 tablespoons of kosher salt: the water should taste as salty as seawater.

Neapolitan Rib & Sausage Ragù with Rigatoni (Ragù di Costicine e Salsiccia alla Napoletana)

Serves six.

For the ragù:

Two 28-ounce cans imported Italian plum tomatoes, preferably San Marzano®

2 pounds baby back pork ribs, trimmed of excessive fat (about 11 ribs)

½ cup extra-virgin olive oil

Kosher salt and freshly ground black pepper

1 medium yellow onion, finely chopped (about 1¼ cups)

2 medium cloves garlic, finely chopped

2 tablespoons chopped fresh flat-leaf parsley

½ teaspoon crushed red pepper flakes; more to taste

2 links mild Italian sausage (about ½ pound) casings removed, meat broken into small pieces

1 cup dry white wine

½ cup tomato paste diluted in ½ cup water

For the pasta:

1 tablespoon unsalted butter

1¼ pounds dried rigatoni

½ cup freshly grated Parmigiano-Reggiano or Pecorino Romano

This ragù gets deep and complex flavor from both baby back pork ribs and mild Italian sausage. Adding a little butter and some grated Parmigiano cheese when you toss the sauce with the pasta rounds out all the flavors beautifully.

Make the ragù: Position a rack in the lower third of the oven and heat the oven to 300°F.

Put one can of tomatoes and their juices in a food processor and process until puréed. Using a spatula or the back of a ladle, press the purée through a medium-mesh sieve set over a bowl to remove the seeds. Purée and strain the other can of tomatoes.

Cut the ribs into 2 or 3 pieces so they fit in a 7- to 8-quart Dutch oven. Heat ¼ cup of the oil in the Dutch oven over medium-high heat. Season the ribs with kosher salt and pepper and add them to the hot oil, fatty side down. Cook until the ribs turn a light golden brown, propping them up as needed against the sides of the Dutch oven to brown them evenly, about 6 minutes. Turn the ribs over and brown them on the other side, about 2 minutes. Transfer the ribs to a large plate, discard the fat, and clean the pan with paper towels.

Heat the remaining ¼ cup oil in the pan over medium heat. Add the onion, garlic, parsley, and red pepper flakes and cook, stirring occasionally, until the onion just begins to color, about 5 minutes. Add the sausage and cook, stirring and breaking up the sausage with a wooden spoon until it's lightly browned, 3 to 4 minutes.

Return the ribs to the pan and stir them around with the savory base. Raise the heat to high and add the wine. Cook, stirring occasionally, until the wine is reduced approximately by half, about 5 minutes. Add the tomatoes and the diluted tomato paste. Season with ½ teaspoon salt and ¼ teaspoon pepper. Stir until the liquid begins to simmer.

Turn off the heat, cover the pan tightly with a lid or heavy-duty aluminum foil, and put it in the oven. Simmer very gently, turning the ribs every half hour, until the sauce has a medium-thick consistency and the meat begins to fall off the bone, about 2½ hours.

Remove the pan from the oven and transfer the ribs and any meat that has fallen off the bone to a cutting board. Use a ladle to skim the fat off the surface of the sauce. When the ribs are cool enough to handle, pull the meat off the ribs. Discard the bones and any fat and connective tissue. Finely chop the meat. Stir the meat back into the sauce and simmer on the stovetop over medium heat, stirring occasionally, to allow the flavors to meld and the sauce to thicken slightly, about 10 minutes. Adjust the seasoning with salt, pepper, and crushed red pepper to taste.

Serve the ragù and pasta: Bring a large pot of well-salted water to a boil. Add the rigatoni and cook according to package directions. Drain. Add the butter to the ragù and then pour in the cooked and drained pasta and Parmigiano or Pecorino. Toss over medium-high heat until the pasta and sauce are well combined. Serve immediately.
—Biba Caggiano

Ribs add succulence

Rather than using ground meat as in a Bolognese sauce, some of the most sumptuous ragùs get their rich consistency and deep flavor from braising meat on the bone—such as baby back ribs—until tender, then shredding the cooked meat and adding it back to the sauce.

Short Rib & Porcini Mushroom Ragù with Gnocchi (Ragù di Manzo e Funghi Porcini)

Serves eight to ten.

1 ounce dried porcini mushrooms (about 1 cup)

Two 28-ounce cans imported Italian plum tomatoes, preferably San Marzano

½ cup extra-virgin olive oil

2 pounds bone-in beef short ribs, trimmed of excess fat

1 pound boneless beef chuck, trimmed of excess fat

Kosher salt and freshly ground black pepper

1 small yellow onion, finely chopped (about 1 cup)

1 small carrot, finely chopped (about 1 cup)

1 small celery stalk, finely chopped (about ½ cup)

1 medium clove garlic, finely chopped

2 ounces thickly sliced pancetta, finely chopped

1 tablespoon chopped fresh flat-leaf parsley

1 cup dry white wine

For the gnocchi:

2 tablespoons unsalted butter

2 pounds uncooked gnocchi

1 cup freshly grated Parmigiano-Reggiano or Pecorino Romano

This ragù gets layers of intense flavor from meaty beef short ribs, pancetta, and dried porcini mushrooms. Plain potato gnocchi are a good foil for the rich sauce; you can find them in vacuum packs in the pasta section or freezer section of most grocery stores.

Position a rack in the lower third of the oven and heat the oven to 300°F.

Soak the mushrooms in 2 cups of warm water for 20 to 30 minutes. With a slotted spoon, transfer the mushrooms to a cutting board and chop them finely. Line a strainer with a coffee filter or two layers of paper towels and strain the mushroom-soaking water into a bowl to get rid of any grit. Set aside both mushrooms and liquid.

Put one can of tomatoes and their juices in a food processor and process until puréed. Using a spatula or the back of a ladle, press the purée through a medium-mesh sieve set over a bowl to remove the seeds. Purée and strain the other can of tomatoes.

Heat ¼ cup of the oil in a 7- to 8-quart Dutch oven over medium-high heat. Season the ribs and beef chuck with kosher salt and pepper and add them to the hot oil. Cook, turning as necessary, until the meat is golden brown on all sides, about 10 minutes. Transfer to a large plate, discard the fat, and clean the pan with paper towels.

Heat the remaining ¼ cup oil in the pan over medium heat. Add the onion, carrot, celery, garlic, and pancetta and cook, stirring frequently, until the vegetables are lightly golden and soft, 7 to 8 minutes. Add the mushrooms and parsley and stir for about 1 minute to blend the ingredients.

Return the meat to the pan and stir to coat with the savory base. Raise the heat to high and add the wine. Cook, stirring occasionally, until the wine is reduced approximately by half, about 5 minutes. Add the tomatoes and ½ cup of the reserved mushroom-soaking water. Season with ½ teaspoon salt and ¼ teaspoon pepper. Stir until the liquid begins to simmer.

Turn off the heat, cover the pan tightly with a lid or heavy-duty aluminum foil, and put it in the oven. Cook, turning the meat every half hour, until the meat is fork tender and the ribs begin to fall off the bone, about 2½ hours.

Remove the pan from the oven and transfer the meat (including any that has fallen off the bone) to a cutting board. Use a ladle to skim the fat off the surface of the sauce. When the meat is cool enough to handle, pull the meat off the ribs. Discard the bones and any fat and connective tissue. Finely chop all the meat. Stir the meat back into the sauce and simmer on the stovetop over medium heat,

stirring occasionally, to allow the flavors to meld and the sauce to thicken slightly, about 10 minutes. Adjust the seasoning with salt and pepper to taste.

Serve the ragù and gnocchi: Bring a large pot of well-salted water to a boil. Add the gnocchi and cook according to package directions. Drain. Add the butter to the ragù and then pour in the cooked and drained gnocchi and Parmigiano or Pecorino. Toss over medium-high heat until the gnocchi and sauce are well combined. Serve immediately. *—Biba Caggiano*

Lamb Shank & Sweet Pepper Ragù with Pappardelle (Ragù di Stinco d'Agnello con Peperoni)

Serves eight to ten.

One 28-ounce can imported Italian plum tomatoes, preferably San Marzano

4 pounds lamb shanks (about 2 large or 3 medium), trimmed of excess fat

Kosher salt and freshly ground black pepper

½ cup all-purpose flour

½ cup extra-virgin olive oil

1 medium yellow onion, finely chopped (about 1½ cups)

2 medium cloves garlic, finely chopped

1 bay leaf

Pinch crushed red pepper flakes

2 medium red bell peppers, seeded and cut into small dice (about 2½ cups)

1 cup dry white wine

¾ to 1½ cups homemade or low-salt canned beef broth

For the pasta:

2 tablespoons unsalted butter

2 pounds dried or fresh pappardelle

¾ cup freshly grated Parmigiano-Reggiano or Pecorino Romano

This ragù is inspired by a traditional one from the southern Italian region of Abruzzi, in which sweet red bell peppers balance the rich gaminess of lamb shanks.

Position a rack in the center of the oven and heat the oven to 300°F.

Put the can of tomatoes and their juices in a food processor and process until puréed. Using a spatula or the back of a ladle, press the purée through a medium-mesh sieve set over a bowl to remove the seeds.

Pat the lamb shanks dry with paper towels and season generously with salt and pepper. Spread the flour in a wide, shallow dish and dredge the shanks lightly in the flour.

Heat ¼ cup of the oil in a 7- to 8-quart Dutch oven over medium-high heat. Add the shanks and cook, turning a few times, until they are golden brown on all sides, 8 to 10 minutes. Transfer the shanks to a large plate, discard the fat, and clean the pan with paper towels.

Heat the remaining ¼ cup oil in the pan over medium heat. Add the onion and cook, stirring frequently, until it's pale gold and soft, about 5 minutes. Add the garlic, bay leaf, and pepper flakes, stir for about 1 minute, and add the bell peppers. Cook, stirring frequently, until the peppers begin to color and soften a little, 4 to 5 minutes.

Return the shanks to the pan and stir them around with the pepper mixture. Increase the heat to high, add the wine, and stir until the wine is reduced approximately by half, 1 to 2 minutes. Add the tomatoes, ¾ cup of broth, and ½ teaspoon salt. Stir until the liquid begins to simmer.

Turn off the heat, cover the pan tightly with a lid or heavy-duty aluminum foil, and put it in the oven. Cook, turning the shanks every half hour or so, until the meat begins to fall off the bone, 2 to 2½ hours.

Remove the pan from the oven and transfer the shanks to a cutting board. When the shanks are cool enough to handle, pull the meat off the bones, discarding any fat and connective tissue. Cut the meat into bite-size pieces. Stir the meat into the sauce and bring it back to a gentle simmer. Cook, stirring a few times, until the sauce has a medium-thick consistency and a rich, reddish color, 5 to 10 minutes. If the sauce seems too dry, stir in some or all of the remaining broth. Discard the bay leaf, adjust the seasoning with salt, and turn off the heat.

Serve the ragù and pasta: Bring a large pot of well-salted water to a boil. Add the pappardelle and cook according to package directions. Drain. Add the butter to the ragù and then pour in the cooked and drained pasta and Parmigiano or Pecorino. Toss over medium-high heat until the pasta and sauce are well combined. Serve immediately. *–Biba Caggiano*

Pork Lo Mein with Seared Scallions & Shiitakes

Serves three to four.

¾ pound boneless pork country-style ribs, cut into ¼-inch-wide strips

2½ tablespoons soy sauce; more to taste

2 tablespoons dry sherry

1 teaspoon cornstarch

2 tablespoons plus 1 teaspoon kosher salt

9 ounces fresh Chinese noodles

5 tablespoons canola or peanut oil

6 ounces scallions (14 to 16 medium), trimmed and cut into 2-inch pieces

3½ to 4 ounces fresh shiitake mushrooms, stemmed, caps thinly sliced (2 cups)

1 tablespoon minced fresh ginger

2 medium cloves garlic, minced

¼ teaspoon crushed red pepper flakes

3 cups thinly sliced Napa cabbage (about 6 ounces)

2 cups mung bean sprouts, rinsed

2 teaspoons Asian sesame oil

Lo mein is a dish made with a type of Chinese egg noodle made from wheat flour. You can usually find the noodles fresh in the produce section of the supermarket. If you can't find something labeled "Chinese" or "Chinese-style noodles," use any kind of thin fresh noodle or pasta.

In a medium bowl, toss the pork with 1 tablespoon of the soy sauce, 1 tablespoon of the sherry, the cornstarch, and ¼ teaspoon of the salt. Refrigerate for at least 15 minutes and up to 1 hour.

Bring 2 quarts of water to a boil in a large pot. Add 2 tablespoons of the salt and cook the noodles, stirring occasionally, until just tender, about 3 minutes. Drain in a colander and run under cold water until the noodles cool to about room temperature. Turn the noodles out onto a baking sheet lined with paper towels to dry.

Heat 1½ tablespoons of the oil in a 12-inch nonstick skillet over medium heat. Add the noodles and cook, tossing occasionally, until golden and slightly crisp, about 6 minutes. Meanwhile, replace the damp paper towels on the baking sheet with dry ones. When golden, transfer the noodles to the dry towels.

Heat another 1½ tablespoons of the oil in the nonstick skillet over medium-high heat until shimmering hot. Add the pork and cook, tossing often, until browned and just cooked through, 2 to 3 minutes. Transfer to a plate or bowl. Pour the remaining 2 tablespoons oil into the skillet and then add the scallions, mushrooms, and ¼ teaspoon of the salt. Cook, stirring occasionally, until browned, 3 to 4 minutes. Add the ginger, garlic, and pepper flakes and cook, stirring, until fragrant, 30 to 60 seconds. Add the cabbage, bean sprouts, and the remaining ½ teaspoon salt. Cook, stirring often, until the cabbage just starts to soften, 1 to 2 minutes.

Add the noodles and pork to the pan and cook, stirring, until heated through, 1 to 2 minutes. Add the remaining 1½ tablespoons soy sauce, the remaining 1 tablespoon sherry, and the sesame oil and cook, tossing the ingredients, for 1 minute more. Serve immediately. Add more soy sauce to taste or pass the soy sauce at the table.

—*Tony Rosenfeld*

Stir-Fried Noodles with Beef & Vegetables

Traditionally, the noodles for this Korean favorite are made of sweet-potato starch, though bean threads, made from mung bean flour and also called cellophane noodles, or thin rice noodles are also fine.

Bring a 3-quart pot of water to a boil. Add the bean threads or rice noodles, remove from the heat, and let sit until just softened (they should still be plenty toothy), about 3 minutes. Drain in a colander and rinse well under cool, running water. Toss with 1 tablespoon of the canola or peanut oil, and spread out on a tray or large plate lined with paper towels.

In a small bowl, mix the soy sauce, sesame oil, rice vinegar, and brown sugar. Trim the beef of excess fat and slice it thinly across the grain. Cut the slices into 2-inch pieces. Season the beef with salt.

Heat 1½ tablespoons of the canola or peanut oil in a 12-inch nonstick skillet or large stir-fry pan over medium-high heat until shimmering hot. Add the beef and cook, stirring, until it loses most of its raw appearance, about 1 minute. Transfer to a large plate.

Add the remaining 1½ tablespoons oil and the vegetables to the pan. Cook, stirring, until they start to soften, about 2 minutes. Reduce the heat to medium and add the beef and the noodles. Stir the soy mixture and drizzle it over all. Cook, tossing until everything is evenly coated with the sauce and the vegetables are cooked through, about 3 minutes. Serve immediately, sprinkled with the sesame seeds. *—Tony Rosenfeld*

Serves four.

3 ounces bean threads (cellophane noodles) or thin rice noodles (see note on the facing page)

¼ cup canola or peanut oil

3 tablespoons soy sauce

1½ tablespoons Asian sesame oil

1½ tablespoons rice vinegar

1 tablespoon light brown sugar

½ pound flank steak

Kosher salt

1 small zucchini (about 6 ounces), halved and thinly sliced crosswise into half circles

1 cup matchstick-cut or grated carrot (1 large carrot)

1 small yellow onion, halved and thinly sliced crosswise into half circles

1 tablespoon toasted sesame seeds

Rice Pilaf with Sage, Parmigiano & Prosciutto

Serves six to eight.

- 2 tablespoons extra-virgin olive oil
- ¼ pound very thinly sliced prosciutto (about 5 slices), cut crosswise into 1-inch-wide strips
- 4 tablespoons unsalted butter
- 3 tablespoons chopped fresh sage
- 4 large cloves garlic, minced (2 tablespoons)
- 3 large shallots, thinly sliced (1 scant cup)
- 1½ cups long-grain white rice
- 1 teaspoon kosher salt; more as needed
- 1 cup dry white wine
- 1½ cups low-salt chicken broth
- 2 ounces Parmigiano-Reggiano, coarsely grated on the large holes of a box grater (about ⅔ cup)

Serve this simple but fragrant pilaf with roast chicken, along with asparagus or fava beans in spring. The prosciutto gets crisped in the olive oil so its salty-sweet flavor infuses the oil, which in turn flavors the rest of the dish.

In a 3-quart heavy-based saucepan with a tight lid, heat the olive oil over medium heat. Cook half the prosciutto in the hot oil, stirring occasionally, until browned and crispy, 1 to 2 minutes. With tongs or a slotted spoon, transfer the prosciutto to a paper towel to drain. Repeat with the remaining prosciutto.

Add 2 tablespoons of the butter to the pan and reduce the heat to low. When the butter has melted, add 2 tablespoons of the sage and cook for a few seconds, and then add the garlic and shallots. Cook, stirring occasionally, until the shallots are soft but not browned, about 5 minutes. Add the rice and salt and stir well to coat each grain with oil. Toast for a full 5 minutes, stirring regularly to keep the grains separated and to prevent them from sticking to the bottom of the pan (the rice may turn opaque before 5 minutes is up, but keep going).

Add the wine, stir well, and cook over medium heat until the wine is mostly reduced, about 3 minutes. Add the chicken broth, stir once, and bring to a boil. Cover, reduce the heat to low, and cook for 18 minutes. Remove the pan from the heat and let sit, still covered, for 5 minutes.

Once the pilaf has rested, remove the lid and fluff the rice with a fork. Cut the remaining 2 tablespoons butter into several pieces and, using the fork, gently fold it into the rice with the remaining 1 tablespoon sage, the Parmigiano, and the cooked prosciutto. Taste for seasoning and adjust as needed. —*Ris Lacoste*

1 The aromatic base

Creating a deeply flavored pilaf begins before you toast the rice. Choose a flavorful fat (for instance, olive oil, butter, or ghee), and then sauté your aromatic ingredients in it. Many delicious pilafs start with nothing more than onions and butter, but you can also add garlic, spices, herbs, and other finely chopped vegetables.

2 The flavorful liquid

Building up the dish's flavor profile continues when you add the liquid. You might choose chicken broth instead of water, or use a bit of both with wine or a fruit juice. As the liquid boils down, it concentrates, infusing the pilaf with intense flavor.

3 The finishing touches

Finally, when you fluff the rice before serving it, you can fold in ingredients that add textural interest as well as flavor. These final mix-ins might be uncooked ingredients, like fresh herbs, nuts, and cheeses, or precooked items like crispy bacon or caramelized onions.

Saffron Rice Pilaf with Red Pepper & Toasted Almonds

Serves six to eight.

2½ cups low-salt chicken broth or water

Pinch of saffron (about 20 threads)

1 tablespoon extra-virgin olive oil

1 medium onion, cut into small dice (1¼ cups)

1 red bell pepper, cored, seeded, and small diced (about 1 cup)

1½ cups long-grain white rice

1 teaspoon kosher salt; more as needed

Pinch of ground cayenne

¼ cup roughly chopped fresh flat-leaf parsley

1 large clove garlic, minced (1½ teaspoons)

¼ cup slivered almonds, toasted

1 tablespoon roughly chopped fresh oregano

The flavors in this dish are reminiscent of paella, making it a great partner for seafood, especially shrimp or mussels. If you can't find fresh oregano, just use 1 teaspoon dried.

On the stovetop or in the microwave, heat the broth until hot. Add the saffron, cover, and let sit for 15 to 20 minutes.

In a heavy-based 3-quart saucepan with a tight lid, heat the oil over medium heat. Reduce the heat to medium low and add the diced onion and bell pepper. Cook, stirring occasionally, until soft but not browned, about 5 minutes. Add the rice, salt, and cayenne, and stir well to coat each grain with oil. Toast for a full 5 minutes, stirring regularly to keep the grains separated and to prevent them from sticking to the bottom of the pan (the rice may turn opaque before 5 minutes is up, but keep going). Reduce the heat to low if there are any signs of scorching. Stir in 2 tablespoons of the parsley and the garlic.

Add the saffron broth, stir once, and bring to a boil over medium heat. Cover, reduce the heat to low, and cook for 18 minutes. Remove from the heat, and let the pilaf sit, still covered, for 5 minutes.

Once the pilaf has rested, remove the lid and fluff the rice with a fork. Using the fork, gently fold in the almonds, the remaining 2 tablespoons parsley, and the oregano. Taste for seasoning and adjust as needed. *—Ris Lacoste*

How to fluff pilaf

Without a doubt, a fork is the best tool for fluffing rice pilaf. A spoon encourages clumping, but a fork's narrow tines gently separate the grains without breaking them, which helps preserve the perfect texture you've taken pains to achieve. Use a light hand, because vigorous stirring could break up the grains and encourage them to cling together.

Here's how to do it: Slip the tines down into the rice alongside the edge of the pan. Gently lift and toss the rice toward the center of the pan. Continue this process as you work your way around the perimeter. Then add your finishing-touch ingredients and gently fold them in with the fork, using a similar gentle fluffing motion.

Rice Pilaf with Spiced Caramelized Onions, Orange, Cherry & Pistachio

Serves six to eight.

4 tablespoons unsalted butter

3 medium onions: 2 sliced (about 3 cups); 1 small diced (about 1¼ cups)

½ teaspoon ground allspice

½ teaspoon ground cinnamon

Pinch ground cloves

1½ teaspoons kosher salt; more as needed

Freshly ground black pepper

1 orange, zest finely grated (about 2½ teaspoons) and juiced (about 6 tablespoons)

¾ cup sweetened dried tart cherries

1½ cups long-grain white rice

¾ cup shelled pistachios, toasted and roughly chopped (3½ ounces)

Toasting the rice in fat a full five minutes before adding liquid will produce dry, separate grains, which is key to perfect pilaf. The flavors of this pilaf are wonderful with curries and with full-flavored fish like salmon.

In a 12-inch heavy-based skillet, melt 2 tablespoons of the butter over medium heat. Add the sliced onions, reduce the heat to medium low, and cook, stirring occasionally, until soft and lightly caramelized, 20 to 25 minutes. Add the allspice, cinnamon, and cloves, and stir well. Reduce the heat to low and cook another 5 minutes, stirring occasionally, to allow the onion to absorb the flavors of the spices and caramelize a bit more. Season with ½ teaspoon of the salt and a few grinds of black pepper. Set aside.

Pour the orange juice over the cherries in a small bowl to hydrate them, if necessary adding enough water to cover completely.

In a heavy-based 3-quart saucepan with a tight lid, melt the remaining 2 tablespoons butter over medium heat. Reduce the heat to medium low and add the diced onion. Cook, stirring occasionally, until soft but not browned, about 5 minutes. Add the rice and the remaining 1 teaspoon salt and stir well to coat each grain with butter. Toast for a full 5 minutes, stirring regularly to keep the grains separated and to prevent them from sticking to the bottom of the pan (the rice may turn opaque before 5 minutes is up, but keep going). Reduce the heat to low if there are any signs of scorching.

Add 2½ cups water, stir once, and bring to a boil over medium heat. Cover, reduce the heat to low, and cook for 18 minutes. Remove from the heat, and let the pilaf sit, still covered, for 5 minutes.

Once the pilaf has rested, remove the lid and fluff the rice with a fork. Strain the cherries and discard the orange juice. Using the fork, gently fold in the cherries, caramelized onions, pistachios, and orange zest. Taste for seasoning and adjust as needed. *–Ris Lacoste*

Southwestern Rice Pilaf

Poblano chiles are about the size of small bell peppers, with glossy dark-green skins and wide shoulders that taper to a point. They're generally mild, with just a bit of zing, but occasionally you can get a hot one, so taste before you use the full amount in any dish. This pilaf makes a delicious accompaniment to steak or chicken fajitas.

In a heavy-based 3-quart saucepan with a tight lid, heat the oil over medium heat. Add the onion, poblano, and garlic and reduce the heat to medium low. Cook for 3 minutes, stirring occasionally. Add the chili powder and cumin and cook, stirring frequently, until the onion is softened and the spices are very fragrant, about 3 minutes.

Add the rice and salt, and stir well to coat each grain with oil. Toast for a full 5 minutes, stirring regularly to keep the grains separated and to prevent them from sticking to the bottom of the pan (the rice may turn opaque before 5 minutes is up, but keep going). Reduce the heat to low if there are any signs of scorching.

Add the chicken broth and tomatoes, stir once, and bring to a boil over medium heat. Cover, reduce the heat to low, and cook for 18 minutes. Remove from the heat and let the pilaf sit, still covered, for 5 minutes. Meanwhile, finely grate 1 tablespoon zest from the lime, and then cut the lime into wedges.

Once the pilaf has rested, remove the lid and fluff the rice with a fork. Using the fork, gently fold in the cilantro, jalapeño, and lime zest. Season to taste with salt. Serve with the lime wedges for spritzing over the rice. *—Ris Lacoste*

Serves six to eight.

- 2 tablespoons extra-virgin olive oil
- 1 medium onion, medium diced (1½ cups)
- 1 medium poblano, stemmed, seeded, and finely diced (½ cup)
- 4 large cloves garlic, minced (2 tablespoons)
- 1½ teaspoons chili powder
- 1 teaspoon ground cumin
- 1½ cups long-grain white rice
- 1 teaspoon kosher salt; more as needed
- 2½ cups low-salt chicken broth
- One 14-ounce can diced tomatoes, drained well
- 1 lime
- ½ cup coarsely chopped fresh cilantro
- 1 jalapeño, stemmed, seeded, and minced

Why long-grain rice?

There are many kinds of rice, but only long-grain white rice is perfect for pilaf. Why? Because of its starch content. Different rice varieties contain different kinds and amounts of starch, and starch content is what ultimately determines whether rice grains become fluffy or sticky as they cook. Long-grain rice is rich in a type of starch (called amylose) that is quite stable and doesn't get sticky during cooking, so the rice cooks up with firm, separate grains. Medium- and short-grain rice varieties, on the other hand, contain high amounts of a different type of starch (called amylopectin), which makes the rice grains become soft and sticky as they cook.

4 Seafood

p130

p156

Braised Cod with Fennel, Potatoes & Littlenecks
(recipe on page 126)

Braised Red Snapper Puttanesca

Serves four.

Four 5-ounce skinless red snapper fillets (about ¾ inch thick)

Kosher salt and freshly ground black pepper

3 tablespoons extra-virgin olive oil

3 medium cloves garlic, minced (about 1 tablespoon)

Two 14½-ounce cans petite-diced tomatoes

2 anchovy fillets, minced

½ cup pitted Kalamata olives, halved lengthwise (about 3 ounces)

3 tablespoons coarsely chopped fresh basil leaves

1 tablespoon capers, rinsed

¼ teaspoon crushed red pepper flakes

1 tablespoon coarsely chopped fresh mint

2 teaspoons red-wine vinegar

Black sea bass makes a good substitute for snapper in this recipe. If you're adventurous, buy a whole fish, and fillet it yourself, with our method on pages 124–126. Remember that cooking times will vary, depending on the thickness and texture of fish, so be sure to sneak a peek before removing the fish from the sauce.

Position a rack in the center of the oven and heat the oven to 325°F. Season the snapper all over with salt and pepper. Let sit at room temperature while you prepare the sauce.

Heat 2 tablespoons of the olive oil in a 12-inch ovenproof skillet over medium-low heat. Add the garlic and cook, stirring, until softened but not golden, about 1 minute. Add the tomatoes and their juice, anchovies, olives, 2 tablespoons of the basil, the capers, and pepper flakes to the pan. Bring the sauce to a brisk simmer and cook, stirring occasionally, until the tomatoes are tender and the juices have reduced to a saucy consistency, about 8 minutes.

Nestle the snapper fillets into the sauce, spooning some on top to keep the fish moist. Drizzle with the remaining 1 tablespoon olive oil. Tightly cover the pan with a lid or aluminum foil and braise in the oven until the fish is almost cooked through, 10 to 15 minutes, depending on thickness.

With a slotted spatula, transfer the snapper to 4 shallow serving bowls. If the sauce seems too thin, simmer over medium-high heat until thickened to your liking. Stir the remaining 1 tablespoon basil and the mint and vinegar into the sauce and spoon it over the fish. *—Allison Ehri Kreitler*

What happens when you go to the store and you can't find fillets, only whole fish? No problem—filleting a snapper (or any other similar fish) is easy if you follow these steps. Just be sure to use your sharpest knife, whether it's a fillet knife or a chef's knife.

A note on fish scales

Before you fillet a whole fish, it should be scaled. Doing the job yourself isn't difficult, but it's messy, because the scales tend to fly all over and you find them in weird places around the kitchen for days after. For this reason, we always ask the fishmonger to do the scaling for us. And actually, a good fishmonger will also fillet the fish for you, but where's the fun in that?

1 Rinse the fish under running water and pat dry. Position it on a cutting board with its back towards you. Using a sharp knife held behind the gills and side fin, cut straight down halfway through the fish to the backbone, being sure to include the meaty spot right behind the top of the head.

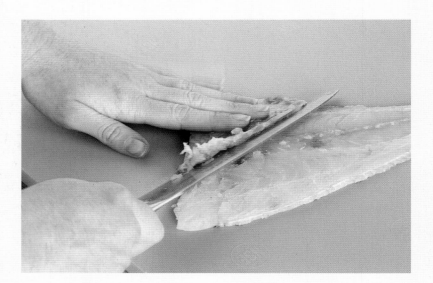

4 Remove the rib bones and belly flap by cutting under the top of the rib bones to the bottom of the fillet at a 45-degree angle. There is some meat here, but on small fish it is minimal. (On larger fish like tuna, this fatty belly is thicker and very flavorful.)

2 Turn the knife parallel to the board (at a 90-degree angle to your first cut) and cut along the spine from head to tail, removing the belly flap with the fillet. You'll need to apply a fair amount of pressure at first to break through the rib bones. As you cut, press down firmly on top of the fish to steady it.

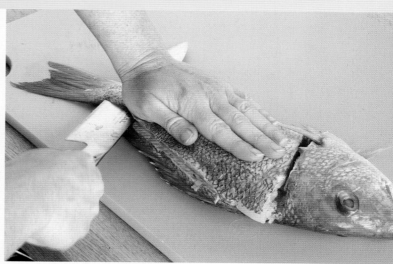

3 Finish removing the fillet by cutting all the way through the skin at the tail. Repeat steps 1 through 3 on the other side of the fish.

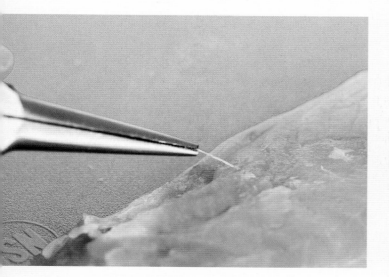

5 Finally, check for pin bones. Some fish have little bones that run along the midline of the fillet and are nearly impossible to see. To remove them, feel along the fillet to locate each bone and then pluck it out with a pair of clean needlenose or fish pliers. Pull the bones out in the direction they are pointing, as you would a splinter.

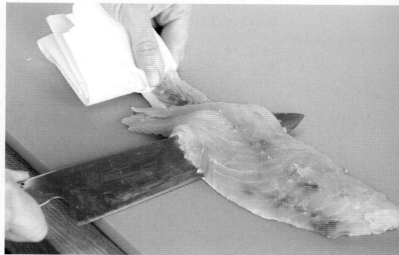

6 Skinning is optional. Put the fillet, skin side down, on the cutting board. Starting at the tail end and holding the knife parallel to the cutting board, slice between the flesh and the skin, as close to the skin as possible, until you can grasp the tail end of the skin with a paper towel. With the knife angled ever so slightly down toward the skin, slice along the skin, using a gentle sawing motion. As you slice, simultaneously pull on the tail skin in the opposite direction to maintain pressure on the cutting edge of the knife. If you miss a spot, trim it away.

Braised Cod with Fennel, Potatoes & Littlenecks

Serves four.

Four 5-ounce cod fillets (preferably 1-inch thick)

Kosher salt and freshly ground black pepper

3 tablespoons extra-virgin olive oil

1 small fennel bulb (about ¾ pound), trimmed (leave core intact) and cut into ½-inch wedges, plus 1 tablespoon chopped fronds for garnish

2 large cloves garlic, finely chopped

1 medium-large shallot, chopped

Two 8-ounce bottles clam juice

8 ounces small baby red or fingerling potatoes, scrubbed and sliced into ⅛-inch-thick coins, ends discarded (about 6 potatoes)

1 large tomato, cut into small dice (12 ounces, about 1½ cups)

2 tablespoons anisette liqueur, such as Pernod or Sambuca

1 bay leaf

1 large sprig fresh thyme

¼ teaspoon roughly chopped or coarsely ground fennel seeds

A generous pinch of saffron, crumbled (about 25 threads)

12 littleneck clams, scrubbed

1½ tablespoons chopped fresh flat-leaf parsley leaves

The subtle flavor of fresh fennel (also called anise) gets a boost from anisette liqueur, giving the whole dish a delicious French feel. Crusty garlic bread is perfect for soaking up the flavorful sauce. You could use halibut in place of the cod.

Position a rack in the center of the oven and heat the oven to 325°F. Season the cod with salt and pepper. Let it sit at room temperature while you prepare the braising mixture.

Heat the olive oil in a 12-inch ovenproof skillet over medium-high heat. Add the fennel wedges, sprinkle with a pinch of salt and pepper and brown on both sides, about 5 minutes total. Remove the pan from the heat and transfer the fennel to a plate. Put the pan over low heat and add the garlic, shallot, ½ teaspoon salt, and ¼ teaspoon pepper. Cook, stirring, until just softened, 1 to 2 minutes.

Add the clam juice, potatoes, tomato, liqueur, bay leaf, thyme, fennel seeds, and saffron to the skillet. Raise the heat to medium and bring to a simmer. Simmer for 3 minutes to start the potatoes cooking. Nestle the cod pieces and clams into the sauce, piling the fennel on top of the fish and making sure all of the potatoes are submerged. Tightly cover the pan with a lid or aluminum foil and braise in the oven until the fish is almost cooked through, 10 to 15 minutes, depending on thickness.

With a slotted spatula, transfer the cod to 4 shallow bowls. Bring the braising liquid, clams, and vegetables to a brisk simmer on top of the stove, cover the pan, and cook until the clams are opened and the vegetables are tender, 3 to 6 minutes more. Divide the opened clams (discard any unopened ones) and vegetables among the bowls. Add the fennel fronds and parsley to the braising liquid in the pan. Bring to a simmer and pour over the fish and vegetables. —*Allison Ehri Kreitler*

tip : To check if your fish is done, use a paring knife to peek between two bits of flesh in the center of the fillet. The very middle should look ever-so-slightly translucent, which means it's almost cooked through. The fish will continue to cook as you finish your sauce, so it'll be perfectly done by the time you're ready to serve it.

Adjusting the thickness of a fillet

Fillets that are ¾ to 1 inch thick work best, but if you can find only long, thin ones, they will do. Score the fish crosswise on the bone side, being sure to cut only halfway through. Flip the fillets over and fold them in half, skin side in, and proceed as if they were thick fillets. As the fish cooks, it will firm up and hold this shape.

Roasted Cod with Lemon-Parsley Crumbs

Serves six.

1 cup panko breadcrumbs

3 tablespoons melted unsalted butter

3 tablespoons finely chopped fresh flat-leaf parsley

2 teaspoons finely grated lemon zest

Kosher salt and freshly ground black pepper

Six 1- to 1½-inch-thick cod fillets (about 6 ounces each)

Cod fillets can vary in thickness by as much as an inch or so. If you get thinner pieces from the tail, you can simply fold them over to double the thickness so they don't cook too quickly and dry out (see page 127 to learn how).

Position a rack in the center of the oven and heat the oven to 425°F.

In a medium bowl, combine the panko, butter, parsley, and lemon zest. Add a pinch of salt and a grind of pepper and stir to evenly distribute the ingredients.

Line a heavy-duty rimmed baking sheet with parchment. Arrange the cod fillets on the baking sheet and season all over with salt and pepper. Divide the panko topping among the fillets, pressing lightly so it adheres. Roast until the breadcrumbs are browned and the fish is mostly opaque (just cooked through), with a trace of translucence in the center (cut into a piece to check), 10 to 12 minutes, depending on the thickness of the fillets. Serve immediately.
—*Molly Stevens*

Sear-Roasted Halibut with Roasted Red Pepper Purée

This dish has the heartiness of a winter meal with the brightness of early spring. Any remaining purée can be kept in your refrigerator for up to five days to use as a finishing sauce for roasted pork loin or sautéed chicken breasts.

Position a rack in the center of the oven and heat the oven to 375°F.

In a blender, combine the red pepper, vinegar, and honey. Turn the blender on, let it run for a few seconds, and then drop the garlic through the feed hole. With the blender still running, slowly pour in the ¼ cup oil and process until the mixture is smooth, about 1 minute, stopping to scrape down the lid and sides of the blender jar as necessary. Season with salt and pepper to taste.

Set the fish skin side down on a plate and season with salt and pepper. Heat the remaining 2 tablespoons oil in a large ovenproof skillet (preferably cast iron) over medium-high heat until shimmering. Put the fish, skin side up, in the skillet and cook until well browned, 3 to 5 minutes. Flip the fish, turn off the heat, and transfer the pan to the oven. Roast until the fish is flaky, moist, and cooked through (use the tip of a paring knife to check), 5 to 7 minutes.

Transfer the fish to dinner plates, spoon about 1 tablespoon purée onto or around each piece, sprinkle with the chives or marjoram, and serve immediately with the remaining purée on the side. *—Maryellen Driscoll*

Serves four.

2½ ounces roasted red pepper (about ½ large jarred roasted peppers)

2 tablespoons sherry vinegar

½ teaspoon honey

1 medium clove garlic, peeled

¼ cup plus 2 tablespoons extra-virgin olive oil

Kosher salt and freshly ground black pepper

Four 6- to 7-ounce center cut, skin-on halibut fillets

1 tablespoon thinly sliced fresh chives or chopped marjoram

Grilled Halibut Steaks with Lemon, Dill & Cucumber Sauce

Serves four to six.

For the sauce:

1 medium English cucumber, peeled and finely diced to yield 2 cups

2 tablespoons fresh lemon juice

½ teaspoon granulated sugar

Kosher salt and freshly ground black pepper

¼ cup extra-virgin olive oil

2 tablespoons minced fresh dill

1 tablespoon minced shallot

2 teaspoons minced fresh mint

For the halibut:

Four to six 1¼ -inch-thick halibut steaks (6 to 8 ounces each)

1½ tablespoons olive oil; more for brushing the grill

1 teaspoon kosher salt

Delicate and light, this sauce—which has a loose texture that's somewhere between a vinaigrette and a salsa—complements almost any grilled fish, but it's especially nice with the clean, mild flavor of halibut.

Make the sauce: Put the cucumber in a medium bowl. Add the lemon juice and the sugar, toss to combine, and season with salt and pepper to taste. Stir in the olive oil, dill, shallot, and mint, and add more salt and pepper if necessary. Let sit for 30 minutes to allow the flavors to marry. Taste for seasoning again just before serving and adjust if necessary.

Grill the halibut: Meanwhile, generously coat both sides of the halibut with the oil and season both sides with salt. Let the fish sit at room temperature for 15 minutes. Clean and oil the grates on a gas grill and heat the grill to medium high, or prepare a medium-hot charcoal fire.

Grill the halibut steaks directly over the heat source (covered on a gas grill, uncovered on a charcoal grill), without touching, until they have good grill marks, 2 to 4 minutes. Flip the steaks and grill until the second sides have good grill marks and the fish is done to your liking, another 2 to 4 minutes. (Check for doneness by slicing into one of the thicker pieces.) Serve immediately with the lemon, dill, and cucumber sauce. *—Maria Helm Sinskey*

Seared Tuna with Fennel Seeds & Caper Brown Butter

Serves four.

1½ tablespoons fresh lemon juice

1 tablespoon capers, drained, coarsely chopped if large

6 tablespoons unsalted butter, cut into six pieces

¼ cup heavy cream

Four 1-inch-thick tuna steaks (6 to 8 ounces each)

1 tablespoon fennel seeds, crushed

¾ teaspoon kosher salt

½ teaspoon freshly ground black pepper

2 tablespoons vegetable oil

The fennel-seed crust makes this quick fish dish a perfect partner for roasted fresh fennel. The tangy-salty capers and nutty brown butter create a bright sauce that cuts through the richness of the tuna steaks.

Put the lemon juice and capers in a 1-quart heatproof measuring cup. Bring the butter and cream to a brisk simmer in a small saucepan over medium heat, whisking often. The mixture will look homogenous at first and then will separate and begin to turn golden brown. Continue to whisk until it turns a dark rust color, about 10 minutes total. Carefully pour the brown butter mixture into the lemon juice; the butter will boil up and sputter. Whisk to combine and return to the saucepan, off the heat.

Sprinkle the tuna on both sides with the fennel seeds, salt, and pepper. Heat the oil in a 10- to 12-inch heavy skillet (preferably cast iron) over medium-high heat until shimmering hot. Sear the tuna on both sides until done to your liking, about 2 minutes per side for medium rare (still raw in the middle) or 3 minutes per side for medium (just pink in the middle). Transfer the tuna to plates. If necessary, quickly reheat the sauce. Serve the tuna drizzled with the sauce. *—Allison Ehri Kreitler*

Tuna Teriyaki with Scallion Salad

If your scallions are large and strong flavored, slice them as thinly as you can and soak them in ice water for 10 to 15 minutes. Dry them before making the salad.

Make the teriyaki sauce: Bring the soy sauce, brown sugar, ginger, and garlic to a boil over medium-high heat in a small saucepan. Boil until the mixture has thickened slightly, about 2 minutes. Stir in ½ teaspoon of the sesame oil.

Broil the tuna: Position an oven rack 5 to 6 inches from the broiler element and heat the broiler to high.

Line the bottom of a broiler pan with foil and replace the perforated top part of the pan. Season the tuna on both sides with the cayenne and arrange on the broiler pan. Broil the tuna for 2 minutes, brush generously with the teriyaki sauce, and broil until the glaze sets, about 2 minutes longer.

Turn the tuna over with a spatula and broil for 2 minutes, brush generously with the teriyaki sauce, and broil until the tuna is pale pink in the center or to desired doneness (cut into a piece to check), about 2 minutes longer. Brush with any remaining teriyaki sauce.

Meanwhile, stir together the scallions, cilantro, vinegar, and the remaining ½ teaspoon sesame oil. Transfer the tuna to serving plates, top with the scallion salad, and serve. *—Lori Longbotham*

Serves four.

6 tablespoons soy sauce

3 tablespoons firmly packed dark brown sugar

1 teaspoon finely grated fresh ginger

1 medium clove garlic, finely chopped

1 teaspoon Asian sesame oil

Four 6-ounce tuna steaks, 1 inch thick

⅛ teaspoon cayenne

8 slender scallions, dark green parts only, trimmed and thinly sliced diagonally (about ¾ cup)

¼ cup fresh cilantro leaves

2 tablespoons rice vinegar

Tips for broiling fish

No preheating is necessary. Not only does the broiler cook food quickly, it heats up in just a few minutes, unlike the oven, which can take 15 to 20 minutes to reach the desired temperature. So just turn it on and get ready to cook.

Be ready to move the pan around. Take a close look at your broiler and see how it releases its heat. If the heat is concentrated right down the center of the oven,

arrange the food right down the center of the broiler pan. Most broilers have hot and cool spots, so be ready to move the broiler pan around to compensate.

Some pieces may cook faster than others. The pieces you're broiling won't be exactly the same size, so they won't cook in the same amount of time; remove what's done and continue to cook anything that needs more time.

Grilled Tuna Steaks with Sun-Dried Tomato, Olive & Caper Relish

Serves four to six.

For the relish:

½ cup finely chopped oil-packed sun-dried tomatoes, drained

¼ cup finely chopped oil-cured olives

5 tablespoons extra-virgin olive oil

2½ tablespoons fresh lemon juice

1 tablespoon chopped capers

1 tablespoon minced fresh flat-leaf parsley

1 tablespoon minced shallot

2 teaspoons minced fresh oregano

½ teaspoon finely grated orange zest

Kosher salt and freshly ground black pepper

For the tuna:

Four to six 1¼-inch-thick tuna steaks (6 to 8 ounces each)

1½ tablespoons olive oil; more for brushing the grill

1 teaspoon kosher salt

For a shortcut, pulse the tomatoes and olives a few times in a food processor and then add the remaining ingredients and pulse to combine. The saltiness of the ingredients in this Mediterranean-inspired relish will vary, so make sure to adjust the seasonings to taste.

Make the relish: Combine all the ingredients, seasoning with salt and pepper to taste. You can make the relish up to 2 days ahead, which will allow the flavors to marry.

Grill the tuna: Generously coat both sides of the tuna with the oil and season both sides with salt. Let the fish sit at room temperature for 15 minutes. Clean and oil the grates on a gas grill and heat the grill to medium high, or prepare a medium-hot charcoal fire.

Grill the tuna directly over the heat source (covered on a gas grill, uncovered on a charcoal grill), without touching, until they have good grill marks, 2 to 4 minutes. Flip the steaks and grill until the second sides have good grill marks and the tuna is done to your liking, another 2 to 4 minutes. (Check for doneness by slicing into one of the thicker pieces.) Serve immediately with the relish. *—Maria Helm Sinskey*

Tips for grilling fish steaks

Grilled fish steaks are a wonderful choice for entertaining because you can grill them to your guests' individual preferences. Follow the tips below, and the steaks will look gorgeous, too.

Begin with a clean, well-oiled grill, and let it heat up. A major culprit behind sticking fish is the debris left on the grates. Clean and oil the grill for best results. Hot grates keep fish from sticking by causing the proteins in the fish to contract and release, so be sure your grates are thoroughly heated before you start to grill.

Don't move the steaks for the first few minutes of cooking. You need to give the side that's facing down time to cook (and contract) before turning the fish.

Use tongs and a spatula to move the fish steaks. Tongs work really well for turning sturdy fish steaks, but sometimes a little unseen debris on the grill rack will cause the fish to stick. If this happens, slide a thin spatula underneath the stubborn spot to release it.

Cut into the fish to check for doneness. Once you've grilled a lot of fish steaks, you'll know by feel when they're done to your liking. If you're not there yet, cut into the side of the fish with a paring knife to see what's going on inside. (Poke it with your finger, too, so you learn what different donenesses feel like—the harder the flesh, the more done it is.)

Grilled Swordfish Steaks with Tarragon-Scented Mayonnaise, Cornichons & Capers

Serves four to six.

For the mayonnaise:

1 large egg

4 teaspoons fresh lemon juice

¾ teaspoon kosher salt; more as needed

Freshly ground black pepper

½ cup extra-virgin olive oil

½ cup canola or vegetable oil

¼ cup finely chopped cornichons (or gherkins)

2 tablespoons chopped capers

1 tablespoon minced shallot

1 tablespoon finely chopped fresh flat-leaf parsley

1 tablespoon chopped fresh tarragon

½ teaspoon sweet paprika

For the swordfish:

Four to six 1¼-inch-thick swordfish steaks (6 to 8 ounces each)

1½ tablespoons olive oil; more for brushing the grill

1 teaspoon kosher salt

This tangy tarragon-infused sauce complements mild but meaty swordfish, adding needed richness to the somewhat dry fish. Most mayonnaise is made with an egg yolk, but this recipe uses a whole egg, which gives the mayonnaise a looser consistency. You can make the sauce with a pasteurized egg if raw eggs are an issue or even with store-bought mayonnaise (use about 1 heaping cup in place of the egg and oils).

Make the mayonnaise: Whisk the egg, lemon juice, salt, and a few grinds of black pepper in a bowl until well combined. Combine the oils and drizzle them into the egg mixture, whisking constantly. Once all the oil is added, the sauce should be shiny and thick. Fold in the remaining ingredients and season with salt and pepper to taste. Refrigerate for up to 1 day before using.

Grill the swordfish: Generously coat both sides of the swordfish steaks with the oil and season both sides with salt. Let the fish sit at room temperature for 15 minutes. Clean and oil the grates on a gas grill and heat the grill to medium high, or prepare a medium-hot charcoal fire. Grill the swordfish steaks directly over the heat source (covered on a gas grill, uncovered on a charcoal grill), without touching, until they have good grill marks, 2 to 4 minutes. Flip the steaks and grill until the second sides have good grill marks and the fish is done to your liking, another 2 to 4 minutes. (Check for doneness by slicing into one of the thicker pieces.) Serve immediately with the tarragon mayonnaise. *—Maria Helm Sinskey*

Grilled Salmon Steaks with Sea Salt, Chile & Lime Butter

Serves four to six.

For the butter:

¼ pound (8 tablespoons) unsalted butter, softened to room temperature

3 tablespoons finely chopped fresh cilantro

2 teaspoons fresh lime juice

1 teaspoon coriander seeds, lightly toasted and coarsely ground

¾ teaspoon freshly grated lime zest

½ teaspoon coarse sea salt, like fleur de sel or sel gris

½ teaspoon piment d'Espelette chile powder or crushed red pepper flakes

¼ teaspoon minced garlic

For the salmon:

Four to six 1¼-inch-thick salmon steaks (6 to 8 ounces each)

1½ tablespoons olive oil; more for brushing the grill

1 teaspoon kosher salt

The subtle spiciness of French Basque piment d'Espelette chile powder is perfect for this butter, though crushed red pepper flakes make a fine substitute. Slice thin rounds from the butter log and top the salmon with a couple of them the second it comes off the grill.

Make the butter: Beat the butter in a small bowl with a spoon to loosen it. Mix in the remaining ingredients until they're evenly distributed. Scrape the butter onto a sheet of parchment or plastic wrap and roll it into a neat log, using the parchment or plastic as a guide. Twist the ends and refrigerate the butter until firm, about 1 hour. Keep the butter chilled until ready to use.

Grill the salmon: Generously coat both sides of the salmon steaks with the oil and season both sides with salt. Let the fish sit at room temperature for 15 minutes. Clean and oil the grates on a gas grill and heat the grill to medium high, or prepare a medium-hot charcoal fire. Grill the salmon steaks directly over the heat source (covered on a gas grill, uncovered on a charcoal grill), without touching, until they have good grill marks, 2 to 4 minutes. Flip the steaks and grill until the second sides have good grill marks and the fish is done to your liking, another 2 to 4 minutes. (Check for doneness by slicing into one of the thicker pieces.) Serve immediately with the flavored butter.

—Maria Helm Sinskey

How to turn a salmon steak into a medallion

Salmon on the grill can be a little tricky because it likes to stick to the grill grates, even grates that are perfectly cleaned and oiled. A salmon steak is less likely than a fillet to stick, but with all the bones, it's not as neat and easy to eat as a fillet.

A salmon medallion, which is a salmon steak that's been boned and tied into a tidy little round, gives you the best of both worlds. Some fish counters sell the medallions ready to go, but if all you can find is a salmon steak, here's how to turn it into a medallion.

1 **Trim the lining** and bones from the belly flaps and divide the steak in half along the backbone. Discard the backbone and belly trimmings.

2 **Run a fingertip** over the salmon flesh on both sides to feel for pin bones; use needlenose pliers or fish tweezers to remove them. Reverse the direction of one side of the steak and nestle the two sides together, yin-yang style.

3 **Make an incision** between the skin and flesh of the thicker end of each salmon piece (shown at knife point above), and then trim just enough skin off the belly flaps (shown at bottom of photo) that the flaps can wrap around and tuck in under the skin of the thicker ends (shown at center left). Tie a piece of butcher's twine around the medallion to hold it together.

Salmon Braised in Pinot Noir

Serves four.

Four 5-ounce skinless salmon fillets (preferably 1 inch thick)

Kosher salt and freshly ground black pepper

2 tablespoons unsalted butter

6 ounces medium-small cremini or white mushrooms, quartered (about 18, 2½ to 3 cups)

1 large celery rib, cut into small dice (about ¾ cup)

2 small carrots, cut into small dice (about ½ cup)

1 small leek, white and light green parts only, cut into medium dice (⅓ to ½ cup), well rinsed

2 teaspoons tomato paste

1 cup Pinot Noir

1 bay leaf

1 large sprig fresh thyme, plus 1 teaspoon chopped fresh thyme leaves

1 cup homemade or low-salt chicken broth

½ cup heavy cream

1 tablespoon chopped fresh flat-leaf parsley

Red-wine sauce for fish? Of course—salmon and Pinot Noir are a classic combo, especially in the Pacific Northwest. Salmon is full-flavored enough to stand up to a red-wine sauce, especially one made with the delicate Pinot Noir. Look for a wine that's fruity but only lightly oaked.

Position a rack in the center of the oven and heat the oven to 325°F.

Season the salmon all over with salt and pepper. Let sit at room temperature while you prepare the sauce.

Melt the butter in a 12-inch ovenproof skillet over medium-high heat. Add the mushrooms and celery and cook, stirring occasionally, until the mushrooms are browned on at least one side, 3 to 5 minutes. Add the carrots and leeks and cook, stirring occasionally, until just softened, about 4 minutes (reduce the heat to medium if the pan starts to get dark). Add the tomato paste and cook, stirring, for 1 minute. Add the Pinot Noir, bay leaf, and thyme sprig, scrape the bottom of the pan with a wooden spoon to release any browned bits, and boil until the wine is reduced by about half, 2 to 4 minutes. Add the chicken broth and cream and bring to a brisk simmer.

Nestle the salmon fillets into the vegetables and pile some of the vegetables on top of the fillets to keep the fish moist. Tightly cover the pan with a lid or aluminum foil and braise in the oven until the fish is almost cooked through, 10 to 15 minutes, depending on thickness.

With a slotted spatula, transfer the salmon to 4 shallow serving bowls. Concentrate the sauce by placing the pan over medium-high heat and boiling until it's thickened to your liking. Discard the bay leaf and thyme sprig. Stir in the chopped thyme and parsley, season to taste with salt and pepper, spoon the sauce over the salmon, and serve. *—Allison Ehri Kreitler*

Grilled Salmon Bundles
with Saffron, Tomatoes & Olives

Serves four.

2 medium plum tomatoes, cored
and cut into medium dice
(about 1 cup)

¼ cup pitted and coarsely
chopped black oil-cured
olives (20 to 25 olives)

¼ cup extra-virgin olive oil

1 tablespoon minced fresh
garlic (3 to 4 medium cloves)

½ teaspoon chopped fresh
thyme

½ teaspoon kosher salt; more
as needed

Pinch of saffron (15 to
20 threads)

Freshly ground black pepper

Four 6-ounce center-cut, skin-on
salmon fillets

Try this different take on grilled salmon: Salmon, tomatoes, and
seasonings are folded into foil packets, which keep the fish moist
and let the flavors of all the ingredients marry as they steam together
on the grill. You can prep the packets up to an hour ahead of grilling.

Heat a gas grill with all burners on high.

In a medium bowl, combine the tomatoes, olives, olive oil, garlic, thyme,
salt, saffron, and pepper to taste.

Set one piece of salmon, skin side down, on a 12x18-inch piece of heavy-
duty foil; sprinkle lightly with salt and pepper. Spoon a quarter of the tomato
mixture over the fish and seal tightly. Repeat to make four packets.

Set the foil packets on the hot grate and cook, with the grill covered, until
the fish is opaque throughout, about 8 minutes (open a packet and cut into
the fish to check). Let the salmon rest for a few minutes before serving.
—*Pam Anderson*

A clean grill means less sticking

It's always a good idea to start with thoroughly cleaned
and oiled grill grates. That way, there's no flavor transfer
from the last thing you grilled, and foods are less likely to
stick to the grates.

To clean the grates, heat them first to soften the stuck-
on gunk and then scrub them with a stiff wire grill brush.
Next, fold a paper towel into a little pad, grasp it with
long-handled tongs, and dip it in some cooking oil. Quickly
swab the grates with the towel, cleaning and oiling them
at the same time. Repeat this step until the grates seem
clean, and then cover the grill briefly to let it heat up again.
If you're grilling something that tends to stick, like fish, give
the grates another swipe of oil just before the food goes on.

Orange-Roasted Salmon with Yogurt-Caper Sauce

Serves six.

2 tablespoons extra-virgin olive oil; more for the baking sheet

Six 1-inch-thick, skin-on center-cut salmon fillets (about 6 ounces each), pin bones removed

1½ teaspoons finely grated orange zest

¾ teaspoon kosher salt; more to taste

Freshly ground black pepper

¾ cup plain whole-milk yogurt

2 tablespoons finely chopped fresh flat-leaf parsley

1½ tablespoons capers, drained, rinsed, and chopped

1 tablespoon fresh orange juice

Salmon is a wonderful fish to roast because its rich, oily flesh doesn't dry out easily. In this recipe, that richness is perfectly balanced by a sauce with bright orange zest, tangy yogurt, and briny capers.

Position a rack in the center of the oven and heat the oven to 400°F. Lightly oil a heavy-duty rimmed baking sheet.

Arrange the salmon, skin side down, on the baking sheet, drizzle with 1 tablespoon of the olive oil, and sprinkle with 1 teaspoon of the orange zest, the salt, and a few grinds of black pepper. Gently rub the seasonings into the fish. Let sit at room temperature while the oven heats.

Combine the yogurt in a small bowl with the remaining 1 tablespoon olive oil, ½ teaspoon orange zest, and the parsley, capers, and orange juice. Stir to combine. Season to taste with salt and black pepper. (The sauce can be made up to several hours ahead and kept refrigerated.)

Roast the salmon until just cooked through, with a trace of bright pink in the center (cut into a piece to check), 10 to 15 minutes. Serve immediately, drizzled with the yogurt sauce. *—Molly Stevens*

Fish steaks vs. fillets

When you're at the fish counter, not only do you have to choose what kind of fish you want, but sometimes you also have to decide whether you want it cut as a fillet or a steak.

A fish steak (top) usually refers to a cross-cut portion of a large fish like salmon or halibut. It comes bone-in and skin-on. It can be confusing, but fillets from big, meaty fish like tuna and swordfish are often referred to as steaks as well, even though they're technically fillets.

A fish fillet (bottom) is one whole, boneless side of a fish. It may be skin-on or skinless. Fillets from large fish like salmon are frequently cut into individual portions, which are also called fillets.

For most cooking, fillets and steaks are essentially interchangeable, and the choice between the two usually comes down to aesthetics and whether or not you feel like dealing with fish bones. On the grill, however, steaks behave better than fillets because the skin and bones help hold the fish together. (And though they're really fillets, meaty fish "steaks" grill well because they're firm to begin with.)

Gravlax

Serves eight to twelve as an appetizer.

1 to 1¼ pounds skin-on salmon
    fillet, preferably center-cut
    and very fresh

4 teaspoons fresh lemon juice

2 teaspoons vodka (optional)

½ cup kosher salt

¼ cup coarsely chopped
    fresh dill

3 tablespoons granulated sugar

2 teaspoons freshly cracked
    black pepper

Discover how satisfying and easy it is to make gravlax, and you'll want to do it again and again. This version is flavored with the traditional lemon and dill, but you can get as inventive as you want with the flavorings as long as you keep the salt amount the same. You can even use more sugar, if you like.

Set a small perforated pan, a flat-bottomed colander or strainer basket, or even a cooling rack or a broiler pan in a baking dish or similar container to catch drippings. Line the perforated pan with a large piece of cheesecloth, allowing the edges to drape over the sides of the pan.

Remove the pin bones from the salmon and put it, skin side down, in the center of the cheesecloth. Brush the lemon juice and vodka (if using) evenly over the salmon. In a small bowl, mix the salt, dill, sugar, and pepper. Pack this cure mixture on top of the salmon in a thick, even layer. Wrap the edges of the cheesecloth around the salmon to loosely bundle it up.

Choose another pan that's roughly the same size as the salmon—a loaf pan, for example—and put it on top of the salmon. Add about 2 pounds of weight to the pan—two 15-ounce food cans work well—to press the salmon and help it exude moisture. Refrigerate for 3 days. Gently brush off and discard the cure.

To serve, slice very thinly at a sharp angle to make wide slices. Well-wrapped gravlax will keep in the refrigerator for about 5 days.

—Allison Ehri Kreitler

Before modern transportation and refrigeration, salmon was dried and smoked—often to a crisp—to preserve it. These days, salmon is still cured and smoked, but the goal is enhanced flavor and texture, not preservation. Different methods produce different results, all of them delicious (and all of them needing refrigeration). Here's a description of what's most widely available.

Gravlax

Gravlax is salmon fillet that's been cured in a mixture of salt and sugar with herbs, spices, citrus, and alcohol (see the recipe on the facing page). In addition to adding flavor, the cure draws moisture from the salmon. Moisture allows bacteria to grow, so reducing the moisture preserves the salmon; the drier it is, the longer it will last. Without the need for preservation, today's gravlax is fairly moist, and because it's not cooked, it has a lovely silky texture and delicate flavor. Thinly sliced gravlax is delicious served on buttered toasts and topped with a little crème fraîche and chives. Avoid using it in cooked dishes where heat might destroy its texture.

Cold-smoked salmon

Cold-smoked salmon begins with a salt cure, usually a flavored brine. The cured salmon is then air-dried in a cool place until the surface develops a shiny layer, called the pellicle, which helps the smoke penetrate. Next, the salmon is put in a special smoker, which keeps the heat low enough that the fish doesn't cook as it's flavored by the smoke. The smoking time ranges from a few hours to a few days, depending on the desired flavor and the smoker. Like gravlax, cold-smoked salmon should not be heated. Its smoky flavor is great with capers, red onion, caviar, and boiled eggs.

Hot-smoked salmon

Hot-smoked salmon may be cured and air-dried like cold-smoked salmon, or it may not be cured at all. But the real difference is that hot-smoked salmon slowly cooks in the smoker, giving it a texture and appearance similar to that of regular cooked salmon. Delicious hot or cold, it makes a wonderful addition to scrambled eggs, pastas, and potato dishes.

Spicy Seared Chipotle Shrimp with Zucchini & Chorizo

Serves three.

½ cup low-salt chicken broth

½ small canned chipotle, seeded and minced, plus 2 tablespoons adobo sauce (from a can of chipotles en adobo)

1 tablespoon tomato paste

1 teaspoon light brown sugar

1 pound shrimp (21 to 25 per pound), peeled, deveined, rinsed, and patted dry

¾ teaspoon kosher salt; more as needed

Freshly ground black pepper

¼ cup extra-virgin olive oil

¼ pound chorizo, cut into ¼-inch dice (scant 1 cup)

1 medium zucchini, cut into ½-inch dice (2 cups)

1 small yellow onion, thinly sliced (1 cup)

½ small red bell pepper, sliced into strips about ¼ inch wide and 2 to 3 inches long (½ cup)

¼ cup chopped fresh cilantro

2 tablespoons fresh lime juice; more as needed

Searing shrimp in a single layer in a very hot pan is the key to the best browning. Arrange the shrimp in a single layer and don't fiddle with them, though it's tempting to keep tossing. You'll build up a flavor base in the pan, so you can use the same one to prepare the sauce for a more intensely flavored dish.

In a measuring cup, whisk together the chicken broth, chipotle, adobo sauce, tomato paste, and brown sugar.

Sprinkle the shrimp with a scant ¼ teaspoon salt and a few generous grinds of black pepper. Put a 12-inch skillet (not nonstick) over medium-high heat for 1½ minutes. Add 2 tablespoons of the oil and once it's shimmering hot, add the shrimp in a single layer. Cook undisturbed until the shrimp browns nicely, about 2 minutes. Flip and brown the second side, about 1½ minutes. Transfer to a large plate. The shrimp should still be a little undercooked.

Add the remaining 2 tablespoons oil and the chorizo to the pan and cook, tossing, until it starts to brown, about 1 minute. Add the zucchini, onion, and red pepper, sprinkle with ½ teaspoon salt, and cook, tossing often, until the zucchini browns in places and is just tender, about 4 minutes.

Add the broth mixture to the skillet and bring to a boil. Reduce the heat to medium low. Stir in the shrimp, about half of the cilantro, and the lime juice. Cook, stirring often, until the zucchini is tender and the shrimp are opaque throughout (cut one in half to check), 2 to 3 minutes. Season to taste with salt, pepper, and more lime juice. Serve immediately, sprinkled with the remaining cilantro. —*Tony Rosenfeld*

Shrimp with Fennel, Tomato & Pernod Sauce

Serves three.

1 pound shrimp (21 to 25 per pound), peeled, deveined, rinsed, and patted dry

¾ teaspoon kosher salt; more as needed

Freshly ground black pepper

¼ cup extra-virgin olive oil

3 cups very thinly sliced fennel (1 small to medium bulb, trimmed and cored first)

3 cloves garlic, smashed

¼ cup Pernod (French anise-flavor liqueur)

One 14½-ounce can petite-diced tomatoes

1 teaspoon chopped fresh thyme

¼ cup chopped fresh flat-leaf parsley

If your fennel bulb seems fibrous, peel the outer layer with a vegetable peeler to eliminate the stringiest parts.

Sprinkle the shrimp with a ¼ teaspoon salt and a few generous grinds of black pepper. Put a 12-inch skillet (not nonstick) over medium-high heat for 1½ minutes. Add 2 tablespoon of the oil and once it's shimmering hot, add the shrimp in a single layer. Cook undisturbed until the shrimp browns nicely, about 2 minutes. Flip the shrimp and brown the second side, about 1½ minutes. Transfer to a large plate. The shrimp should still be a little undercooked.

Reduce the heat to medium. Add the remaining 2 tablespoon oil and the fennel and garlic. Sprinkle with ½ teaspoon salt and cook, tossing often, until the fennel is very soft and golden brown in places, 6 to 8 minutes.

Carefully add the Pernod (it may flame up) and cook, stirring, until any flames die out and the Pernod has almost evaporated, about 1 minute. Add the tomatoes and their juice, the thyme, and about half the parsley.

Bring to a boil and then reduce the heat to a gentle simmer and cook for 3 minutes to meld the flavors. Add the shrimp, and cook, tossing, until it's opaque throughout (cut one in half to check), 1 to 2 minutes. Season to taste with salt and pepper. Serve immediately, sprinkled with the remaining parsley.
—Tony Rosenfeld

tip: It's hard to tell when shrimp are done by just looking at them. So here's what to do: Cut a shrimp in half at the thickest part. It should look creamy white and opaque throughout, and the texture should be firm and springy but still moist. If it's a little translucent, cook a minute longer.

Hot Garlicky Shrimp
with Asparagus & Lemon

Serves three.

1 pound shrimp (21 to 25 per pound), peeled, deveined, rinsed, and patted dry

¾ teaspoon kosher salt; more as needed

Freshly ground black pepper

1 lemon

6 tablespoons extra-virgin olive oil

4 medium cloves garlic, thinly sliced

¾ pound asparagus, bottoms snapped off, halved lengthwise if thick, and cut into 2-inch lengths (2 cups)

⅛ to ¼ teaspoon crushed red pepper flakes

⅔ cup low-salt chicken broth

½ teaspoon cornstarch

Bigger shrimp are great because they offer a buffer against overcooking. When you buy shrimp, look for a count—such as 21 to 25 per pound—as opposed to "jumbo" or "large", which are not standardized terms.

Sprinkle the shrimp with a scant ¼ teaspoon salt and a few generous grinds of black pepper. Using a peeler, gently shave the zest in strips from the lemon, taking care not to get any of the bitter white pith.

Squeeze the lemon to get 1 tablespoon juice.

Put a 12-inch skillet (not nonstick) over medium-high heat for 1½ minutes. Add 2 tablespoons of the oil and once it's shimmering hot, add the shrimp in a single layer. Cook undisturbed until the shrimp browns nicely, about 2 minutes. Flip the shrimp and brown the second side, about 1½ minutes. Transfer to a large plate. The shrimp should be a little undercooked.

Reduce the heat to medium, add the remaining 4 tablespoons oil and the garlic and cook, tossing, until the garlic starts to sizzle steadily, about 30 seconds. Add the asparagus, lemon zest, and red pepper flakes, sprinkle with ½ teaspoon salt and cook, tossing often, until the garlic is golden brown and the asparagus looks blistery in places, 2 to 3 minutes. Add the chicken broth, cover with the lid ajar, and cook until the asparagus is just tender, 1 to 2 minutes.

In a small dish, whisk together the cornstarch with 1 tablespoon water, stir into the asparagus mixture, and bring to a boil. Stir in the shrimp, reduce the heat to low, and cook, tossing, until the shrimp is opaque throughout (cut one in half to check), 1 to 2 minutes. Stir in the 1 tablespoon lemon juice and then add salt, pepper, and additional lemon juice to taste. Serve immediately.

—Tony Rosenfeld

Red Curry with Shrimp & Sugar Snap Peas

Serves four.

2 tablespoons vegetable oil

2 tablespoons jarred or homemade red curry paste (see recipe on page 226)

15-ounce can unsweetened coconut milk

1 cup low-salt chicken broth, fish broth, or water

1 pound shrimp (21 to 25 per pound) peeled and deveined

2 cups sugar snap peas (7 to 8 ounces), trimmed

5 wild lime leaves, torn or cut into quarters (optional)

2 tablespoons fish sauce

1 tablespoon palm sugar or light brown sugar

½ teaspoon kosher salt

A handful of fresh Thai or Italian basil leaves

Hot cooked rice or rice noodles for serving

1 long, slender fresh red chile (such as red jalapeño or serrano), thinly sliced on the diagonal (optional)

When you use curry paste from a jar, this Thai-inspired dish comes together quickly enough even for busy weeknights, yet the dish is so fragrant and complex, you'll feel like you've spent hours making something exotic.

Heat the oil in a 2- to 3-quart saucepan over medium heat until a bit of curry paste just sizzles when added to the pan. Add all the curry paste and cook, pressing and stirring with a wooden spoon or heatproof spatula to soften the paste and mix it in with the oil, until fragrant, about 2 minutes.

Add the coconut milk and broth and bring to a simmer. Simmer, stirring often, for 5 minutes, allowing the flavors to develop.

Increase the heat to medium high and let the curry come to a strong boil. Add the shrimp, sugar snap peas, and half the lime leaves (if using), and stir well. Cook, stirring occasionally, until the shrimp curl and turn pink, about 2 minutes. Add the fish sauce, sugar, and salt and stir to combine. Remove from the heat.

Tear the basil leaves in half (or quarters if they are large), and stir them into the curry, along with the remaining lime leaves (if using). Let rest for 5 minutes to allow the flavors to develop.

Serve hot or warm with rice or noodles, garnished with the chile slices (if using). *—Nancie McDermott*

Selecting the best shrimp

Wild Wild shrimp tend to have a sweeter, more pronounced flavor and a firmer texture than the farmed variety. If you're lucky enough to find some wild-caught shrimp (frozen shrimp will be labeled wild or farmed), grab them, as only about 20% of shrimp sold in the United States is wild-caught.

Frozen There's very little truly "fresh" shrimp to be had in the United States. Most supermarkets simply defrost frozen shrimp and put them on ice at the fish counter. There's no telling how long they've sat around, so buying shrimp that's still frozen is a better way to ensure freshness. Until a few years ago, this meant buying a solid block of frozen shrimp in ice. Now you can buy individually quick frozen, or IQF, shrimp

in 1- or 2-pound plastic bags and defrost as many as you need quickly (it takes only 15 or 20 minutes) when you're ready to use them.

Not treated with STP Many shrimp these days are soaked in a saltwater solution called STP (sodium tripolyphosphate), which helps shrimp maintain its moisture during processing and cooking. This may not sound like such a bad thing, but this solution can give shrimp a saltier flavor and a bit of a spongy texture. To avoid shrimp that contains STP, check the ingredient list on bags of frozen shrimp. If you're buying from a fish counter, ask if it's been treated. If you can find only STP-treated shrimp, be sure to reduce the salt in the recipe.

Shrimp Skewers with Smoky Pimentón Vinaigrette

Serves six; yields 12 skewers.

36 shrimp (21 to 25 per pound; about 1½ pound total), peeled (tail segment left on) and deveined

Twelve 8-inch bamboo skewers, soaked in water

1 recipe Pimentón Vinaigrette (see recipe below)

Shrimp skewers cook very quickly and are perfect for an entertaining menu focused around your backyard barbeque. Skewering the shrimp the day before and marinating them earlier in the day will give you time to enjoy your own party instead of getting stuck in the kitchen. The smoky vinaigrette is used as a marinade here, but would be delicious as a dressing for grilled and sliced flank steak on another night.

Thread three shrimp onto each skewer. Lay the skewers in a large Pyrex® baking dish (or other large nonreactive container) and pour the pimentón vinaigrette over the skewers, turning them to coat completely. Marinate for at least 30 minutes in the refrigerator.

Heat a gas grill to medium high or prepare a medium-hot charcoal fire. Grill the skewers (covered on a gas grill, uncovered on a charcoal grill), flipping once, until the shrimp are just cooked through, about 4 minutes total.
—Allison Ehri Kreitler

Pimentón Vinaigrette

Pimentón is smoked Spanish paprika. You can find it in specialty food stores or online. This can be made up to 2 days ahead and refrigerated.

Yields about ½ cup.

1 large clove garlic

Generous ½ teaspoon kosher salt

¼ cup extra-virgin olive oil

1½ tablespoons fresh lemon juice

1 tablespoon sherry vinegar

1 teaspoon sweet (dulce) pimentón

½ teaspoon freshly ground black pepper

Chop the garlic, sprinkle it with the salt, and mash it into a paste with the side of a chef's knife (or use a mortar and pestle). In a medium bowl, mix the garlic paste, oil, lemon juice, vinegar, pimentón, and pepper. —Allison Ehri Kreitler

Curried Coconut Shrimp

Serves four.

½ cup coarsely shredded coconut, preferably unsweetened

3 tablespoons canola or peanut oil

1 medium yellow onion, finely diced

2 tablespoons coarsely chopped ginger

1 teaspoon kosher salt; more to taste

2 teaspoons Madras hot curry powder

¾ cup canned diced tomatoes with their juices

¾ cup coconut milk

Freshly ground black pepper

1 pound shrimp (26 to 30 or 21 to 25 per pound), peeled and deveined

⅓ cup chopped fresh cilantro

2 tablespoons fresh lime juice

You get a double layer of coconut flavor in this quick curry, with coconut milk as the base of the sauce, and a sprinkling of toasted shredded coconut as a garnish. Unsweetened coconut is sometimes found in the natural foods section of the grocery store.

In a 12-inch skillet over medium heat, toast the coconut, tossing often, until lightly browned, 2 to 5 minutes. Transfer to a plate.

Heat 1½ tablespoons of the oil in the skillet over medium heat until shimmering hot. Add the onion and ginger, sprinkle with ½ teaspoon of the salt, and cook, stirring, until softened, 3 to 5 minutes. Add the curry powder and cook, stirring, for 1 minute. Add the tomatoes and coconut milk and cook, stirring, until the mixture reduces slightly, 3 to 5 minutes. Transfer to a blender and purée. Season to taste with salt and pepper.

Toss the shrimp with the remaining ½ teaspoon salt and several grinds of pepper. Rinse and dry the skillet. Set over medium-high heat until hot, 1 minute. Add the remaining 1½ tablespoons oil and once it's shimmering hot, add the shrimp. Cook without touching for about 2 minutes, allowing the shrimp to brown nicely. Flip and cook until they turn almost completely pink (but are not quite cooked through), about 1½ more minutes.

Add the curry sauce and simmer, stirring, until the shrimp are cooked through and the sauce is hot, 1 to 2 minutes. Stir in half of the cilantro and half of the lime juice. Season to taste with more salt, pepper, and the remaining lime juice. Serve sprinkled with the toasted coconut and the remaining cilantro. —*Tony Rosenfeld*

5 Poultry

p200

p190

**Roast Chicken with
Rosemary-Lemon Salt
(recipe on page 198)**

Orange Chicken with Scallions

Serves two to three.

1 large navel orange

1 tablespoon soy sauce

1 tablespoon rice vinegar

2 teaspoons light brown sugar

⅛ teaspoon crushed red pepper flakes

1 pound boneless, skinless chicken breasts, cut into 1-inch cubes

¾ teaspoon kosher salt

2 large egg whites

⅓ cup cornstarch

3 to 4 tablespoons canola or peanut oil

4 scallions, trimmed and thinly sliced (keep whites and greens separate)

Great stir-fries are easy, if you use a few simple tricks: First, cut the ingredients uniformly so they cook evenly. Use a stir-fry pan, or use a heavy skillet with a large surface area, which will give the ingredients enough space to sear properly. And make sure your pan is truly hot before cooking so the ingredients will brown but not stick.

Using a vegetable peeler, shave the zest from the orange in long, wide strips. If necessary, remove any large patches of bitter white pith from the zest strips with a paring knife. Juice the orange into a small bowl and mix with the soy sauce, rice vinegar, brown sugar, and red pepper flakes.

Sprinkle the chicken with ½ teaspoon of the salt. In a mini chopper or food processor, process the egg whites, cornstarch, and the remaining ¼ teaspoon salt until smooth. In a medium bowl, toss the chicken with the cornstarch batter.

Heat 2 tablespoons of the oil in a 12-inch nonstick skillet or large stir-fry pan over medium-high heat until shimmering hot. Using tongs, transfer about half the chicken to the pan. Reduce the heat to medium and cook, flipping every minute or so, until the chicken browns and crisps all over and is firm to the touch, 3 to 4 minutes. With clean tongs, transfer to a paper-towel-lined plate. Add the remaining 1 tablespoon oil to the skillet (or 2 tablespoons oil if the pan seems very dry) and repeat the cooking process with the remaining chicken; transfer to the plate.

Put the orange zest strips in the skillet and cook, stirring, until they darken in spots, 15 to 30 seconds. Stir the orange juice mixture and add it to the pan. Let it boil for about 10 seconds and then add the chicken and the scallion whites. Cook, stirring often, until the sauce reduces to a glaze and the chicken is just cooked through—check by cutting into a thicker piece—1 to 2 minutes. If the chicken isn't cooked through but the glaze is cooking away, add a couple tablespoons of water and continue cooking. Serve sprinkled with the scallion greens. *—Tony Rosenfeld*

Buttermilk Country Fried Chicken with Cucumber Salad

Serves two.

¼ cup halved and very thinly sliced red onion

1 very small clove garlic

Kosher salt

1 tablespoon canola or vegetable oil, plus 1 to 1¼ cups for frying

¾ cup plus 2 tablespoons buttermilk

1½ teaspoons fresh lemon juice

1 tablespoon chopped fresh dill

Freshly ground black pepper

½ English cucumber, halved lengthwise, seeded, and thinly sliced crosswise (about 1 heaping cup sliced)

¾ cup all-purpose flour

2 boneless, skinless chicken breast halves (about ¾ pound total), pounded to an even thickness (about ½ inch thick)

These fried chicken breasts are a lot quicker to make than old-fashioned fried chicken, but just as delectably crunchy, with a slight tang of buttermilk.

Put the onion in a small bowl, cover it with very hot water, and let it sit for 15 minutes. Roughly chop the garlic, sprinkle it with a generous pinch of salt, and mash it into a paste with the side of a chef's knife. In a medium bowl, whisk the mashed garlic, 1 tablespoon oil, 2 tablespoons buttermilk, the lemon juice, dill, ¼ teaspoon salt, and a few grinds of pepper. Toss the cucumber in the bowl with the dressing. Drain the onion, toss it with the cucumber salad, and let sit to allow the flavors to meld.

Put the flour in a shallow bowl and, in another shallow bowl, mix the remaining ¾ cup buttermilk with 1 teaspoon salt. Season the chicken with ¾ teaspoon salt and ¼ teaspoon pepper. Dip the chicken in the buttermilk and then dredge it in the flour. (You can let the chicken sit in the flour while the oil heats; gently shake off excess flour before cooking.)

Choose a skillet (preferably cast iron) that's large enough to fit the chicken. Pour in oil to a depth of ¼ inch (about 1 cup for a 10-inch skillet or 1¼ cups for an 11-inch skillet). Heat over medium-high heat. When the oil is shimmering and the chicken sizzles briskly when a corner is dipped in the oil, cook the chicken until golden brown on both sides, 2 to 3 minutes per side. Transfer the chicken to paper towels and pat lightly to absorb excess oil. Sprinkle the chicken with a pinch of salt and serve it with the cucumber salad. *—Allison Ehri Kreitler*

Grilled Thai Chicken Breasts with Herb-Lemongrass Crust

Before chopping the lemongrass, be sure to cut off the spiky green top and enough of the bottom to eliminate the woody core. Peel off a few of the outer layers until you're left with just the tender heart of the stalk. Though these breasts are incredible served hot off the grill, they're also delicious served cold, either plain or sliced on top of a salad.

Combine 1¼ cups of the cilantro with the coconut milk, lemongrass, basil, chiles, garlic, salt, brown sugar, pepper, and coriander in a food processor or blender and purée until smooth. Arrange the chicken breasts in a nonreactive baking dish or other vessel large enough to accommodate them in a snug single layer. Pour the marinade over the breasts and turn to coat them well. Cover and refrigerate for at least 2 hours and up to 1 day.

Heat a gas grill to medium high or prepare a medium-hot charcoal fire. Grill the chicken (covered on a gas grill) until it has good grill marks on the first side, 4 to 5 minutes. Flip the chicken (cover a gas grill) and continue to cook until firm to the touch and completely cooked through (check by making a slice into one of the thicker breasts), 5 to 6 more minutes. Transfer to a platter and let rest for 5 minutes. Sprinkle with the remaining ¼ cup cilantro and serve with the lime wedges. *—Tony Rosenfeld*

Serves twelve.

- 1½ cups chopped fresh cilantro (leaves and tender stems)
- ¾ cup coconut milk
- ¼ cup finely chopped lemongrass (from about 2 stalks)
- 12 fresh basil leaves
- 3 Thai bird chiles, 2 jalapeños, or 2 medium serranos, stemmed, seeded, and finely chopped
- 3 cloves garlic, minced
- 1½ tablespoons kosher salt
- 2 teaspoons packed light brown sugar
- 1½ teaspoons freshly ground black pepper
- ¾ teaspoon ground coriander
- 12 boneless, skinless chicken breast halves (5 to 5½ pounds), trimmed (remove tenderloins if still attached)
- 2 limes, cut into wedges for serving

Chicken Breasts Stuffed with Prosciutto, Parmesan & Sun-Dried Tomatoes

Serves two.

3 tablespoons freshly grated
Parmigiano-Reggiano

2 tablespoons finely chopped
prosciutto

2 tablespoons finely chopped,
well-drained sun-dried
tomatoes

1 teaspoon finely chopped
fresh sage or ¼ teaspoon
dried sage

1 tablespoon plus 1 teaspoon
unsalted butter, softened

Kosher salt and freshly ground
black pepper

2 boneless, skin-on chicken
breast halves

1 tablespoon olive oil

This chicken, with its crisp skin, tender meat, and savory filling, will surely become a favorite. Make a double or even triple batch of the stuffing, freeze it in batches in a zip-top bag, and simply pull it out at the last minute for a quick dinner. The small amount of filling will thaw in a few minutes by soaking the bag in cold water.

Heat the oven to 450°F.

In a small bowl, combine the Parmigiano, prosciutto, sun-dried tomatoes, sage, and 1 tablespoon of the butter; mix until well blended. Taste and season with pepper and possibly more salt; the mixture should be highly seasoned.

Gently slide your index finger under the skin of one chicken breast to create a small pocket. Scoop up some of the filling and push it into the pocket, spreading it as evenly as possible. Do this in a few places until you've used half the filling and covered the top of the breast, but be careful not to completely detach the skin from the meat. Stretch the skin over the filling and breast as evenly as possible. Repeat with the second breast. Chill in the freezer for about 5 minutes to let the filling firm up.

Heat a cast-iron or other heavy-based ovenproof skillet on the stove over medium-high heat. Season both sides of the chicken with salt and pepper. When the pan is hot, add the oil and the remaining 1 teaspoon butter. When the butter stops foaming, add the chicken breasts, skin side down. Don't try to move them for at least 1 minute or the skin might tear. After 1 minute or so, you can move them around to be sure they're not sticking. Cook until the skin side is well browned, about 4 minutes.

Carefully slide a thin spatula under the chicken and flip it over, taking care not to rip the skin. Put the pan in the hot oven and continue cooking until the chicken is no longer pink inside, about 10 minutes, or until an instant-read thermometer registers 165°F at the thickest part. Take the breasts from the oven, let them rest for 3 to 5 minutes tented with foil, and then serve immediately. *—Martha Holmberg*

Crispy Chicken Breasts with Lemon & Capers

Serves four.

4 small boneless, skinless chicken breast halves (6 to 7 ounces each), trimmed of excess fat

¾ cup freshly grated Parmigiano-Reggiano

5 tablespoons capers (preferably nonpareils), rinsed, patted dry, and chopped

2 tablespoons chopped fresh thyme

3 tablespoons extra-virgin olive oil

2 tablespoons Dijon mustard

1 lemon, zest finely grated, cut into wedges

½ teaspoon kosher salt

½ teaspoon freshly ground black pepper

3½ cups Toasted Breadcrumbs (see recipe at right)

You'll need to make a double batch of breadcrumbs for this recipe so you might want to use two pans so you can make both batches at the same time.

Heat the oven to 450°F. Put a flat rack on a large rimmed baking sheet lined with foil.

With a meat pounder or a heavy skillet, lightly pound the chicken between two sheets of plastic wrap to even out the thickness of the breasts.

In a large bowl, mix ¼ cup of the Parmigiano, 2½ tablespoons of the capers, 1 tablespoon of the thyme, and the oil, mustard, lemon zest, salt, and pepper. Squeeze one or two of the lemon wedges to get 1 tablespoon juice and add to the mixture, along with 2 tablespoons water. Add the chicken and toss to coat well. You can proceed directly to coating the chicken breasts with crumbs, or let them marinate in the fridge for up to 24 hours.

Put the breadcrumbs in a large shallow dish and toss with the remaining ½ cup Parmigiano, 2½ tablespoons capers, and 1 tablespoon thyme. Working with one piece at a time, transfer the chicken to the dish of crumbs, scoop some crumbs on top, and press well a couple of times so the crumbs adhere to both sides. Transfer to the rack on the baking sheet.

Bake the chicken until it's firm to the touch and registers 165°F on an instant-read thermometer, about 20 minutes. Serve immediately with the remaining lemon wedges for squeezing over the chicken. —*Tony Rosenfeld*

Toasted Breadcrumbs

These breadcrumbs form the base for the coating in the crispy chicken at left and on pages 172 and 173. You can cook up a batch in advance to save time; they'll keep for up to 3 days in an airtight container at room temperature. Or if you want to whip up a few batches of crumbs, you can store them in a zip-top bag in your freezer for a couple of months.

Yields about 2 cups.

About ½ pound fresh white bread, preferably a firm country loaf (to yield 4 cups coarse crumbs)

2 tablespoons extra-virgin olive oil or melted unsalted butter

¼ teaspoon kosher salt

Tear or cut the bread into 1- to 2-inch pieces. Put a few handfuls into the bowl of a food processor (the bread shouldn't be crowded or squished), and pulse into coarse crumbs, including smaller pieces the size of oatmeal flakes and larger pieces about the size of small peas. Pour the

crumbs into a large bowl. Repeat until you have made 4 cups of breadcrumbs.

Toss the breadcrumbs with the olive oil or butter and the salt. Set a large (preferably 12-inch), heavy-based skillet (cast iron is great) over medium heat. Add the breadcrumbs and cook, stirring or tossing often—they should sizzle and make a steady popping noise—until they start to color and crisp, about 5 minutes. Reduce the heat to medium low and continue to cook, stirring, until the crumbs dry out and crisp and have browned nicely, about 6 minutes.

Let cool; the crumbs will continue to crisp as they cool.

—Tony Rosenfeld

1 **Pound** just enough to even out the thickness so the chicken will cook evenly (don't make them too thin). If tenderloins are attached, remove, bread, and bake them with the breasts (they'll cook faster).

2 **Flavor** the chicken with sticky ingredients that will help the breadcrumbs adhere to the meat.

3 **Coat** with precooked crumbs that are already very crisp.

4 **Bake** in a hot oven until browned and cooked through.

tip: Pack on the crumbs. The crumbs in the recipes on pages 168, 172, and 173 are coarser than your average breadcrumbs, so it takes a little extra force to get the crumbs to adhere. Pat a healthy amount of breadcrumbs on top of the chicken and then use the heel of your hand and a firm rotating motion to press the crumbs onto the chicken. Don't shake off the excess when transferring the breasts to the baking sheet; you want to keep as many crumbs on the chicken as possible.

Crispy Cheddar & Jalapeño–Coated Chicken Breasts

Serves four.

4 small boneless, skinless chicken breast halves (6 to 7 ounces each), trimmed of excess fat

1 cup plain yogurt, preferably whole-milk

1 tablespoon chopped fresh thyme

1 tablespoon light brown sugar

2 teaspoons chili powder

1 teaspoon garlic powder

1 teaspoon kosher salt

½ teaspoon freshly ground black pepper

2 cups Toasted Breadcrumbs (see recipe on page 169)

¼ pound tortilla chips, crushed into coarse crumbs (about 1⅓ cups)

¼ pound sharp Cheddar, grated (about 1 lightly packed cup)

½ to ⅔ cup sliced jarred jalapeños, chopped and patted dry

1 lime, cut into wedges

You can pound the chicken and immerse it in the flavor bath the day before you plan to cook it. The results will be excellent because the flavors will really sink into the meat.

Heat the oven to 450°F. Put a flat rack on a large rimmed baking sheet lined with foil.

With a meat pounder or a heavy skillet, lightly pound the chicken between two sheets of plastic wrap to even out the thickness of the breasts.

In a large bowl, mix the yogurt with half of the thyme, the brown sugar, chili powder, garlic powder, salt, and pepper. Add the chicken and toss to coat well. You can proceed directly to coating the chicken breasts with crumbs, or let them marinate in the fridge for up to 24 hours.

Put the breadcrumbs in a large shallow dish and toss with the tortilla chips, Cheddar, jalapeños, and the remaining thyme. Working with one piece at a time, transfer the chicken to the dish of crumbs, scoop some crumbs on top, and press well so the breadcrumbs adhere to both sides. Transfer to the rack on the baking sheet.

Bake the chicken until it's firm to the touch and registers 165°F on an instant-read thermometer, about 20 minutes. Serve immediately with the lime wedges for squeezing over the chicken. *—Tony Rosenfeld*

Herbed Chicken Breasts with a Crispy Black Olive & Parmigiano Crust

The olives, Parmigiano, and sun-dried tomatoes give this crust a wonderful savory essence and a healthy dose of salt, too, so you may want to reduce or omit the salt from the breadcrumbs recipe, if you like.

Heat the oven to 450°F. Put a flat rack on a large rimmed baking sheet lined with foil.

With a meat pounder or a heavy skillet, lightly pound the chicken between two sheets of plastic wrap to even out the thickness of the breasts.

In a large bowl, mix the oil and mustard with half of the thyme, half of the rosemary, and the salt and pepper. Add the chicken and toss to coat well. You can proceed directly to coating the chicken breasts with crumbs, or let them marinate in the fridge for up to 24 hours.

Put the breadcrumbs in a large shallow dish and toss with the olives, Parmigiano, sun-dried tomatoes, and the remaining thyme and rosemary. Working with one piece at a time, transfer the chicken to the dish of crumbs, scoop some crumbs on top, and press well a couple of times so the crumbs adhere to both sides (these crumbs will be a little wet, so really press them on). Transfer to the rack on the baking sheet.

Bake the chicken until it's firm to the touch and registers 165°F on an instant-read thermometer, about 20 minutes. Serve immediately with the lemon wedges for squeezing over the chicken. *—Tony Rosenfeld*

Serves four.

4 small boneless, skinless chicken breast halves (6 to 7 ounces each), trimmed of excess fat

2 tablespoons extra-virgin olive oil

2 tablespoons whole-grain mustard

4 teaspoons chopped fresh thyme

2 teaspoons chopped fresh rosemary

½ teaspoon kosher salt

½ teaspoon freshly ground black pepper

2 cups Toasted Breadcrumbs (see recipe on page 169)

1 cup pitted Kalamata olives, rinsed, patted dry, and chopped

¾ cup freshly grated Parmigiano-Reggiano

3 tablespoons chopped oil-packed sun-dried tomatoes (about 3 large tomato halves; pat dry before chopping)

1 lemon, cut into wedges

Chinese Five-Spice-Crusted Duck Breasts

Serves four.

**4 boneless duck breast halves
with skin (2 to 2½ pounds)**

**1½ teaspoons Chinese five-
spice powder**

¾ teaspoon kosher salt

**¼ teaspoon freshly ground
black pepper**

Duck shouldn't just be enjoyed at a restaurant, nor only on special occasions. Duck breasts are widely available at grocery stores (sometimes in the freezer section), and a duck breast is as easy to cook as a pork chop. This duck would go nicely with a wild rice pilaf with toasted almonds and sautéed Asian greens seasoned with a touch of sesame oil.

Trim the visible fat and silverskin from the flesh side of the duck. If the tenderloins are still on the breasts, leave them on. Don't trim the skin side; simply score the duck skin in a crosshatch pattern to allow the fat to cook out. Mix the five-spice powder with the salt and pepper in a small bowl. Gently rub the mixture all over the duck.

Heat a 12-inch skillet over medium-low heat and put the duck, skin side down, in the skillet. Slowly render the fat from the skin without moving the duck breasts. After 15 minutes, tilt the pan and carefully spoon off as much fat as possible. Cook until the skin is dark golden brown and crisp, about 25 minutes total.

Flip the breasts with a metal spatula (carefully loosen the skin if it's stuck to the pan). Increase the heat to medium and finish cooking the duck until the second side is golden and the duck is done to your liking, another 3 to 7 minutes, depending on thickness. (An instant-read thermometer should register 135°F for medium doneness, which will still be pink and juicy.)

Transfer the duck breasts to a cutting board and let rest, skin side up, for about 5 minutes before serving either whole or sliced on an angle into medallions. *—Allison Ehri Kreitler*

Roasted Chicken Thighs with Late-Summer Vegetables & Pan Sauce

Serves three to four.

6 skin-on, bone-in chicken thighs (2½ to 3 pounds)

Kosher salt and freshly ground black pepper

3 tablespoons extra-virgin olive oil

½ pound green beans, stem ends trimmed (2 cups)

10 ounces cherry or grape tomatoes (2 cups)

½ large sweet onion (like Vidalia or Walla Walla) or red onion, cut into ½-inch-thick slices

½ cup pitted Niçoise or Kalamata olives

2 large cloves garlic, sliced about ⅛ inch thick

¾ cup dry white wine

1 teaspoon unsalted butter (optional)

½ cup loosely packed fresh basil leaves, sliced into ½-inch strips

Feel free to improvise with the selection of vegetables, depending on what's fresh in your market. Yellow wax beans, thick slices of red bell pepper, or tender summer squash would also be lovely in this colorful dish.

Position two racks near the center of the oven and heat the oven to 425°F. Heat a 10- to 11-inch heavy, ovenproof skillet over medium-high heat. Generously season the chicken on both sides with salt and pepper. Pour 1 tablespoon of the oil into the hot skillet and swirl to coat. Arrange the chicken thighs skin side down in the pan and cook until the skin is golden brown, about 7 minutes. Turn the chicken over. If a lot of fat has accumulated, carefully spoon it off and discard.

While the chicken browns, toss the beans, tomatoes, onion, olives, and garlic in a large bowl with the remaining 2 tablespoons oil. Season with ¾ teaspoon salt and several grinds of pepper and spread the vegetables on a rimmed baking sheet.

Put the skillet of chicken and the baking sheet with the vegetables in the oven, with the chicken on the higher rack. Roast the chicken until a thermometer inserted in the center of a thigh registers 170°F, 18 to 20 minutes. Continue to roast the vegetables until very soft and beginning to brown, 8 to 12 minutes more.

Meanwhile, remove the skillet from the oven and transfer the chicken to a plate. Spoon off and discard as much fat as possible from the chicken juices, add the wine, set over high heat, and boil until reduced to about ¼ cup sauce, 4 to 6 minutes; it should be syrupy and concentrated in flavor. Swirl in the butter, if using.

Remove the vegetables from the oven and toss them with the basil. Divide the vegetables among four plates. Arrange one or two chicken thighs on the vegetables and drizzle with the pan sauce. Serve immediately.
—Martha Holmberg

Lime Chicken with Poblano Sour Cream

Serves four.

4 large poblano chiles

1 large lime

½ cup sour cream or Mexican crema

2 tablespoons chopped fresh cilantro, plus a few sprigs for garnish (optional)

2 teaspoons kosher salt; more to taste

1 tablespoon ground coriander

1 teaspoon ground cumin

½ teaspoon freshly ground black pepper

8 medium (5- to 6-ounce) bone-in, skin-on chicken thighs, trimmed

3 tablespoons extra-virgin olive oil

Real Mexican crema will give this dish a more authentic flavor than plain sour cream, though either is fine. Look for crema in the dairy case or near the tortillas in supermarkets. Making your own is fun and easy; see the recipe on the facing page.

Position an oven rack 5 to 6 inches from the broiler element and heat the broiler to high. Line the bottom of a broiler pan with foil and replace the perforated top part of the pan. Broil the poblanos, turning 3 times, until blackened, 12 to 15 minutes total. Put the poblanos in a medium bowl, top with a dinner plate, and let stand for 5 minutes.

Meanwhile, cut the lime in half. Cut one half into wedges and squeeze the other half to get 2 teaspoons juice. Measure the juice into a small bowl and stir in the sour cream or crema and the chopped cilantro.

Transfer the poblanos to a cutting board to cool a bit, then peel away the burned skin, discard the stems and seeds, and cut into ½-inch dice. Add to the sour cream mixture and stir to combine. Season to taste with salt.

In a small bowl, combine the 2 teaspoons salt with the coriander, cumin, and pepper. Coat the chicken with the oil and season on both sides with the spice mixture. Put the chicken skin side down on the broiler pan and broil until well browned, 7 to 10 minutes. Turn the chicken over with tongs and continue to broil, checking frequently, until the chicken is dark brown and cooked through (an instant-read thermometer should register at least 165°F), 4 to 6 minutes more. If the chicken threatens to burn before it's cooked through, move the pan to a lower rack.

Transfer the chicken to serving plates, spoon the poblano sour cream on the side, and garnish with cilantro sprigs, if using, and the lime wedges for squeezing over the chicken. Serve hot. —*Lori Longbotham*

Buy tangy Mexican crema, or make it yourself

Crema is the Mexican version of French crème fraîche. Both are slightly soured and thickened cream, milder and less thick than American sour cream, with crema being the thinnest. You can buy crema in Mexican markets or even in some supermarkets, but it's easy to make it yourself, and the result has a smoother flavor than that of the commercially prepared version.

Homemade Crema (Mexican Sour Cream)

Yields about 1 cup.

Use crema as you would sour cream, dolloping or drizzling it on soups, tacos, potatoes, or anything else that needs a little tang. Start with pasteurized cream if you can find it—it makes a richer, thicker crema than ultrapasteurized cream does. It will keep for about 2 weeks in the refrigerator, continuing to thicken as it ages.

1 cup heavy cream (pasteurized or ultrapasteurized)

1 tablespoon buttermilk (with active cultures)

In a small saucepan, warm the cream over medium-low heat to about 95°F, just enough to take off the chill. If it goes over 100°F, let it cool before continuing.

Stir in the buttermilk and transfer to a clean glass jar. Set the lid loosely on top of the jar—don't tighten—and let sit in a warm spot, such as near the stove or on top of the fridge, until the cream starts to thicken, 18 to 24 hours. Stir, tighten the lid, and refrigerate until the cream is thicker and thoroughly chilled, 12 to 24 hours more. Stir well before using. The crema should have a thick but pourable consistency.

Grilled Five-Spice Chicken Thighs with Soy-Vinegar Sauce & Cilantro

Serves four to six.

- 2 tablespoons Chinese five-spice powder
- 1 tablespoon plus 1 teaspoon dark brown sugar
- 1 teaspoon garlic powder
- ¾ teaspoon kosher salt
- 2 tablespoons soy sauce
- 2 teaspoons rice vinegar
- 1 teaspoon Asian sesame oil
- ¼ teaspoon crushed red pepper flakes
- 2½ pounds boneless, skinless chicken thighs (about 8 large, 10 medium, or 12 small), trimmed of excess fat
- 2 tablespoons vegetable oil; more for the grill
- 3 tablespoons chopped cilantro

Boneless, skinless chicken thighs offer all the benefits of boneless chicken breasts—convenience and fast cooking—without the tendency to turn tasteless and dry, thanks to their slightly higher fat content.

Mix the five-spice powder, the 1 tablespoon sugar, the garlic powder, and the salt in a small bowl. In another bowl, mix the soy sauce, vinegar, sesame oil, red pepper flakes, and remaining 1 teaspoon sugar.

Put the chicken in a shallow pan, drizzle with the vegetable oil, and toss to coat evenly. Sprinkle the spice mixture over the chicken; toss and rub to coat thoroughly.

Prepare a hot charcoal fire or heat a gas grill with all burners on medium high for 10 minutes. Clean the hot grate with a wire brush and then lubricate it with an oil-soaked paper towel. Put the chicken on the grate and grill (covered on a gas grill or uncovered over a charcoal fire) until one side has dark grill marks, 5 to 6 minutes for large thighs or 4 to 5 minutes for medium and small thighs. Turn and continue to grill until well marked on the other sides and cooked through, 5 to 6 minutes longer for large thighs or 4 to 5 minutes for medium and small thighs.

Move the thighs to a serving dish. Drizzle with about half of the soy mixture, sprinkle with the cilantro, and toss to coat. Let rest for 4 to 5 minutes, tossing once or twice. Serve hot, warm, or at room temperature, with the remaining soy mixture passed at the table. *—Pam Anderson*

Quick and succulent grilled chicken thighs

Unfold the boneless chicken thighs, remove any large pockets of fat, and spread the pieces flat on the hot grill.

Don't turn the thighs for 4 to 6 minutes, so that they develop nice grill marks. To check for doneness, look for the chicken thighs to shrink and plump up a bit when they're ready to be taken off the grill.

Grilled Rosemary Chicken Skewers with Sweet & Sour Orange Dipping Sauce

Serves four to six.

- 1 tablespoons plus 1 teaspoon minced fresh rosemary
- 2 teaspoons dark brown sugar
- 2 teaspoons kosher salt
- 1 teaspoon freshly ground black pepper
- 1 teaspoon crushed red pepper flakes
- 2 tablespoons vegetable oil; more for the grill
- 2½ pounds boneless, skinless chicken thighs (about 8 large, 10 medium, or 12 small), trimmed of excess fat, sliced into 1½-inch-wide strips
- 1 cup orange marmalade
- ¼ cup rice vinegar

Chicken thighs lend themselves to kebabs, which make a nice change of pace on the grill. Just put a few slices of chicken on each skewer and serve as an hors d'oeuvre, or serve full skewers with rice and a salad as a fresh and light main dish.

In a small bowl, mix the 1 tablespoon rosemary with the brown sugar, salt, pepper, and red pepper flakes. In a shallow pan, drizzle the oil over the chicken and toss to coat. Sprinkle the chicken evenly with the rosemary mixture.

Warm the marmalade, vinegar, and remaining 1 teaspoon rosemary in a small saucepan over low heat until just warm; set aside in a warm spot.

Prepare a hot charcoal fire or heat a gas grill with all burners on medium high for 10 minutes. Thread the chicken onto skewers (soak wood skewers in water for at least 20 minutes first), folding each strip in half as you skewer it. If some strips are very thick, cut them in half crosswise rather than folding them so that all the pieces of chicken are roughly the same size. Clean the hot grate with a wire brush and then lubricate it with an oil-soaked paper towel.

Grill the skewers, turning them every 4 to 5 minutes as dark grill marks form, until cooked through, 12 to 15 minutes total.

Serve hot, warm, or at room temperature with individual bowls of warm marmalade dipping sauce. *—Pam Anderson*

Grilled Tandoori-Style Chicken Thighs

Serves four to six.

1½ tablespoons ground cumin

1½ teaspoons curry powder

1½ teaspoons kosher salt

1 teaspoon garlic powder

½ teaspoon ground ginger

¼ teaspoon cayenne

2 tablespoons vegetable oil;
  more for the grill

3 tablespoons red-wine vinegar

½ cup regular or nonfat plain
  yogurt

2½ pounds boneless, skinless
  chicken thighs (about 8 large,
  10 medium, or 12 small),
  trimmed of excess fat

3 tablespoons chopped cilantro

The longer you marinate the chicken thighs in this yogurt-based mixture, the more succulent and tangy they become, but even a short swim through the marinade will add flavor. Serve these with a basmati rice pilaf.

Mix the cumin, curry powder, salt, garlic powder, ginger, and cayenne in a medium bowl. Heat the oil in an 8-inch skillet over low heat. Stir the spices into the oil and heat until they bubble and become fragrant, 30 to 60 seconds. Return the spice blend to the bowl and stir in the vinegar and then the yogurt. Add the chicken thighs and toss to coat evenly. Let sit for 10 minutes or cover and marinate in the refrigerator for up to 12 hours.

When ready to cook, prepare a hot charcoal fire or heat a gas grill with all burners on medium high for 10 minutes. Clean the hot grate with a wire brush and then lubricate it with an oil-soaked paper towel. Put the chicken on the grate and grill (covered on a gas grill or uncovered over a charcoal fire) until one side has dark grill marks, 5 to 6 minutes for large thighs or 4 to 5 minutes for medium and small thighs. Turn and continue to grill until well marked on the other sides and cooked through, 5 to 6 minutes longer for large thighs or 4 to 5 minutes for medium and small thighs. Move the thighs to a platter and let rest for 4 to 5 minutes. Sprinkle with the chopped cilantro before serving.
—Pam Anderson

Indonesian Grilled Chicken Thighs with Mango-Peanut Salsa

Try to find the small, yellow ataulfo mango, sometimes called a Champagne mango, which has beautifully smooth, fiber-free flesh that's easy to dice. The flavor is as fine as the texture—sweet and full of tropical perfume.

Mix the ginger, coriander, turmeric, and garlic powder in a medium bowl. Heat 2 tablespoons of the oil in an 8-inch skillet over low heat. Add the spices to the hot oil and heat until they bubble and become fragrant, 30 to 60 seconds. Return the spice blend to the bowl; stir in the chile paste, brown sugar, and salt. The mixture will be thick and pasty. Add the chicken and toss to coat evenly.

In a medium bowl, mix the mango, bell pepper, peanuts, scallions, cilantro or mint, jalapeño, and the remaining 1 tablespoon oil. Add the lime juice to taste. Set aside. (You can season the chicken and make the salsa up to 2 hours ahead and refrigerate.)

Prepare a hot charcoal fire or heat a gas grill with all burners on medium high for 10 minutes. Clean the hot grate with a wire brush and then lubricate it with an oil-soaked paper towel. Put the chicken on the grate and grill (covered on a gas grill or uncovered over a charcoal fire) until one side has dark grill marks, 5 to 6 minutes for large thighs or 4 to 5 minutes for medium and small thighs. Turn and continue to grill until well marked on the other sides and cooked through, 5 to 6 minutes longer for large thighs or 4 to 5 minutes for medium and small thighs.

Move the thighs to a platter, let rest for 4 to 5 minutes, and serve hot, warm, or at room temperature with the salsa alongside. *–Pam Anderson*

Serves four to six.

1 tablespoon ground ginger

1 tablespoon ground coriander

1½ teaspoons turmeric

1½ teaspoons garlic powder

3 tablespoons vegetable oil; more for the grill

1 tablespoon Asian chile paste (like sambal oelek)

1 tablespoon dark brown sugar

2 teaspoons kosher salt

2½ pounds boneless, skinless chicken thighs (about 8 large, 10 medium, or 12 small), trimmed of excess fat

2 cups small-diced fresh mango

½ cup small-diced red bell pepper (from 1 small pepper)

½ cup salted peanuts, coarsely chopped

⅓ cup thinly sliced scallions (white and green parts of 4 to 5 scallions)

3 tablespoons chopped fresh cilantro or mint, or a combination

1 tablespoon seeded, minced jalapeño

2 to 3 tablespoons fresh lime juice

Green Curry with Chicken & Eggplant

Serves four.

1 pound boneless, skinless chicken thighs (4 large)

2 small Japanese eggplants or 2 very small Italian eggplants (about 4 ounces each)

2 tablespoons vegetable oil

1½ to 2 tablespoons jarred or homemade green curry paste

One 15-ounce can unsweetened coconut milk

1 cup low-salt chicken broth

5 wild lime leaves, torn or cut into quarters (optional)

2 tablespoons fish sauce

1 tablespoon palm sugar or light brown sugar

¼ teaspoon kosher salt

A handful of fresh Thai or Italian basil leaves

Hot cooked rice or rice noodles for serving

1 long, slender fresh red chile (such as red jalapeño or serrano), thinly sliced on the diagonal (optional)

tip: In these recipes, the traditional ingredients palm sugar and Thai basil can be replaced with easier-to-find light brown sugar and Italian basil. Wild lime leaves have no good substitution, though, so leave them out if you can't find them.

Green curry paste tends to be spicier than red. If you make your own curry paste, it may be even hotter than the jarred paste, depending on the type of chiles you use. To make sure you don't go too high on the heat scale, start with the lesser amount of paste and add more to taste.

Trim the chicken and cut it into bite-size chunks. Trim the eggplant, cutting away stems and bottoms. Quarter each lengthwise, and then slice crosswise at 1-inch intervals.

Heat the oil in a 2- to 3-quart saucepan over medium heat until a bit of curry paste just sizzles when added to the pan. Add all the curry paste and cook, pressing and stirring with a wooden spoon or heatproof spatula to soften the paste and mix it in with the oil, until fragrant, about 2 minutes.

Increase the heat to medium high and add the chicken. Spread it in a single layer and cook undisturbed until it starts to brown around the edges, 1 to 2 minutes. Stir and continue cooking until most of the chicken is lightly browned, 1 to 2 minutes.

Add the coconut milk and chicken broth and stir well, scraping the bottom of the pan to release the browned bits. Add the eggplant and half the lime leaves (if using) and bring to a simmer.

Simmer, adjusting the heat as needed and stirring occasionally, until the chicken is completely done and the eggplant is tender, 8 to 10 minutes.

Add the fish sauce, sugar, and salt and stir. Remove from the heat. Tear the basil leaves in half (or quarters if they are large), and stir them into the curry, along with the remaining lime leaves (if using). Let rest for 5 minutes to allow the flavors to develop.

Serve hot or warm with rice or noodles, garnished with the chile slices (if using). —*Nancie McDermott*

Spicy Fried Chicken

Serves four to six.

9 ounces (2 cups) all-purpose flour

½ cup plain low-fat yogurt

2 tablespoons chili powder

2½ teaspoons kosher salt; more as needed

2 teaspoons Bell's® Poultry Seasoning

2 teaspoons onion powder

2 teaspoons freshly ground black pepper

½ teaspoon celery seed

½ to ¾ teaspoon cayenne

2½ cups vegetable oil

8 chicken drumsticks, skin removed

The spiced coating for these juicy drumsticks is what Shake 'N Bake® only dreams of being. If you use a large sauté pan (ideally 12 inches), you'll be able to fry all your chicken in one batch; otherwise, use two pans.

Put the flour in a large, sturdy brown paper bag and the yogurt in a medium bowl. To the flour, add 1 tablespoon of the chili powder, 2 teaspoons of the salt, 1 teaspoon each of the poultry seasoning, onion powder, and pepper, and ¼ teaspoon each of the celery seeds and cayenne. Roll the top of the bag closed and shake to combine.

To the yogurt, add the remaining 1 tablespoon chili powder, the remaining 1 teaspoon each poultry seasoning, onion powder, and pepper, ½ teaspoon of the salt, the remaining ¼ teaspoon celery seeds, and ¼ to ½ teaspoon cayenne. Mix well.

In an 11- or 12-inch straight-sided sauté pan or cast-iron skillet, heat the vegetable oil over medium heat.

Add the drumsticks to the yogurt mixture and stir and toss (with your hands or tongs) to coat completely. Put 4 of the drumsticks in the bag with the flour mixture, close the bag, and shake vigorously (over the sink in case any flour escapes) to coat well. Shake off excess flour, put the drumsticks on a plate, and repeat with the remaining chicken.

Put the drumsticks in the hot oil, cover, and fry until they're golden brown on the bottom, 5 to 7 minutes. Turn each drumstick and continue to fry, uncovered, turning occasionally as needed to brown evenly, until golden brown and cooked through, 5 to 10 minutes longer (cut into a piece to check). Put the drumsticks on a wire rack set over paper towels to drain and sprinkle all over with salt while still hot. Serve hot, warm, or at room temperature. *—Pam Anderson*

Jerk Chicken Drumsticks

Scotch bonnet chiles are authentic, but they're very hot and can be hard to find; the habanero chile is a good substitute. If you want to tame the heat, use less habanero or Scotch bonnet but don't substitute a less spicy variety.

In a food processor, pulse the scallions, chile, vinegar, thyme, garlic, allspice, salt, and pepper to a thick paste. Transfer the paste to a large bowl, add the chicken, and toss to coat. Let stand for 10 minutes.

Position an oven rack in the center of the oven and heat the broiler to high. Line the bottom of a broiler pan with foil and replace the perforated top part of the pan. Oil the pan or coat with cooking spray. Arrange the chicken on the broiler pan. Season generously on all sides with salt.

Broil the chicken in the center of the oven, turning once after about 10 minutes, until fully cooked and nicely browned in spots, about 20 minutes total. Transfer to a platter and serve. –*Lori Longbotham*

Serves five to six.

10 thin scallions, white and tender green parts, coarsely chopped

1 Scotch bonnet or habanero chile, seeded and coarsely chopped

2 tablespoons distilled white-wine vinegar

1 tablespoon fresh thyme leaves

3 medium cloves garlic, chopped

1¼ teaspoons ground allspice

1 teaspoon kosher salt; more as needed

½ teaspoon freshly ground black pepper

10 chicken drumsticks (3½ pounds)

Vegetable oil or cooking spray for the pan

Roasted Chicken Legs with Lemon & Green Olives

Serves six.

6 chicken leg quarters (drumsticks and thighs connected; 4 to 5 pounds)

3 tablespoons extra-virgin olive oil; more as needed

1 teaspoon dried thyme

1 teaspoon kosher salt

¼ teaspoon crushed red pepper flakes

1 small lemon, scrubbed, halved lengthwise, seeded, and sliced into ⅛-inch-thick half moons (discard the ends)

Heaping ½ cup unpitted green olives, preferably Picholine or Lucques

This dish gets complex flavor from good-quality green olives—which are at once buttery and briny—and the roasted lemon slices. Be sure to tell your guests that the olives have pits, and encourage them to eat the roasted lemon slices, rind and all. They add a nice sour-bitter counterpoint to the rich chicken meat. If Meyer lemons are in season, by all means use them here.

Position a rack in the center of the oven and heat the oven to 450°F.

If portions of the backbone are still attached to the chicken quarters, cut them off and discard. Pat the chicken dry with paper towels. In a small bowl, combine the olive oil, thyme, salt, and red pepper flakes. Using your fingers, rub all of the seasoned oil over all the chicken pieces, carefully separating the skin from the meat and rubbing the oil under the skin as well. Arrange the legs skin side up (not overlapping) on a heavy-duty rimmed baking sheet. Roast the chicken for 20 minutes.

Meanwhile, put the lemon slices and olives in a small bowl. When the chicken has roasted for 20 minutes, take the pan out of the oven and spoon a little of the fat from the pan over the lemons and olives (or use a little fresh olive oil). Scatter the lemons and olives on the baking sheet around but not on top of the chicken, trying to keep the lemon slices away from the edge of the pan where they might burn.

Continue to roast until the chicken juices run clear when pierced with a knife and an instant-read thermometer inserted in a thigh registers 170°F, another 20 to 25 minutes. Transfer the chicken, olives, and lemon slices to a platter and serve. *—Molly Stevens*

Moroccan Chicken with Olives & Preserved Lemons

Serves four.

For the charmoula:

1 medium onion, finely diced (to yield about 1 cup)

About 10 sprigs fresh cilantro, leaves and stems finely chopped; more chopped leaves for garnish

Small bunch fresh flat-leaf parsley, leaves and stems finely chopped

1 teaspoon paprika

½ teaspoon ground ginger

¼ teaspoon turmeric

¼ teaspoon ground cumin

¼ teaspoon kosher salt

¼ teaspoon freshly ground black pepper

⅛ to ¼ teaspoon cayenne

Small pinch saffron (about 10 threads), crushed

For the chicken:

¼ cup olive oil

One 3-pound chicken, cut into eight pieces

1 preserved lemon (see recipe on the facing page), most of the pulp removed; the rind cut into thin strips

1 cup red-brown unpitted olives, such as Gaetas

This quintessentially Moroccan dish calls for browning the chicken first and then marinating it in charmoula, a fragrant North African marinade, before slowly stewing everything together. The entire stew may be cooked up to two days ahead and gently reheated. Traditional preserved lemons must be made about a month ahead, but you can buy them in jars at many specialty stores.

Make the charmoula: In a large bowl, mix the onion, cilantro, parsley, and spices.

Cook the chicken: In a deep skillet or a Dutch oven, heat the oil on medium-high heat. Cook the chicken in two batches until browned on all sides, about 3 minutes per side, transferring the pieces to the bowl with the charmoula as they're done. Pour off and discard most of the oil in the pan, leaving a film on the bottom. Toss the chicken to coat it.

Pour ¼ cup water into the pan over medium heat and scrape up any browned bits. Remove the pan from the heat and add the chicken so it's mostly in a single layer. Scrape out the bowl of charmoula, adding the contents to the pan. Add ¾ cup water and bring to a simmer over medium heat. Reduce the heat to medium low and add the lemon strips and olives. Cover and simmer, turning the chicken occasionally, until the chicken is cooked through and very tender, 10 to 15 minutes. If it's not saucy but dry, add more water and cook for another 10 to 15 minutes. Transfer the chicken to a platter. Simmer the sauce, uncovered, for about 3 minutes. Spoon the sauce over the chicken and sprinkle with the cilantro leaves. *—Kathy Wazana*

Preserved Lemons

Preserved lemons have a taste and texture that cannot be replicated: sour, salty and almost sweet at the same time. As a result of the long curing time (one month), the rind becomes soft and edible, with a kind of pungency that imparts the delicious taste of Morocco to any dish. To use, rinse the lemons briefly to remove excess salt. You can use both the pulp and rind, or the rind alone, cutting it into quarters, strips, or small pieces.

Yields six to eight preserved lemons.

¼ to ⅓ cup coarse sea salt or kosher salt
6 to 8 lemons (organic, if possible), well washed

Sterilize a 1-quart mason jar or run it through the dishwasher. Coat the bottom of the jar with a thin layer of salt.

Cut each lemon lengthwise into quarters to within about ½ inch of the base, keeping it attached at the stem end.

Holding a lemon over a bowl, press a generous amount of salt into the exposed flesh. Close up the lemon and roll it in more salt to coat the skin. Put the salted lemon in the jar and continue with the remaining lemons, pushing each lemon down tightly to release some of the juice and fill all the space. Pack the jar to within ¼ inch of the top. If the released juice doesn't cover the fruit, top it off with more squeezed lemon juice before closing the jar.

Keep the jar in a cabinet or on a shelf for four weeks, turning the jar every day. To use, rinse the amount of lemon needed under water. Store the opened jar in the refrigerator or another cool place. The lemons will keep for at least six months as long as they're always completely covered with juice—the acidity and salinity prevent bacterial growth. If the juice level falls too low, top it up with more fresh lemon juice. Remove the lemons from the jar with a clean wooden spoon (not your fingers) to avoid introducing any impurities from your hands.

—Kathy Wazana

Chicken with Vinegar & Onions

Serves four to six.

3 tablespoons unsalted butter

2 medium-small yellow onions, thinly sliced (about 2½ cups)

Kosher salt and freshly ground black pepper

3 tablespoons Champagne vinegar

One 4-pound chicken, cut into 8 pieces (or 2 bone-in, skin-on breasts and 4 bone-in, skin-on thighs)

½ cup all-purpose flour

2 tablespoons extra-virgin olive oil

½ cup dry white wine, such as Sauvignon Blanc or Pinot Gris

2 teaspoons chopped fresh tarragon leaves

2 tablespoons crème fraîche (or heavy cream)

tip: For a deeply flavored sauce, let it reduce. Leave the lid off the skillet slightly ajar to let some steam escape during cooking. This concentrates the liquid for a more intense sauce, and it also ensures that the liquid doesn't boil or simmer too hard, which would overcook the chicken.

As the chicken cooks, it simmers in its own juices, creating a very concentrated, rich sauce. This dish can be made a day or two ahead, but don't add the last teaspoon of tarragon. Reheat gently in a covered baking dish in a 325°F oven for about 30 minutes, adding a few tablespoons of water or chicken broth if the chicken appears dry. Sprinkle with the tarragon at the last minute and serve.

In a 12-inch skillet, melt 2 tablespoons of the butter over medium heat. Add the onions, sprinkle with a couple of big pinches of salt and a few grinds of pepper, and stir to coat the onions. Cover, reduce the heat to medium low, and continue to cook, stirring occasionally, until the onions are tender and lightly browned, about 20 minutes. Scrape them into a small bowl and set the skillet over medium-high heat. Add 1 tablespoon of the vinegar and stir with a wooden spoon to dissolve any browned bits on the bottom of the pan. Pour the vinegar into the onions and set the skillet aside.

If using chicken parts, cut each breast crosswise into two equal-size portions and trim any excess fat or skin from the thighs. Rinse and pat dry.

Spread the flour in a pie plate, and season the chicken pieces with salt and pepper. Set the skillet over medium-high heat and add the olive oil and the remaining 1 tablespoon butter. While the butter melts, dredge half of the seasoned chicken pieces in the flour, shaking off the excess. Set them skin side down in the skillet. Brown, turning once, until the skin is crisp and the chicken is evenly browned, 6 to 8 minutes total. Lower the heat if the chicken or the drippings threaten to burn. Transfer the chicken pieces to a pan or platter and repeat with the remaining chicken.

When all the chicken is browned, pour off all of the fat. Return the skillet to medium-high heat, add the wine, and scrape the bottom of the pan with a wooden spoon to dissolve the drippings. Add the remaining 2 tablespoons vinegar, the sautéed onions, and 1 teaspoon of the tarragon. Return the chicken pieces, skin side up, to the skillet, arranging them in a single snug layer. Partially cover, leaving a small gap for the steam to escape, and lower the heat to maintain a low simmer. Continue to simmer gently, turning every 10 minutes, until the chicken is tender and cooked through, about 30 minutes total.

Transfer the chicken to a platter. Increase the heat to a more rapid simmer, and stir in the crème fraîche (or cream); the sauce may appear broken at first, but it will come together. Taste for salt and pepper. Add the remaining 1 teaspoon tarragon and spoon over the chicken to serve. *—Molly Stevens*

Mustard-Crusted Roast Chickens

Serves six to eight.

1 cup Dijon mustard

½ cup minced shallots (about 2 large)

¼ cup minced garlic (12 to 16 cloves)

2 tablespoons chopped fresh thyme

Kosher salt and freshly ground black pepper

2 whole chickens, about 3½ pounds each, wingtips trimmed and excess fat removed

5 tablespoons extra-virgin olive oil for drizzling

This pair of succulent chickens is a hands-off main course that not only lets you get the rest of your meal going, but is also eminently satisfying. The mustard rub for the chicken gets crusty and delicious as the chickens roast to a golden nut brown. Let the chickens rest for at least 10 minutes before you carve them, just the right amount of time to finish preparing the other dishes you're serving.

In a small bowl, combine the mustard, shallots, garlic, and thyme, along with 2 teaspoons salt and 2 teaspoons pepper.

Clean out the cavities of the chickens. Set the chickens on a large dish and, using your hands, rub the mustard paste all over the outside (top and bottom) of the chickens. The coating should be generous but not gloppy. Rub any remaining paste into the cavities. Refrigerate, uncovered and breast side up, for several hours or overnight.

Heat the oven to 450°F. Put the chickens on a rack in a large roasting pan, a rimmed baking sheet, or two smaller pans. (If the chickens wind up on different oven racks, rotate them occasionally during roasting.) Sprinkle a little salt and pepper over the chickens and then drizzle each with 1½ tablespoons of the olive oil. Roast for 25 minutes. Remove the roasting pan from the oven and drizzle each chicken with another 1 tablespoon oil. Reduce the oven temperature to 350°F, rotate the pan, and continue roasting another 25 minutes. Baste each chicken with fat from the pan. Rotate the pan and roast until the chickens are deep golden brown, crusty, and cooked through, another 30 to 45 minutes. The chickens are done when an instant-read thermometer inserted in the thickest part of the thigh reads 170° to 175°F and the juices run clear. Remove the chickens from the oven and let rest for 10 minutes before carving.

Carve the chicken, taking care to disturb the mustard crust as little as possible. Arrange the pieces on one or two platters and bring to the table.
—*Tom Douglas*

Roast Chicken with Rosemary-Lemon Salt

See photo on page 161.

One whole chicken serves four for dinner; the second yields enough to make two additional meals.

2 medium lemons

2 tablespoons plus 1 teaspoon kosher salt

2 tablespoons chopped fresh rosemary

1 teaspoon freshly ground black pepper

Two 4-pound chickens, giblets and excess fat discarded

¼ cup unsalted butter, melted

For a very flavorful roast chicken, liven up plain kosher salt by mixing it with some fresh rosemary and lemon zest; use the food processor to help release the flavorful oils from the zest and the rosemary. A clever idea is to roast two chickens; serve one on Sunday and turn the other into delicious weeknight meals

Finely grate the zest from the lemons. In a food processor or mini chopper, combine the zest with the 2 tablespoons salt, the rosemary, and black pepper. Pulse several times to combine.

Sprinkle each chicken with this salt mixture both inside and outside the cavity and between the skin and the breast meat (use your fingers to gently open up a pocket between the two). Cut 1 of the lemons in half and stuff a half in the cavity of each bird. Reserve the remaining lemon for another use. Set the chickens on a wire rack atop a rimmed baking sheet, and refrigerate uncovered for at least 4 hours and up to 24 hours.

About 30 minutes before you're ready to roast the chickens, set an oven rack in the middle position and heat the oven to 425°F. Take the chickens out of the refrigerator and brush the butter uniformly over the skin. Sprinkle each chicken with ½ teaspoon salt. Set each chicken, breast side up, on 1 or 2 racks (preferably a large nonadjustable V-rack) in a large roasting pan. Let the chickens sit at room temperature while the oven heats.

Roast the chickens until the breasts are nicely browned and crisp, about 40 minutes. Gently flip each chicken (using tongs to clutch the inside of the cavity and the side of the bird) and roast until an instant-read thermometer inserted into the thickest part of the thigh registers 165°F to 170°F, about 20 minutes more. Let rest for 5 minutes before carving one of the chickens into pieces. *—Tony Rosenfeld*

Tips for moist meat & crisp skin

Salt the chicken ahead. Salting seasons the bird, of course, but if you can do it a day, or even a few hours, ahead, you'll get more flavorful meat and crisper skin. You can also flavor the salt with herbs and zest.

Use a rack. A V-shaped roasting rack cradles the chicken and allows its juices to drip away, leaving even the bottom skin crisp.

Start breast side up and flip halfway through. Starting with the breast up ensures brown, crispy skin. Turning the bird over keeps the breast moist while the slower-cooking legs finish roasting.

How much meat from a 4-pound bird?

You can expect one roast chicken to serve four people nicely for dinner. A whole second bird should yield about 5 cups of meat, enough to make the recipes on pages 200 and 202.

LEFTOVER AMOUNT	YIELD (sliced or diced)
1 whole chicken	5 cups
½ chicken	2½ cups
1 breast	1 cup
1 leg (drumstick and thigh)	1 cup

Twice as nice: roast two chickens, save one for meals later in the week

Handling tips

After serving the first chicken for dinner, wrap the leftovers in plastic wrap. Let the second chicken cool to room temperature and wrap in plastic as well. If it's well wrapped and refrigerated, the chicken will stay relatively moist and tender for up to 4 days. Here are a few more pointers for making the most of your leftover chicken.

Don't carve until you have to. Sliced, diced, and otherwise cut-up chicken dries out and spoils faster than a whole one, so keep the chicken whole or in big pieces.

Discard the skin. The crisp skin of a warm roast chicken is wonderful, but once it's cold, the skin tends to become unpleasantly rubbery.

Match the meat to the preparation. Dark-meat leftovers tend to have a richer flavor and retain their moisture, so they're perfect for cooked dishes. White-meat leftovers are more apt to dry out when reheated, so their delicate flavor and texture do better in sandwiches and salads.

Keep the cooking to a minimum. As leftover chicken is already cooked (and as chicken is lean to start with, particularly the breast), it's best to avoid further cooking. Whenever possible, try to fold the chicken in at the end just to warm it up.

Coconut Rice with Chicken & Snow Peas

Serves four.

1½ cups jasmine rice or long-grain white rice

3 tablespoons minced fresh ginger

¼ cup canola oil

¾ cup unsweetened coconut milk (preferably not "lite")

¾ teaspoon kosher salt

3 tablespoons soy sauce

2 tablespoons rice vinegar

1 tablespoon light brown sugar

2 teaspoons cornstarch

2 large green or red jalapeños, cored, seeded, and finely diced

½ pound snow peas (about 3 cups), trimmed

2½ to 3 cups diced leftover roast chicken (preferably dark meat)

⅓ cup chopped fresh cilantro

The rich coconut rice is the perfect counterpoint to a quick chicken stir-fry in a soy-jalapeño sauce. For color, add some red bell pepper to the stir-fry. You could also sprinkle with some toasted coconut as a finishing touch. You can use the leftover meat from a chicken you roast at home, or from a store-bought rotisserie chicken.

Rinse the rice in three changes of cold water, or until the water becomes only slightly cloudy from the rice. Drain well in a sieve.

Heat 1½ tablespoons of the ginger with 2 tablespoons of the oil in a small (2-quart) saucepan over medium-high heat until it begins to sizzle steadily and becomes fragrant, 1 to 2 minutes. Add the rice and cook, stirring, until the grains and ginger start to brown in places, about 2 minutes. Stir in the coconut milk, 1¾ cups water, and the salt. Bring to a boil and then reduce to a simmer. Cook until the liquid has reduced to about the same level as the top of the rice, 5 to 7 minutes. Cover, reduce the heat to low, and cook without disturbing the rice until the liquid is absorbed and the rice is tender, 15 minutes.

Meanwhile, whisk together the soy sauce, rice vinegar, brown sugar, and cornstarch in a small bowl. Stir in ½ cup water and set aside.

In a large skillet over medium-high heat, cook the jalapeños and the remaining 1½ tablespoons ginger in the remaining 2 tablespoons oil until they sizzle steadily for about 30 seconds. Add the snow peas and cook until bright green and browned in places, about 1 minute. Whisk the soy mixture to recombine and add it and the chicken to the skillet. Cook, stirring, until the sauce thickens and the chicken just heats through, about 2 minutes. Stir in half of the cilantro, reduce the heat to low, and cook for another 2 minutes.

Fluff the rice with a fork and serve with the chicken and snow peas, sprinkled with the remaining cilantro. —*Tony Rosenfeld*

Soft Chicken Tacos with the Works

Serves four to six.

2 large ripe avocados, pitted

2 limes, 1 juiced and 1 cut into wedges

1½ teaspoons kosher salt; more as needed

¼ teaspoon freshly ground black pepper; more as needed

2 tablespoons extra-virgin olive oil

1 small yellow onion, finely diced

1 teaspoon chili powder

Scant ⅛ teaspoon ground cinnamon

One 14½-ounce can petite-diced tomatoes, drained

1 medium canned chipotle chile, finely diced, plus 1 to 2 tablespoons adobo sauce (from a can of chipotles en adobo)

2½ to 3 cups leftover roast chicken, shredded or cut into thin strips

12 small corn tortillas, warmed

6 ounces queso fresco or feta, crumbled (1⅓ cups)

3 cups thinly sliced red cabbage (about 6 ounces)

⅔ cup fresh cilantro leaves, washed and patted dry

Look for chipotles en adobo in the Mexican food section of the grocery store; leftovers will keep nicely in the fridge for several weeks. Red cabbage adds color to these tacos, but green cabbage will still provide the crucial crunch.

Mash the avocados with the lime juice in a medium bowl. Season with about 1 teaspoon of the salt and the pepper, or to taste.

Set a large, heavy-based skillet over medium heat. Add the oil and onion, sprinkle with the remaining ½ teaspoon salt, and cook, stirring, until softened and translucent, about 6 minutes. Add the chili powder and cinnamon and cook, stirring, for 30 seconds. Add the tomatoes, chipotle, and adobo sauce and cook, stirring, for 5 minutes, mashing the tomatoes with a wooden spoon. Stir in the chicken, cover, reduce the heat to low, and cook until the chicken heats through, about 10 minutes. Taste and season with salt and pepper if needed.

Let diners assemble their own tacos by spreading the warm tortillas with the avocado and then topping with the chicken, cheese, cabbage, cilantro, and a squeeze of juice from the lime wedges. *—Tony Rosenfeld*

Shredding cabbage can be quick

Whether you're preparing cabbage for a sauté, a salad, or a soup, more often than not you'll be shredding it. For large quantities, use a food processor fitted with a slicing blade, but for small amounts, it's quick to shred by hand.

Quarter and core the head of cabbage. Thinly slice each quarter crosswise, keeping the fingertips of your guiding hand curled under so you don't cut them. If the quarter gets too awkward to hold, flip it onto another side and finish slicing.

Roasted Cornish Game Hens with Wildflower Honey & Orange

Serves six to eight.

3 Cornish game hens (1½ to 2 pounds each)

6 tablespoons plus ⅓ cup dry white wine, such as Sauvignon Blanc or Pinot Grigio

1½ tablespoons honey (preferably wildflower honey)

1½ tablespoons chopped fresh thyme

2 bay leaves, preferably fresh, each torn into about 4 pieces

Pinch of crushed red pepper flakes

1 medium orange

1 small yellow onion, cut crosswise into ¼-inch-thick slices

1 tablespoon kosher salt

Freshly ground black pepper

3 tablespoons unsalted butter, melted, for basting, plus 1 tablespoon butter, not melted, for the sauce

1 cup low-salt chicken broth

Cornish game hens work so beautifully for entertaining. They're a nice departure from chicken, and they don't require any last-minute carving. Marinating in honey and basting with butter adds flavor and encourages the skin to brown, but sometimes the hens can use a flash under the broiler to finish.

Discard the giblets from the hens (if there are any) or reserve for another use. Using kitchen shears, cut along both sides of the backbones and remove them. Then cut each hen in half along the breastbone. Trim off the wingtips and put the hens in a large bowl.

In a small bowl, combine the 6 tablespoons wine, honey, thyme, bay leaves, and red pepper flakes and stir to dissolve the honey (it's all right if it doesn't dissolve completely).

Using a vegetable peeler, peel the zest from the orange in large strips, letting the strips drop into the bowl with the hens. Add the honey mixture and the sliced onion to the bowl. Toss well, cover, and refrigerate for at least 4 hours or overnight, tossing the hens occasionally.

About half an hour before cooking, remove the hen halves from the marinade and gently pat them dry, trying not to disturb the thyme clinging to them. Arrange the hens on a heavy-duty rimmed baking sheet and let sit at room temperature for 30 minutes. (Discard the remaining marinade.) Position a rack in the top third of the oven and heat the oven to 450°F.

When ready to roast, season the hen halves on both sides with the salt and several grinds of pepper. Turn them skin side up. Roast the hens, basting occasionally with the melted butter and rotating the pan for even browning as needed, until an instant-read thermometer inserted into the meaty part of a thigh registers 175° to 180°F (be careful not to hit the bone), about 30 minutes.

If the skin is somewhat pale, baste the hens, turn the broiler to high, and broil, rotating the pan frequently, until the hens are nicely golden, about 2 minutes. (Watch carefully to prevent burning.) Transfer the hens to a serving platter and tent with aluminum foil.

While the rimmed baking sheet is still hot, add the remaining ⅓ cup wine and use a wooden spoon to scrape the browned bits from the bottom of the pan. Pour the wine and juices into a small saucepan and add the chicken broth. Boil the sauce over high heat until it thickens ever so slightly, 2 to 3 minutes; it should be more like a jus than a thick sauce. Off the heat, whisk in the remaining 1 tablespoon butter. Taste and add salt and pepper, if needed. Keep warm.

To serve, pour a small amount of the sauce on and around the hens and pass the remainder at the table. —*Tasha DeSerio*

Herb-Butter Roasted Turkey

Serves twelve, with leftovers.

For the brine:

2½ gallons water

2½ cups kosher salt

1 cup maple syrup

24 bay leaves

24 cloves garlic, peeled

⅓ cup whole black peppercorns

2 small bunches fresh flat-leaf parsley (about 4 ounces)

1 small bunch fresh sage (about 1 ounce)

1 small bunch fresh thyme (about ⅔ ounce)

6 medium sprigs fresh rosemary

Zest and juice of 4 large lemons (remove the zest in long strips with a vegetable peeler)

For the turkey:

14- to 16-pound natural turkey (preferably fresh)

1 recipe Three-Herb Butter (see recipe on page 209), slightly softened

2 tablespoons kosher salt

2 tablespoons freshly ground black pepper

4 tablespoons unsalted butter, melted

The star of any Thanksgiving dinner is, of course, the turkey. This one is slathered with a delicious herb butter that makes it incredibly flavorful and succulent. But to make sure that it's as moist and juicy as possible (especially the breast meat, which tends to dry out in the oven), you should brine it for several hours in water, salt, and lots of aromatics. Not only do the aromatics infuse the turkey with flavor, but brining also helps the meat absorb moisture before cooking, so it ends up juicier once it's roasted.

Two days ahead, prepare the brine: Put all of the brine ingredients in a 5-gallon stockpot with a lid. Cover and bring to a boil over high heat. Reduce the heat to medium low and simmer for 5 minutes. Remove from the heat, cool to room temperature, cover the pot, and refrigerate the brine until cold, preferably overnight.

One day ahead, brine the turkey: If already loose, trim the tail from the turkey. Otherwise, leave it attached. Remove and discard the giblets. Keep the neck and tail in the refrigerator. Rinse the turkey and put it in the pot with the brine. Refrigerate for 8 to 24 hours before roasting the turkey.

Prepare and roast the turkey: Position a rack in the bottom of the oven and heat the oven to 350°F. Remove the turkey from the brine and discard the brine. Rinse the turkey well, pat it dry, and set it in a large flameproof roasting pan. Gently slide your hand between the breast meat and skin to separate the skin so you can apply the herb butter. Slice the herb butter into ¼-inch-thick rounds and distribute them evenly between the skin and breast meat, completely covering the breast. Maneuver a few pieces between the skin and legs, too. Next, with your hands on the outside of the turkey, massage the butter under the skin to distribute it evenly and break up the round pieces so the turkey won't look polka-dotted when it's done.

Sprinkle 1 tablespoon of the salt and 1 tablespoon of the pepper in the cavity of the turkey. Tie the legs together. Fold the wings back and tuck the tips under the neck area. Flip the turkey onto its breast, pat the back dry, and brush with some of the melted butter. Sprinkle with some of the remaining salt and pepper. Flip the turkey over, pat dry again, brush all over with the remaining butter, and sprinkle with the remaining salt and pepper.

Put the reserved neck and tail in the pan with the turkey. Cover the pan very tightly with foil and put in the oven, legs pointing to the back of the oven, if possible (the legs can handle the higher heat in the back better than the breast can). Roast undisturbed for 2 hours and then uncover carefully (watch out for escaping steam). Continue to roast, basting every 15 minutes with the drippings that have collected in the pan, until an instant-read thermometer inserted in the thickest part of both thighs reads 170° to 175°F and the juices run clear when the thermometer is removed, 45 minutes to 1 hour more for a 15-pound turkey.

Remove the turkey from the oven. With a wad of paper towels in each hand, move the turkey to a serving platter, cover with foil to keep warm, and set aside. Discard the neck and tail; reserve the drippings in the roasting pan. Let the turkey rest for 30 minutes while you make the Pinot Noir Gravy on page 210. *—Ris Lacoste*

1 **Brine the turkey** in water, salt, and aromatics. The meat absorbs moisture (and flavor), so it doesn't dry out while roasting.

2 **Rub herb butter** between the skin and meat. When the butter melts, it infuses the turkey with flavor and creates rich drippings for basting.

3 **Cover with foil** during the first 2 hours of roasting to further help the meat stay tender and juicy.

Three-Herb Butter

The butter can be made up to 1 week ahead and refrigerated or up to 2 months ahead and frozen. If frozen, take the butter out of the freezer and store in the refrigerator a day before you plan to use it.

Yields about 1¼ cups.

½ pound (1 cup) unsalted butter, at room temperature

½ cup finely chopped shallots (about 3 ounces)

½ cup dry white wine

¼ cup chopped fresh flat-leaf parsley (from about 1 ounce parsley sprigs)

¼ cup chopped fresh thyme leaves (from about ¾ ounce thyme sprigs)

¼ cup chopped fresh sage leaves (from about ½ ounce sage sprigs)

In a 10-inch skillet, melt 1 tablespoon of the butter over medium heat until it begins to foam. Add the shallots and cook until soft and fragrant, stirring occasionally, about 3 minutes. Add the wine and boil until it's completely evaporated, 5 to 8 minutes. Stir in the parsley, thyme, and sage and cook until fragrant, 2 minutes more. Transfer to a medium bowl and refrigerate. When well chilled, put the remaining butter in the bowl of a mixer fitted with the paddle attachment. Add the herb mixture and beat on medium speed until blended, about 1 minute.

On a large piece of plastic wrap, shape the herb butter into a log. Wrap in the plastic and refrigerate.
—Ris Lacoste

Brining produces succulent turkey, but requires some planning

To brine your turkey you either need space for a 5-gallon pot in your refrigerator or you can cook the brine in a smaller pan and proceed with one of the alternative methods below. The brine should be prepared 2 days before the Thanksgiving dinner and the turkey actually brined the day before.

Space-saving brining tips

With your refrigerator stuffed full of food around Thanksgiving time, you might be challenged to fit a large brining pot in there as well. And if you don't own such a large pot or bucket, you have a double conundrum. Here are a couple of alternative space-saving approaches to brining:

Use roasting or brining bags. Brining the turkey in a jumbo plastic bag uses less space and less brine than a pot does. Look in kitchen shops for turkey brining bags, and follow the instructions on the package. Or use the plastic turkey-cooking bags found in the plastic wrap and foil section of the supermarket. Just double up the bags (for leak protection) and add the turkey, breast side down. Put the bagged turkey in a roasting pan or bowl (again, for leak protection) and add enough brine to fill the inner bag about halfway up the turkey. Then tightly close the opening of each bag with a twist-tie, eliminating as much air as possible from the inner bag to force the brine to surround the turkey, and refrigerate.

Brine in a cooler. Using a clean cooler means the turkey won't be in the fridge at all—nice if you're really crunched for space. The challenge here is that you need to add ice to keep the turkey cold, but you don't want the melting ice to dilute your brine too much. To offset the ice-melt, use ½ cup extra kosher salt in your brine. Make sure the brine is refrigerator-cold before pouring it over the turkey in the cooler. Add enough ice to submerge the turkey in brine—you'll need 5 to 10 pounds, depending on the cooler. Store the cooler in the coldest location you can think of. If that happens to be outdoors, put it in a place where animals can't get to it, like a screened porch or your car.

Pinot Noir Gravy for Roast Turkey

Serves twelve.

2½ ounces (5 tablespoons) unsalted butter

2½ ounces (½ cup) all-purpose flour

Reserved drippings from Herb-Butter Roasted Turkey (see recipe on page 206)

4 cups Turkey Broth (see recipe on the facing page) or low-salt chicken broth

1½ cups Pinot Noir

Kosher salt

Freshly ground black pepper

Any light-bodied fruity red wine that's not too oaky will be fine in this gravy.

Melt the butter in a small saucepan over medium-high heat until foaming. Add the flour and quickly whisk it into the butter until it's completely incorporated. Cook, whisking constantly, until the roux smells toasty and darkens slightly to a light caramel color, about 2 minutes. Watch carefully, as you don't want it to get too dark. Remove from the heat and set aside.

Pour the reserved turkey drippings into a clear, heatproof container, preferably a fat separator cup. (Don't rinse the roasting pan.) Let sit until the fat rises to the top, and then pour out 1 cup of the juices (or remove and discard the fat with a ladle and measure 1 cup of the juices). Combine the juices with the turkey or chicken broth.

Set the roasting pan on top of the stove over two burners on medium heat. Add the Pinot Noir and simmer, scraping the pan with a wooden spoon to release any stuck-on bits, until the wine has reduced by half, about 5 minutes. Add the broth mixture and simmer to meld the flavors, about 5 minutes. Whisk in the roux a little at a time until you have reached your desired thickness (you may not want to use it all). Adjust the seasoning with salt and pepper to taste. Strain through a fine sieve and transfer to a serving vessel. *—Ris Lacoste*

Turkey Broth

The turkey broth can be made up to 4 days ahead and refrigerated or up to 2 months ahead and frozen.

Yields 6 to 7 cups.

1½ to 2 pounds turkey parts, such as backs, wings, or legs

1 large onion (about 12 ounces), coarsely chopped

4 large ribs celery (about 9 ounces), coarsely chopped

2 small carrots (about 4 ounces), coarsely chopped

2 cups dry white wine

6 cups low-salt chicken broth

Half a small bunch fresh flat-leaf parsley (about 1 ounce)

Half a small bunch fresh sage (about ½ ounce)

Half a small bunch fresh thyme (about ⅓ ounce)

3 bay leaves

1 tablespoon whole black peppercorns

Position a rack in the center of the oven and heat the oven to 350°F. Put the turkey parts in a small roasting pan (approximately 9x13 inches) along with the onion, celery, and carrots and roast until the meat is well

browned, 1 to 1¼ hours. Transfer the turkey parts and vegetables to a 4-quart saucepan.

Add the wine to the roasting pan and scrape any browned bits with a wooden spoon to release them into the wine. Pour the wine into the saucepan and add the chicken broth, herbs, bay leaves, and peppercorns. Bring to a boil over medium-high heat, reduce the heat to medium low or low, and simmer gently until the meat is falling off the bone, 30 to 40 minutes, skimming occasionally to remove the fat and foam that rise to the top. Strain the broth through a fine sieve, cover, and refrigerate until ready to use. Remove any solidified fat before using. *—Ris Lacoste*

An easy wine gravy in three steps

1 **Make a roux** by adding flour to melted butter and whisking until golden brown. This will be your thickener.

2 **Pour wine** into the roasting pan and reduce it to add flavor and character to the gravy. Then pour in the broth and the drippings.

3 **Whisk the roux** into the gravy a little at a time to thicken it just the way you like it.

6
Beef, Lamb & Pork

p224

p244

Grilled Flank Steak with Sesame Sauce & Grilled Scallions (recipe on page 214)

Grilled Flank Steak with Sesame Sauce & Grilled Scallions

See photo on page 213.

Serves four.

1½ pounds flank steak

1½ teaspoons kosher salt

½ teaspoon freshly ground
  black pepper

¼ cup plus 1 tablespoon
  soy sauce

¼ cup canola oil; more for
  the grill

¼ cup minced fresh ginger

1½ tablespoons minced garlic

3 tablespoons rice vinegar

2 tablespoons Asian sesame oil

1½ tablespoons light or dark
  brown sugar

2 teaspoons cornstarch

20 scallions (preferably thick
  ones), roots trimmed

1 tablespoon sesame seeds,
  toasted

Flank steak can be so luscious and beefy, but only if you don't overcook it. Pay attention when at the grill to keep the meat rare or medium rare, and be sure to let the steak rest properly before slicing.

Season the flank steak with 1 teaspoon of the salt and the pepper. Mix 1 tablespoon of the soy sauce, 1 tablespoon of the canola oil, 2 tablespoons of the ginger, and 1 tablespoon of the garlic in a large zip-top plastic bag. Add the steak and turn and massage it in the bag to cover it with the marinade. Refrigerate for at least 4 hours or as long as overnight.

Heat 1½ tablespoons of the canola oil and the remaining 2 tablespoons ginger and ½ tablespoon garlic in a small saucepan over medium heat until the ginger and garlic sizzle steadily and just begin to brown around the edges, about 3 minutes. Add ⅓ cup water, the remaining ¼ cup soy sauce, and the rice vinegar, sesame oil, and brown sugar. Bring to a boil over medium-high heat. In a small bowl, whisk the cornstarch with 2 teaspoons of water and stir it into the soy mixture. Cook until it returns to a boil and thickens slightly, about 1 minute. Remove from the heat and set aside.

Heat a gas grill to medium high or prepare a fire on a charcoal grill with a medium-hot and a low zone. Rinse the scallions but do not dry them. Toss the scallions with the remaining 1½ tablespoons canola oil and ½ teaspoon salt.

Clean and oil the grill grates. Grill the steak (over the hotter zone if using charcoal), covered, until it has good grill marks, 5 to 6 minutes. Flip and reduce the heat to medium if using a gas grill or transfer the steak to the cooler part of the charcoal fire. Cook, covered, until the steak is done to your liking, 4 to 5 minutes for medium rare (cut into the steak to check). Transfer to a large cutting board, brush with about a third of the sesame sauce, and let rest for 5 to 10 minutes.

While the steak rests, clean and oil the grill grates, set the scallions on the grill (over the cooler zone if using charcoal), and cook until they have good grill marks, 2 to 4 minutes. Flip and cook until they're tender, 2 to 4 minutes. Transfer to a large platter and drizzle with a couple of tablespoons of the sesame sauce.

Slice the steak thinly and serve with the scallions, a drizzle of the remaining sesame sauce, and a sprinkling of sesame seeds. —*Tony Rosenfeld*

Argentine Spice-Rubbed Flank Steaks with Salsa Criolla

Chimichurri is the star salsa of the Argentine grill, but the lesser known salsa criolla can be just as exciting. Full of onions, red peppers, and herbs, the mixture is a light but intensely flavorful condiment for grilled steak.

In a small bowl, mix about two-thirds of the garlic paste with 1 tablespoon of the thyme, 2 teaspoons of the black pepper, the chili powder, brown sugar, and 1½ tablespoons of the salt. Arrange the steaks on a rimmed baking sheet and pat the spice rub all over them. Cover and let sit for at least 4 hours and up to 1 day in the refrigerator.

In a 1-quart sealable container, combine the tomato, onion, red pepper, oil, and vinegar with ¼ cup water, and the remaining garlic paste, 1 tablespoon thyme, 2 teaspoons salt, and 1 teaspoon black pepper. Shake well. Refrigerate for up to 1 day before serving.

Heat a gas grill to medium high or prepare a hot charcoal fire. Grill the steaks (covered on a gas grill) until they have good grill marks on the first side, 4 to 5 minutes. Flip the steaks; if using a gas grill, reduce the heat to medium and cover the grill. Continue to cook until done to your liking (make a slit in the steaks to take a peek), 4 to 5 minutes more for medium rare.

Let the steaks rest on a cutting board for 5 to 10 minutes and then slice thinly across the grain. Stir or shake the salsa criolla and serve with the steaks. *—Tony Rosenfeld*

Serves twelve.

- 3 cloves garlic, minced and mashed to a paste with a pinch of salt
- 2 tablespoons chopped fresh thyme
- 1 tablespoon freshly ground black pepper
- 1 tablespoon chili powder
- 2 teaspoons brown sugar
- 1½ tablespoons plus 2 teaspoons kosher salt
- 4½ pounds flank steak (about 3 medium steaks), trimmed of excess fat
- 1 large ripe tomato, cored, seeded, and finely diced (about 1¼ cups)
- 1 medium yellow onion, minced (about 1⅓ cups)
- ½ red bell pepper, cored, seeded, and minced (about ½ cup)
- ½ cup extra-virgin olive oil
- ⅓ cup white-wine vinegar

Steak & Eggs Rancheros

Serves two.

1 tiny clove garlic

Kosher salt

1 small tomato, cut into small dice

½ avocado, cut into small dice

¼ cup Salsa Criolla (see recipe on page 215), drained

¼ jalapeño, minced

2 tablespoons chopped fresh cilantro

Freshly ground pepper

1 tablespoon vegetable oil

Two 6-inch corn tortillas

2 large eggs

Four ½-inch-thick slices cooked flank steak, warmed in the microwave or in a skillet

¼ cup crumbled feta

This beefed-up version of the Mexican breakfast dish huevos rancheros (ranch-style eggs) is great for lunch or dinner, too. Use leftover Argentine Spice-Rubbed Flank Steak with Salsa Criolla (see recipe on page 215) for the best flavor, but any cooked steak and salsa will work fine.

Peel and chop the garlic. Sprinkle the garlic with a generous pinch of kosher salt and mash it into a paste with the side of a chef's knife. In a small bowl, combine the garlic with the tomato, avocado, leftover salsa, jalapeño, and 1 tablespoon of the cilantro. Season to taste with salt and pepper.

Have two dinner plates and a stack of paper towels ready. Heat the oil in a 10-inch nonstick skillet over medium-high heat. Using tongs, fry the tortillas one at a time until just golden and slightly crisp, about 30 seconds per side, and transfer to the paper towels. Reduce the heat to medium low and let the skillet cool down a bit. Meanwhile, blot the excess oil from the tortillas with the paper towels. Sprinkle each tortilla with a pinch of salt. Put one tortilla on each plate.

Crack the eggs into the skillet. Season with salt and pepper, cover, and cook until the yolks' edges have just begun to set, 2 to 3 minutes. (The eggs should cook gently, so lower the heat if needed.)

While the eggs are cooking, divide half the salsa between the tortillas. Divide the steak between the tortillas and top with the remaining salsa. Separate the eggs with the edge of a spatula, if needed. Slide one egg onto each tortilla. Sprinkle with the remaining 1 tablespoon cilantro and the feta. Serve immediately. —*Allison Ehri Kreitler*

Fried eggs made easy

A fried egg makes a great topper for any hash. Fried eggs are easier to cook if not crowded in the pan; if you're frying a lot, keep them warm by undercooking them slightly and holding them on an oiled baking sheet in a 200°F oven.

Sunny side up

Crack an egg into a cup. Heat about 2 teaspoons butter or oil in a small nonstick skillet over medium heat. When the fat is hot, slip in the egg, season it with salt and pepper, and turn the heat to medium low or low. Cook until done to your liking, 1 to 2 minutes, basting the egg white with the fat to help it set.

Over easy

Begin cooking as you would for sunny-side-up eggs but rather than basting the egg, flip it gently with a spatula after the first side has set and continue to cook for another minute or until done to your liking.

Steak with Three-Chile Sauce

Serves four.

For the sauce:

1 ancho chile

1 pasilla chile

1 chipotle chile (from a can of chipotles en adobo)

3 tablespoons extra-virgin olive oil

1⅓ cups medium-chopped white onion (1 medium-small onion)

2 cloves garlic, chopped

¼ cup loosely packed fresh cilantro

1 tablespoon brandy

¾ cup low-salt beef broth

¾ teaspoon dark brown sugar

Heaping ¼ teaspoon kosher salt; more to taste

For the steaks:

Four ½-inch-thick boneless rib-eye, New York strip, or T-bone steaks (6 to 8 ounces each)

Juice from 1 large lime (about ¼ cup)

Kosher salt and freshly ground black pepper

1 tablespoon extra-virgin olive oil

½ cup (2 ounces) grated Oaxaca cheese (or mozzarella)

⅓ cup (1½ ounces) grated cotija, anejo, or anejo enchilado cheese (or crumbled feta)

For this dish, the earthy combination of three of Mexico's most distinctive chiles creates a nuanced result that is not nearly as hot as you might expect. Much of the spiciness is cut by the cheeses, leaving only the subtle heat that real chile aficionados love.

Make the sauce: Set a dry 10-inch skillet over medium heat for 2 minutes. Toast the ancho and pasilla chiles in the skillet for about 20 seconds on each side; don't let them scorch. Remove the stems, seeds, and ribs from the chiles. Soak the chiles in a bowl of hot water for about 20 minutes; drain them and put them in a blender. Add the chipotle.

Heat 1 tablespoon of the oil in the 10-inch skillet over medium heat. Add the onions and cook, stirring frequently, until soft and golden brown, lowering the heat as necessary to prevent scorching, about 10 minutes. Add the garlic and cook for 1 minute. Put the onions and garlic in the blender, along with the cilantro, brandy, and ¼ cup water. Blend to a smooth paste, adding additional water as necessary, 1 tablespoon at a time, to purée the ingredients. Transfer the chile paste to a small bowl.

Heat the remaining 2 tablespoons olive oil in a small saucepan over medium-high heat. When the oil is just beginning to smoke, add the chile paste. Cook, stirring constantly to incorporate it into the oil, until it's very thick, 2 to 4 minutes; reduce the heat if necessary to prevent burning. Reduce the heat to medium and gradually stir in the broth. Add the brown sugar and salt. Simmer until the mixture is the consistency of a medium-thick sauce, 1 to 2 minutes. Season to taste with salt.

Cook the steaks: Position a rack 4 inches from the broiler element and heat the broiler on high. Drizzle both sides of the steaks with the lime juice and season all over with salt and pepper. Heat an 11- or 12-inch skillet, preferably cast iron, over medium-high heat, add the olive oil, and sear two of the steaks on one side, about 2 minutes. Turn the steaks and sear them on the other side, and then continue cooking, lowering the heat as needed, until they're done to your liking, about 2 minutes on the second side for medium rare. Transfer the steaks to a rimmed baking sheet and repeat with the remaining two steaks.

When all the steaks are cooked, turn the heat to medium, pour the chile sauce into the skillet, and stir to incorporate any browned bits and juices from the meat. Sprinkle some of the Oaxaca (or mozzarella) cheese on each steak, spoon some sauce over them, and then top them with some of the cotija or anejo (or feta) cheese. Put the baking sheet under the broiler to melt the cheese, about 1 minute, and serve immediately. *–James Peyton*

Introducing Mexican cheeses

Oaxaca cheese (far left) is a soft cow's milk variety that melts easily. It's widely available in supermarkets in the Southwest and is now increasingly found across the country. It is delicious on pizzas, over nachos, or in grilled cheese sandwiches. Mozzarella makes the best substitute.

Cotija (bottom right) and anejo (top right) cheeses are aged, crumbly, slightly salty cheeses traditionally made from cow's milk. Anejo enchilado is coated with a mild chile powder. These cheeses are excellent in pasta and salads and make a tasty garnish for tacos, quesadillas, and refried beans. Feta is the best substitute.

Spicy Beef with Peanuts & Chiles

Serves four.

1 pound flank steak, thinly sliced on the diagonal against the grain

2 tablespoons soy sauce

2 teaspoons fish sauce

¼ teaspoon kosher salt; more to taste

2 tablespoons fresh lime juice

1 tablespoon light brown sugar

¼ cup salted peanuts

2 large shallots, coarsely chopped

2 Thai or serrano chiles, stemmed and coarsely chopped (don't seed)

3 tablespoons canola or peanut oil

⅓ cup coarsely chopped fresh cilantro

3 tablespoons chopped fresh basil

This quick stir-fry is of course delicious served on rice, but you could also top a bowl of noodles with it or, for a lighter approach, a bed of crunchy chopped romaine lettuce.

Toss the steak with 1 tablespoon of the soy sauce, 1 teaspoon of the fish sauce, and the salt. Combine the remaining 1 tablespoon soy sauce and 1 teaspoon fish sauce with 1 tablespoon of the lime juice and the brown sugar and set aside.

Pulse the peanuts, shallots, and chiles in a food processor until finely chopped. Transfer to a small bowl.

Set a 12-inch skillet over medium-high heat until hot, about 1 minute. Add 1½ tablespoons of the oil and once it's shimmering, add the beef. Cook, stirring, until the beef just loses its raw appearance, about 2 minutes. Transfer to a plate.

Reduce the heat to medium, add the remaining 1½ tablespoons oil and the shallot mixture, sprinkle with salt, and cook, stirring, until the shallots are soft, about 2 minutes.

Return the beef to the pan. Stir the soy mixture and add it, along with half of the cilantro and basil, and cook, stirring to let the flavors meld, 2 minutes. Season to taste with salt and serve sprinkled with the remaining lime juice, cilantro, and basil. *—Tony Rosenfeld*

Sizing up shallots

Shallots are a great way to bring a mellow oniony flavor to your cooking without the biting astringency of a regular onion. We particularly like to use them raw in vinaigrettes or cooked in pan sauces.

The size of shallots is quite variable, and some shallots have more than one lobe. When we call for a medium shallot, we're referring to a ¾ to 1 ounce shallot, regardless of how many lobes it has. A medium shallot yields about 2 tablespoons finely chopped or ¼ cup thinly sliced. One lobe of a large double-lobed shallot may be equivalent to a medium shallot.

A medium shallot (shown life-size here) is quite a bit larger than a quarter and weighs a little less than an ounce.

A wide range of chile varieties is readily available in the United States nowadays, and each offers a different flavor and heat level. Adding further possibilities are the different forms in which you can find chiles: fresh, canned, dried, and powdered. By using a combination of chile types and forms, you can go beyond just adding heat to a dish to create a surprisingly mild, balanced, and interesting flavor.

Dried chiles offer concentrated flavors that often differ so much from the fresh versions that they are given new names. For example, a dried poblano chile is called an ancho. The ancho (right) remains mild but takes on an entirely different, fruity, raisin-like flavor. Pasilla chiles (left) are dried chilacas. Dried chiles are often rehydrated before use and then blended with a little liquid to form a paste.

Canned chiles are often easier to find than fresh ones, although the available varieties are limited. Canned chipotle chiles store well and are easier to work with than dried. Chipotles are jalapeños which are smoke-dried and then packed with a tangy tomato sauce that absorbs their flavor and heat. They come out of the can soft and ready to use, and the seeds and veins are much easier to remove than they are in their dried form.

Chile powders are made from dried chiles. They differ from the spice jars labeled "chili powder" in that they are ground solely from a specific type of chile. Chili powder is a mix of ground chiles with the addition of spices like garlic powder and cumin. Pure chile powders allow you to add the most nuanced hit of flavor and heat to a dish. Ancho chile powder, for example, has a mild, fruity flavor, moderate heat level, and is good with steaks as well as in black beans dishes and mole sauce.

Steak with Red Onion, Wine & Port Sauce

The easy sauce reduction elevates a simple steak to a sophisticated dinner. The sauce can be made ahead and kept refrigerated for several days. Don't use a red wine that's very oaky, such as many cabernet sauvignons, because that oaky flavor will become too concentrated during cooking.

Make the sauce: Combine the wine and port with the onions, mushrooms, garlic, chile, parsley, and thyme in a 3- or 4-quart saucepan. Bring to a boil and then simmer very briskly until the liquid is reduced by half, about 10 minutes. Add the broth and reduce by half again, about 13 minutes. Strain the liquid and discard the solids. Clean the saucepan and return the strained liquid to the pan. Reduce until there is just over ⅓ cup liquid remaining, about 5 minutes. The sauce may be prepared to this point up to 2 days ahead. Refrigerate if working more than a few hours ahead.

Grill or broil the steaks: Prepare a medium-high gas or charcoal fire or heat the broiler on high. Season the steaks with salt and pepper and grill or broil until they are cooked to your liking. Medium rare takes about 1½ minutes per side; medium, 2 minutes per side. Let rest while you finish the sauce.

Bring the wine reduction to a simmer. Remove from the heat and whisk in the butter. Season to taste with salt. Spoon a tablespoon or so of sauce over each steak. *—James Peyton*

Serves four.

For the sauce:

1½ cups dry red wine

½ cup ruby port

3 cups thinly sliced red onion (1 large)

4 medium white or cremini mushrooms, chopped (about ¾ cup)

3 cloves garlic, coarsely chopped

1 large chipotle chile (from a can of chipotles en adobo), seeds removed

1 tablespoon chopped fresh flat-leaf parsley

1 teaspoon dried thyme

2 cups low-salt beef broth

3 tablespoons cold unsalted butter, cut into ½-inch pieces

Kosher salt

For the steaks:

Four ½-inch-thick boneless rib-eye, New York strip, or T-bone steaks (6 to 8 ounces each)

Kosher salt and freshly ground black pepper

Red Country-Style Curry with Beef, Shiitakes & Edamame

Serves four.

1 pound flank steak

5 ounces fresh shiitake mushrooms

2 tablespoons vegetable oil

3 tablespoons jarred or homemade red curry paste (see recipe on page 226)

2¾ cups low-salt chicken broth

5 wild lime leaves, torn or cut into quarters (optional)

1½ cups frozen shelled edamame (soy beans), thawed

3 tablespoons fish sauce

1 tablespoon palm sugar or light brown sugar

¼ teaspoon kosher salt; more to taste

A handful of fresh Thai or Italian basil leaves

Hot cooked rice or rice noodles for serving

1 long, slender fresh red chile (such as red jalapeño or serrano), thinly sliced on the diagonal (optional)

Wild lime leaves add a distinctive southeast Asian flavor to this curry, but don't fret if you can't find them (they're mostly available in Asian stores)—a juicy lime wedge squeezed over each portion will bring the requisite zing to the dish. When I make this curry with store-bought curry paste and no lime leaves, I like to serve it with lime wedges on the side to squeeze over all.

Slice the beef across the grain ¼ inch thick and then cut the slices into 1½- to 2-inch-long pieces.

Trim and discard the stems from the shiitakes; slice the caps ¼ inch thick (you should have 1½ to 2 cups).

Heat the oil in a 2- to 3-quart saucepan over medium heat until a bit of curry paste just sizzles when added to the pan. Add all the curry paste and cook, pressing and stirring with a wooden spoon or heatproof spatula to soften the paste and mix it in with the oil, until fragrant, about 2 minutes.

Increase the heat to medium high and add the beef. Spread it in an even single layer and cook undisturbed until it just begins to lose its pink color, about 1 minute. Turn the beef and continue cooking, stirring occasionally to coat it with the curry paste, until most of the beef no longer looks raw, 1 to 2 minutes.

Stir the shiitakes into the beef. Add the chicken broth and stir again. Add half the lime leaves (if using), and bring to a simmer. Simmer gently, stirring occasionally, until the shiitakes are tender and the beef is cooked through, about 5 minutes.

Add the edamame, stir well, and cook for about 1 minute, just to blanch them. Add the fish sauce, sugar, and salt and stir to combine. Remove from the heat. Tear the basil leaves in half (or quarters if they are large), and stir them into the curry, along with the remaining lime leaves (if using). Let rest for 5 minutes to allow the flavors to develop. Season to taste with salt.

Serve hot or warm with rice or noodles, garnished with the chile slices (if using). *—Nancie McDermott*

Red Curry Paste

Yields 1 scant cup.

½ cup small dried hot red chiles
(such as Thai bird chiles or
chiles de arbol)

1 large dried red New Mexico
chile (optional)

1 tablespoon coriander seeds

1 teaspoon cumin seeds

5 whole black peppercorns

3 stalks fresh lemongrass

¼ cup chopped shallots

2 tablespoons chopped garlic

1 tablespoon chopped fresh
or frozen galangal or
fresh ginger

1 tablespoon coarsely chopped
cilantro root (root plus about
1 inch of stem) or chopped
cilantro stems and leaves

1 teaspoon finely chopped dried
wild lime peel (soak in warm
water before chopping) or
lime zest

1 teaspoon kosher salt

1 teaspoon shrimp paste
(optional)

Jarred pastes are ideal for busy weeknights, but if you have a little more time, try making curry paste from scratch. It may require a trip to an Asian market for a few ingredients, but it's worth it—homemade curry paste will give your curries a more complex, nuanced flavor. And what's great is that you can make curry paste on a weekend, refrigerate or freeze it, and use it later to whip up a quick curry. Thai curry paste is traditionally made using a sturdy granite mortar and pestle, but a food processor works fine. This curry paste will have a softer texture than the fudge-textured curry pastes you find in stores because of the water you add to help the blades move.

Open the chiles, breaking off their stems and shaking out and discarding most of their seeds. Break the pods into pieces. (Large chiles will be somewhat pliable, while small ones will be brittle.) Combine the chile pieces in a medium bowl and add warm water to cover them. Set aside to soak for about 30 minutes.

Meanwhile, put the coriander seeds in a small, dry skillet over medium-high heat. Cook, shaking the pan, until they darken to a golden brown color and become fragrant, 2 to 3 minutes. Transfer to a small plate.

Let the skillet cool for a few minutes and then toast the cumin seeds in the same way until nicely browned and fragrant, 1 to 2 minutes. Transfer to the plate with the coriander seeds.

Put the coriander, cumin, and peppercorns in a small spice grinder and finely grind. Transfer to a plate and set aside.

Chop off and discard the grassy tops of the lemongrass, leaving about 4 inches, including the rounded base and root end. Discard any dry or discolored outer leaves and trim off the root end to leave a smooth base just under the plump bulb. Slice crosswise into thin rounds and then chop coarsely; transfer to a medium bowl.

Drain the chiles well and add them to the bowl of chopped lemongrass along with the shallots, garlic, galangal, cilantro root, dried lime peel or lime zest, salt, and shrimp paste (if using). Add the ground spices and stir gently to combine.

Transfer to a food processor, add 1 or 2 tablespoons cold water, and process to an almost-smooth paste. If the paste hasn't come together, add more water, 1 tablespoon. at a time. Scrape the paste into a jar, cover tightly, and refrigerate for up to 5 days, or freeze in 1- to 2-tablespoon-size portions for up to 1 month.

To make green curry paste: Use ½ cup finely chopped unseeded fresh hot green chiles (such as Thai bird chiles or serranos), instead of the dried red chiles. (You won't need to soak them.) *–Nancie McDermott*

1 **Heat a little vegetable oil,** add the curry paste, and stir, pressing the paste against the bottom of the pan. This will coat it with hot oil and make it "bloom," releasing complex aromas and flavors.

2 **Add meat and vegetables** to the pan and stir to coat them with the curry paste. If you're using fish or vegetables that cook quickly, add them later.

3 **Pour in the broth** and the coconut milk, if using, and simmer to cook the ingredients through and to build flavor.

4 **Finish with fish sauce** brown sugar, salt, and torn basil leaves after adding any quick-cooking ingredients, like shrimp.

Beef Stew with Red Wine & Carrots (Daube de Boeuf aux Carottes)

Serves six.

One 3-pound boneless beef chuck roast

2 tablespoons extra-virgin olive oil

2 slices thick-cut bacon, cut into ½-inch pieces

Kosher salt and freshly ground black pepper

8 ounces shallots (8 to 10 medium), thinly sliced (about 2 cups)

2 tablespoons brandy, such as Cognac

2 tablespoons tomato paste

2 to 3 cloves garlic, finely chopped (2 to 3 teaspoons)

2 teaspoons herbes de Provence

2 cups hearty red wine, such as Côtes de Provence or Côtes du Rhône

One 14½-ounce can whole, peeled tomatoes

4 strips orange zest (2½ inches long, removed with a vegetable peeler)

1 pound slender carrots, peeled and cut into ¾- to 1-inch chunks (about 2 cups)

¼ cup coarsely chopped fresh flat-leaf parsley

Very simply, a daube (pronounced dohb) is a red wine–based beef or lamb stew. The most famous is the Provençal daube, seasoned with local herbs and a bit of orange zest. When buying meat for this type of stew, your best bet is to select a small chuck roast and cut it yourself. Most butchers and meat markets cut their stew meat way too small for a proper daube, which should be a knife-and-fork affair—meaning the chunks are larger than bite size. This dish can be made up to three days ahead. Reserve the chopped parsley and don't bother skimming the surface fat. Instead, transfer the cooled stew to a bowl or baking dish, cover tightly, and refrigerate. Before reheating, lift off the layer of solid fat that will be on the surface. Reheat gently in a 325°F oven in a covered baking dish, stirring once, for about 30 minutes, or until hot. Taste for salt and pepper and add the parsley just before serving.

Using your fingers and a thin knife, pull the roast apart along its natural seams. Trim off any thick layers of fat. Carve the roast into 1½- to 2-inch cubes and arrange them on a paper-towel-lined tray to dry.

Position a rack in the lower third of the oven. Heat the oven to 325°F.

Heat the oil and bacon together in a 7- or 8-quart Dutch oven over medium heat, stirring occasionally, just until the bacon is browned but not crisp, 5 to 6 minutes. With a slotted spoon, transfer the bacon to a small plate. Season about one-third of the beef with salt and pepper, and arrange the cubes in a sparse single layer in the pot to brown. Adjust the heat so the beef sizzles and browns but does not burn. Cook until all sides are a rich brown, a total of about 10 minutes. Transfer to a large plate or tray, and season and brown the remaining beef in 2 more batches.

When all the beef chunks are browned, pour off all but about 1 tablespoon of drippings, if necessary. Set the pot over medium-high heat, add the shallots, season with a large pinch of salt and several grinds of pepper, and sauté until they just begin to soften, about 1 minute. Add the brandy and let it boil away. Add the tomato paste, garlic, and herbes de Provence, stirring to incorporate, and sauté for another 1 minute. Add the wine, stirring and scraping the bottom of the pan with a wooden spoon to dislodge the caramelized drippings, and bring to a boil. Pour in the liquid from the tomatoes, holding the tomatoes back with your hand. Then one by one, crush the tomatoes with your hand over the pot and drop them in. Add the orange zest and return the beef (along with accumulated juices) and bacon to the pot. Finally, add the carrots, bring to a simmer, cover, and slide into the oven.

Cook the stew, stirring every 45 minutes, until the meat is fork-tender (taste a piece; all trace of toughness should be gone), 2 to 3 hours. Before serving, skim off any surface fat (if there is any), taste for salt and pepper, and stir in the parsley.
—*Molly Stevens*

Custom cut your own stew meat

Rather than buying already cut-up stew meat, buy a whole chuck roast and cut it into 1½- to 2-inch cubes. These larger chunks won't dry out during the long braise, and they make the stew more satisfying to eat.

Classic American Pot Roast

Serves six to eight.

For the roast:

One 4-pound boneless beef chuck pot roast

Kosher salt and freshly ground black pepper

2 tablespoons vegetable oil

5 ounces thick-sliced bacon, cut into ½-inch squares (to yield 1 cup)

¾ cup peeled and finely chopped carrots

¾ cup peeled and finely chopped celery, with leaves

Kosher salt and freshly ground black pepper

2 sprigs fresh flat-leaf parsley

2 sprigs fresh thyme

1 or 2 bay leaves

A few whole cloves

Several whole peppercorns

1½ cups fresh apple cider

3 cups homemade or low-salt chicken or beef broth

For the vegetable garnish:

3 to 4 carrots, peeled and cut into ¾-inch chunks to yield about 2 cups

2 cups whole frozen pearl onions, thawed

2 cups ¾-inch chunks of peeled potatoes (yellow, red, or fingerling; avoid russets) or peeled turnips

Splash of cider vinegar

¼ cup chopped fresh flat-leaf parsley

With pot roast, the parts are transformed into a greater whole as the juices mingle, and the liquid bastes the meat. If you're making the pot roast ahead, it's very easy to degrease the sauce. Simply remove the fat that solidified on top of the sauce after it was refrigerated.

Set a rack on the lower third of the oven and heat the oven to 300°F. Select a 5- to 6-quart Dutch oven or other large, heavy-based pot with a tight-fitting lid. Tie the chuck roast into a snug shape using kitchen twine. Pat it dry with paper towels and season with salt and pepper. In the Dutch oven, heat the oil over medium-high heat. Brown the meat thoroughly on all sides, turning with tongs, about 5 minutes per side. The meat should sizzle but not scorch; stay close by and adjust the heat accordingly. Transfer the meat to a large plate.

Lower the heat to medium, add the bacon, and cook until just browned and beginning to crisp, 5 to 8 minutes. Remove the pot from the heat. With a slotted spoon, transfer the bacon to the plate with the beef. Spoon 2 tablespoons of the fat from the pan into a small dish and discard the rest.

Evaluate the drippings on the bottom of the pot. It's fine if they're very dark, almost black, but if there are any scorched bits, wipe these out with a wadded paper towel (if in doubt, taste a fleck—as long as it doesn't taste acrid, it's fine). Return the pot to medium heat and add the 2 tablespoons reserved bacon fat. Add the carrots and celery, season with salt and pepper, and cook until starting to soften, about 5 minutes.

Tie the parsley, thyme, bay leaves, cloves, and peppercorns in a small cheesecloth sachet. Add the sachet to the pot. Add the apple cider, stirring with a wooden spoon to scrape up any remaining drippings on the bottom of the pot if necessary. Bring to a boil over high heat and cook until the liquid has reduced to about 2 tablespoons. Add the chicken or beef broth and bring to a simmer.

Return the beef, bacon, and any juices that have accumulated to the pot with the braising liquid. Return the liquid to a simmer, cover the pot with a sheet of parchment, pushing down so the paper touches the meat. There's no need to cut a circle; the paper should be crumpled and will extend over the rim. Set the lid in place. Slide the pot into the oven and braise for 2 hours, turning the roast with tongs after 1 hour.

Add the vegetable garnish and finish cooking: Turn the roast once more and then scatter the carrots, pearl onions, and potatoes (or turnips) into the liquid around the roast and continue braising, covered with the parchment and with the lid, until the meat is fork tender, about an hour longer. Test for doneness by spearing the meat toward the center with a carving fork; when you pull out the fork (carefully), if it lifts the meat with it, let it cook for another 20 to 30 minutes.

Transfer the pot roast and chunky vegetables to a shallow platter (don't worry if a few finely chopped aromatics come along too); tent with foil. Strain the sauce into a measuring cup, discarding the spent aromatics and sachet of flavorings. Let the fat rise to the surface and spoon it off. Wipe out the braising pot with a paper towel.

Bring the strained, degreased juices to a simmer over medium heat. Taste and evaluate. If the flavor seems weak, simmer vigorously over medium-high heat to reduce the volume and concentrate the flavor, 5 to 15 minutes; season to taste with salt and pepper. Whisk in the cider vinegar and parsley.

Snip the strings from the pot roast and carve the meat across the grain into ¼- to ½-inch slices. Arrange the meat on a serving platter. Ladle about half the sauce over all, garnish with the vegetables, and serve, passing the remaining sauce at the table. *—Molly Stevens*

Fennel & Rosemary Beef Tenderloin with Creamy Mustard Sauce

Serves six to eight.

1 tablespoon extra-virgin olive oil

1 tablespoon finely chopped fresh rosemary

1½ teaspoons ground fennel seeds

1 teaspoon kosher salt; more to taste

½ teaspoon freshly cracked black pepper

2½- to 3-pound beef tenderloin roast, excess fat trimmed

½ cup crème fraîche

2 tablespoons Dijon mustard

2 teaspoons fresh lemon juice

A roasted tenderloin is always luxurious, but it needn't be time-consuming to prepare. This cut gets jazzed up with a simple spice rub and a whisk-together mustard sauce for serving.

Position a rack in the center of the oven and heat the oven to 375°F.

In a small bowl, combine the olive oil, rosemary, fennel seeds, salt, and pepper. Stir to make a paste. Pat the beef dry with paper towels and rub the paste all over the surface of the meat. If necessary, tie the roast at 1½-inch intervals. (The roast can be seasoned and refrigerated up to 4 hours in advance.)

Put the roast on a rack on a small, rimmed baking sheet or in a shallow roasting pan. Roast until an instant-read thermometer inserted in the center reads 120°F for rare, 125° to 130°F for medium rare, or 135°F for medium, 40 to 50 minutes.

Meanwhile, in a small bowl, whisk together the crème fraîche, mustard, and lemon juice. Season lightly with salt to taste.

Transfer the roast to a carving board (preferably with a well for collecting juices) and let it rest, uncovered, for 10 to 15 minutes before carving it into ⅓- to ½-inch-thick slices. Serve the beef, passing the mustard sauce at the table (it is also excellent cold, spread on leftover roast beef sandwiches).
—*Molly Stevens*

Calibrate your instant-read thermometer

An instant-read thermometer is a must-have tool for checking temperatures and gauging the doneness of all sorts of things. Because you rely on your thermometer for accuracy, it's a good idea to check its calibration occasionally and adjust it as need be.

To check the calibration, bring a small pan of water to a rolling boil and take the water's temperature; it should be 212°F or a few degrees less, depending on your altitude and air pressure. (For the boiling point in your location, visit www.virtualweberbullet.com/boilingpoint.html.)

If the calibration is off, you can adjust a standard (analog) thermometer by turning the hex nut under the thermometer's face with pliers (photo at left). If the nut resists, use a second set of pliers to grip the sides of the face and turn the tools in opposite directions.

There are only a few models of digital thermometers that can be adjusted. Some calibrate automatically, and others need manual adjustment; follow the manufacturer's instructions for your model.

Beef Tenderloin with Wild Mushroom Stuffing & Port Wine Sauce

Serves eight to ten.

For the sauce:

1¼ ounces (2½ tablespoons) unsalted butter

1 large shallot, finely chopped (about ¼ cup)

One 750-ml bottle tawny port (about 3¼ cups)

2 sprigs fresh thyme

2½ cups low-salt chicken broth

1 ounce dried porcini mushrooms

2 teaspoons all-purpose flour

1 teaspoon good-quality balsamic vinegar; more to taste

Kosher salt and freshly ground black pepper

For the roast:

4-pound beef tenderloin roast, preferably center-cut (see pages 236–237 for more information)

Kosher salt and freshly ground black pepper

Don't be scared off by the liver in this stuffing. It's really there just to bind it and add a rich background note; you won't even notice it. Use a good mix of interesting mushrooms, but if you're stuck with just creminis, that's okay—they have a fine flavor, too.

Make the sauce: Melt 1 tablespoon of the butter in a 3- to 4-quart (preferably 8-inch-wide) saucepan over medium-low heat. Add the shallot and cook until softened, about 5 minutes. Add the port and the thyme sprigs and bring to a boil over high heat. Reduce the heat to maintain a brisk simmer and cook until the port has reduced to a syrupy texture, about 30 minutes—you should have about ½, cup including the shallot.

Meanwhile, bring the chicken broth to a simmer in a small saucepan. Off the heat, add the porcini and let them soak for 15 minutes. With a slotted spoon, transfer the porcini to a small bowl. Strain the soaking liquid through a fine sieve lined with a paper towel or coffee filter.

Add the soaking liquid and half of the porcini (about ⅓ cup) to the port reduction (save the remaining porcini for the stuffing). Bring the sauce to a boil over high heat. Reduce the heat to maintain a brisk simmer and cook until it has reduced to 1⅓ cups, about 15 minutes. Strain the sauce through a fine strainer, pressing on the solids. You should have about 1 cup sauce. Set aside until the roast is done. (The sauce can be made to this point and refrigerated up to 2 days ahead. If not making the stuffing ahead, refrigerate the remaining soaked porcini separately.)

Make the stuffing: Soak the currants in hot water for 10 minutes. Drain and put them in a food processor. Add the reserved soaked porcini. Heat 1 tablespoon of the oil in a 10-inch skillet over medium heat. Pat the chicken liver dry and cook on both sides until browned on the outside and just a little pink inside, 3 to 4 minutes total. Transfer to a plate, let cool slightly, and then add to the food processor. Process until finely chopped.

Heat the remaining 1 tablespoon oil in the skillet over medium-high heat. Add the mushrooms, salt, and pepper. Cook, stirring occasionally, until they look wilted and shrunken, 2 to 3 minutes. Add the shallot and garlic and continue to cook, stirring, until the mushrooms are tender and beginning to brown, 3 to 4 more minutes. Add the chicken broth and scrape the bottom of the pan with a wooden spoon to loosen any brown bits. If the liquid doesn't evaporate right away, boil until it does. Remove the pan from the heat and let cool slightly.

Add the sautéed mushrooms, butter, parsley, Cognac or Armagnac, lemon juice, thyme, and lemon zest to the liver mixture in the food processor. Pulse to form a chunky paste and season to taste with additional salt and pepper.

Scrape the stuffing onto a large piece of plastic wrap and shape it into a log a few inches longer than the roast. Tightly roll the stuffing up in the plastic wrap and twist the ends to form a very tight log. Twisting the ends of the plastic will compress the stuffing so that it's just a bit shorter than the roast. Freeze until firm, about 2 hours and up to 2 days.

Stuff and cook the roast: Trim the silverskin and excess fat from the tenderloin. Butterfly the tenderloin by slicing it lengthwise almost but not completely in half, so that you can open it like a book. Unwrap the stuffing and center it along one half of the roast. Fold the roast back up to its original shape and tie at 1- to 2-inch intervals with butcher's twine. (The roast can be stuffed and refrigerated up to 1 day in advance.)

Let the roast sit at room temperature for 1 hour (2 hours if the stuffing is frozen solid). Position a rack in the bottom third of the oven and heat the oven to 500°F. Let the remaining 1½ tablespoons butter for the sauce soften at room temperature.

Season the roast generously with salt and pepper and put it on a flat rack set in a roasting pan or heavy-duty rimmed baking sheet. Roast for 15 minutes and then reduce the oven temperature to 325°F. Continue to roast the beef until a meat thermometer inserted into the center of the meat (not the stuffing) registers 125°F for rare or 130°F for medium rare, 30 to 45 minutes more. Move the roast to a carving board and let it rest, loosely tented with foil, for 15 minutes.

Finish the sauce: While the roast rests, bring the sauce to a simmer in a small saucepan over medium-low heat. Mix the softened butter with the flour to form a paste and whisk it into the sauce. Simmer the sauce to thicken slightly and cook off any raw flour taste, about 3 minutes. Whisk in the vinegar. Season to taste with salt, pepper, and additional vinegar.

Plate and serve: Remove the strings from the roast and slice it into 8 to 10 medallions. Put a medallion on each plate and drizzle the sauce around the beef. *—Allison Ehri Kreitler*

For the stuffing:

1 tablespoon dried currants

2 tablespoons canola oil

1 small chicken liver, fat trimmed and lobes separated (1½ to 2 ounces)

½ pound mixed fresh shiitake, oyster, and hen-of-the-woods mushrooms, stemmed and sliced ¼ inch thick (use all 3 varieties if you can find them; otherwise, try to use at least 2)

1 teaspoon kosher salt; more to taste

¼ teaspoon freshly ground black pepper; more to taste

1 small shallot, finely chopped (a heaping tablespoon)

2 medium cloves garlic, finely chopped (about 2 teaspoons)

¼ cup low-salt chicken broth

1 ounce (2 tablespoons) unsalted butter, cut into 4 pieces and softened at room temperature

1 tablespoon chopped fresh parsley

1½ teaspoons Cognac or Armagnac

1 teaspoon fresh lemon juice

½ teaspoon chopped fresh thyme

¼ teaspoon finely grated lemon zest

Buying a beef tenderloin that's perfect for stuffing

Beef tenderloin is a widely available cut of meat. Try to get a center-cut piece (often referred to as a Châteaubriand) because it's evenly thick from end to end, which makes for easy stuffing and even cooking. A 4-pound center-cut piece, however, comes from a very large tenderloin, which can be hard to find. If you have this problem, then it's fine to use the butt end (the fatter end) of the tenderloin. Just note that there's another piece of meat attached to the side of the butt end, so when you're butterflying the meat, cut through this extra piece first and then into the longer tenderloin piece (see top right photo).

Make sure to tell your butcher that you don't need your roast tied, and ask him to remove the "chain"—a slender, fatty piece of meat that runs along the entire side of the tenderloin. A good butcher should sell you a solid, nicely trimmed piece of meat without any gouges or slashes; the tenderloin is a pricey cut, so don't settle for a piece that's not in good condition.

Cut along the length of the tenderloin about two-thirds of the way through, so you can open it up like a book.

Center your stuffing on one half of the meat, fold the roast to its original shape, and tie with butcher's twine at 1- to 2-inch intervals.

Lamb Chops with Lemon, Thyme & Mustard Butter

Serves four.

4 tablespoons unsalted butter, softened

1 teaspoon whole-grain Dijon mustard

1 teaspoon fresh thyme leaves, lightly chopped

¾ teaspoon finely grated lemon zest

⅛ teaspoon kosher salt; more as needed

⅛ teaspoon freshly ground black pepper; more as needed

8 lamb loin chops (1½- to 2-inch-thick chops; about 3 pounds), trimmed

Whole-grain mustard, sometimes labeled *moutarde à l'ancienne,* adds just a bit more texture and tang than regular Dijon. Serve the chops with sautéed haricots verts and tiny boiled potatoes.

In a small bowl, mash together the butter, mustard, thyme, zest, salt, and pepper until well combined. Refrigerate until ready to use.

Position an oven rack 5 to 6 inches from the broiler element and heat the broiler to high. Line the bottom of a broiler pan with foil and replace the perforated top part of the pan. Arrange the chops on the pan. Season both sides of the lamb generously with salt and pepper. Broil until the first side is well browned, about 8 minutes. Turn the chops over with tongs and continue to broil until they're well browned and the center is cooked to your liking, 3 to 5 minutes longer for medium rare (cut into a chop near the bone to check).

Transfer the lamb to serving plates and top each chop with a dab of the flavored butter. Serve hot. *—Lori Longbotham*

Lamb Chops Crusted with Fennel & Black Pepper

Serves four.

2 teaspoons fennel seeds, lightly crushed

1¼ teaspoons ground coriander

1 teaspoon dried rosemary, chopped

1 teaspoon kosher salt

¾ teaspoon garlic powder

¾ teaspoon freshly cracked black pepper

8 lamb loin chops, about 1 inch thick (4 to 5 ounces each)

1½ tablespoons extra-virgin olive oil

The fragrant spice and herb coating gets toasted by the broiler, making it even more flavorful. For a delicious finger-food hors d'oeuvre, use the same rub on tiny frenched rib chops.

Position a rack 4 inches from the broiler element and heat the broiler to high.

In a small bowl, combine the fennel seeds, coriander, rosemary, salt, garlic powder, and pepper; mix well. Brush the lamb chops with the olive oil to coat. Press an equal amount of the spice mix on both sides of the chops and let them sit for 10 minutes.

Coat a broiler pan with oil or nonstick cooking spray. Set the lamb chops on the pan and broil until the first side is well browned, about 5 minutes. Flip the chops and continue to cook until the second side is well browned and the center is cooked to your liking (cut into a chop near the bone to check), about another 5 minutes for medium rare. *—David Bonom*

Rack of Lamb with Ancho-Honey Glaze

The glaze for this dinner-party dish is full of delicious contrasts—sweet honey, tangy vinegar, fruity orange juice, plus the earthiness and heat from the ancho chile powder. Lamb handles all those flavor beautifully. Serve with herb-flecked couscous or rice pilaf alongside.

Position a rack in the center of the oven and heat the oven to 425°F. Line a small roasting pan or rimmed baking sheet with foil (to make it easier to clean the glaze from the pan).

If necessary, trim the lamb so that only a thin layer of fat remains, being careful not to remove all the fat. Arrange the lamb bone side down in the roasting pan, interlocking the bone ends if necessary to make them fit. Season each rack generously with salt and pepper.

In a small bowl, combine the honey, vinegar, cumin, ancho chile powder, and a pinch each of salt and pepper. Brush the surface of the meat with about half (¼ cup) of the glaze.

Roast, brushing the lamb after 10 minutes and then again every 5 minutes with the glaze that has begun to caramelize on the roasting pan, until an instant-read thermometer inserted close to but not touching the bones reads 125°F for rare or 130° to 135°F for medium rare, about 20 minutes for rare and 25 minutes for medium rare.

Meanwhile, pour the remaining glaze into a small saucepan, add the orange juice and garlic, and bring to a simmer over medium-high heat. Simmer until reduced to a slightly syrupy glaze, about 7 minutes. Add the herbs, if using.

Let the lamb rest for about 5 minutes. Cut between the bones to carve the racks into chops and drizzle each chop with a little of the glaze before serving.
—*Molly Stevens*

Serves six.

2 racks of lamb (each 1¼ to 1½ pounds with 7 to 8 ribs), trimmed, or frenched

Kosher salt and freshly ground black pepper

⅓ cup honey

2 tablespoons red-wine vinegar

1½ teaspoons ground cumin, preferably toasted

1 teaspoon ancho chile powder

½ cup orange juice

1 clove garlic, minced

1 tablespoon finely chopped fresh mint, parsley, basil, or cilantro (optional)

Broiled Lamb Skewers with Baby Arugula & Lemon Vinaigrette

Serves two.

2 tablespoons fresh lemon juice

2 teaspoons sour cream

1 small clove garlic, minced

Kosher salt

¼ cup plus 1 tablespoon extra-virgin olive oil

¾ pound boneless lamb shoulder chops or lamb leg steaks, trimmed of extra fat and cut into 1-inch cubes (1½ cups)

Coarsely ground black pepper

4 ounces baby arugula (about 4 cups)

½ cup very thinly sliced red onion (½ small)

¼ cup crumbled feta or blue cheese (1 ounce)

Savory chunks of lamb, fresh greens, pungent onions, and the creamy tang of feta make this quick dinner like a super-elegant Greek gyro. If you're using bamboo skewers, soak them in water for 30 minutes before threading them.

Position an oven rack 4 inches from the broiler element and heat the broiler to high. In a small bowl, combine the lemon juice, sour cream, garlic, and a pinch of salt. Slowly whisk in the ¼ cup olive oil.

In a medium bowl, combine the lamb with the 1 tablespoon olive oil, ½ teaspoon salt, and ¼ teaspoon pepper. Toss to coat evenly. Thread the lamb onto four small (8-inch) bamboo or metal skewers.

Put the skewers on a broiler pan and broil the lamb, flipping once, until browned on the outside but still pink inside (medium doneness), 2 to 4 minutes per side. Transfer the skewers to a small, shallow baking dish. Whisk the vinaigrette to recombine and pour 3 tablespoons of it over the skewers, turning to coat.

In a medium bowl, toss the arugula and onion with enough of the remaining vinaigrette to lightly coat (you may not need it all). Season with salt and pepper to taste. Pile the greens on two plates, top each salad with two lamb skewers, sprinkle with the cheese, and serve immediately. *—Maryellen Driscoll*

Grilled Herb-Crusted Leg of Lamb with Fresh Mint Sauce

Boneless leg of lamb is the perfect cut for feeding a crowd. It's large, wonderfully flavorful, easy to prepare, and cooks to varied donesses. Butterflying (or further flattening out) this cut and gently pounding it will make it more uniform for cooking.

At least 1 day ahead, marinate the lamb: Set the lamb flat on a large cutting board. Trim any excess fat and then make deep horizontal slices into the thicker parts and open like a book to make an even thickness all around. Lay a piece of plastic wrap on top of the lamb and using a meat mallet or the bottom of a heavy skillet, pound to flatten slightly and make the thickness more uniform. Cut the meat into 2 or 3 more-manageable pieces. Sprinkle all over with 1 tablespoon of the salt and 1 teaspoon of the pepper.

In a small bowl, mix the mustard, garlic, thyme, rosemary, and the remaining 1 tablespoon salt and 1 teaspoon pepper. Spread all over the lamb, transfer to a large nonreactive dish, cover, and refrigerate for at least 24 hours and up to 2 days.

Just before grilling, make the sauce: In a medium bowl, whisk ¼ cup water with the sugar, salt, and pepper—they don't have to dissolve completely. Stir in the mint, vinegar, and oil. Let sit while the lamb grills. Taste and season with more sugar, salt, and pepper if needed. (The sauce should have a sharp, acidic tang to complement the rich lamb.)

Grill the lamb: Heat a gas grill to medium high or prepare a charcoal fire with hot and medium-hot areas. Put the lamb on the grill (on the hotter part if using a charcoal fire) and cook (covered on a gas grill) without disturbing it until it's nicely browned, 6 to 8 minutes. Flip, reduce the heat on the gas grill to medium (or move to the cooler part of the charcoal fire), and cook until an instant-read thermometer inserted into a thicker part of the lamb registers 130°F for medium rare, 5 to 8 more minutes.

Transfer the lamb to a cutting board, tent with foil, and let rest for 10 minutes. Slice thinly across the grain and serve with the mint sauce.

—Tony Rosenfeld

Serves ten to twelve.

For the lamb:

1 large or 2 small boneless legs of lamb (about 5½ pounds)

2 tablespoons kosher salt

2 teaspoons freshly ground black pepper

¼ cup Dijon mustard

4 large cloves garlic, finely chopped (about 2 tablespoons)

2 tablespoons chopped fresh thyme

2 tablespoons chopped fresh rosemary

For the sauce:

2 tablespoons granulated sugar; more as needed

1 teaspoon kosher salt; more as needed

½ teaspoon freshly ground black pepper; more as needed

1 cup chopped fresh mint (about 1 bunch)

¼ cup white-wine vinegar; more as needed

2 tablespoons olive oil

Braised Lamb Shanks with Garlic & Vermouth

Serves six.

6 lamb shanks (¾ to 1 pound each)

Kosher salt and freshly ground black pepper

2 tablespoons extra-virgin olive oil

1 cup dry white vermouth, preferably Vya® or Noilly Prat®

2 bay leaves

2 heads garlic, separated into cloves (unpeeled)

2 teaspoons fresh lemon juice; more as needed

¼ cup chopped fresh herbs, preferably a mix of mint and parsley (chervil and chives are also good)

In this dish, the shanks are cooked with dry white vermouth and a few bay leaves to give the braising liquid an elusive, herbaceous flavor that permeates the meat and intensifies the dish. The dish can be made up to three days ahead. After braising, transfer the shanks to a baking dish. Strain and season the sauce as directed in the recipe. Pour a little sauce over the shanks to moisten. Refrigerate shanks and sauce separately. Before serving, reheat the chilled sauce, pour it over the shanks in the baking dish, cover the dish with foil, and warm in a 325°F oven for about 30 minutes. Finish with the herbs and black pepper, and serve.

Position a rack in the lower third of the oven and heat the oven to 325°F. If necessary, trim any excess fat from the lamb shanks, but don't trim away the thin membrane that holds the meat to the bone. Season the shanks all over with salt and pepper.

Heat the oil over medium heat in a large Dutch oven or other heavy braising pot large enough to accommodate the lamb shanks in a snug single layer. When the oil is shimmering, add half the shanks and brown them on all sides, 12 to 15 minutes total. Set the browned shanks on a platter. Repeat with the remaining shanks. When all the shanks are browned, pour off and discard the fat from the pan.

Set the pan over medium-high heat and add the vermouth. As it boils, stir with a wooden spoon to dissolve any drippings. Return the shanks to the pan, arranging them as best you can so they fit snugly. Tuck the bay leaves in between the shanks and scatter the garlic over them. Cover and braise in the oven, turning the shanks every 45 minutes, until fork-tender, 1½ to 2 hours.

Transfer the shanks to a platter and cover with foil to keep warm. Tilt the braising pot to pool the juices at one end and skim off and discard any surface fat. Pour what remains in the pot into a medium-mesh sieve set over a bowl. Discard the bay leaves. With a rubber spatula, scrape over and press down on the garlic cloves so the pulp goes through but not the skins; be sure to scrape the pulp clinging to the bottom of the strainer into the sauce. Whisk in the lemon juice. Taste and add salt, pepper, and more lemon juice if needed. To serve, pour the sauce over the shanks and shower them with the chopped herbs and a little freshly ground pepper. —*Molly Stevens*

Creating a rich but grease-free sauce

After the long braise, the garlic cloves are tender enough to push through a sieve, creating a flavorful purée that thickens the pan sauce. Don't forget to scrape the pulp clinging to the bottom of the strainer.

Lamb throws off a considerable amount of fat as it cooks, so be sure to take the time to thoroughly skim the sauce before serving. Better yet, braise the shanks a day or two before you plan to serve them, and store them and the braising liquid in the refrigerator. When it comes time to reheat and serve, simply lift the solidified fat from the surface of the sauce. The dish will have even more flavor after a day or two.

Pork Tenderloin with Sage & Marsala Sauce

Serves four.

1 large pork tenderloin (1¼ to 1½ pounds), trimmed and cut in half crosswise

½ teaspoon kosher salt

¼ teaspoon freshly ground black pepper

2 teaspoon pink peppercorns, crushed (optional)

2 tablespoons unsalted butter

1 tablespoon extra-virgin olive oil

½ cup sweet Marsala

1 tablespoon chopped fresh sage leaves

Fried sage leaves (see below), for garnish (optional)

The classic Italian combo of sage and Marsala comes together in a quick sauce for tender slices of pork. Let the tenderloin rest for a few minutes before cutting, for the most succulent texture. Serve this dish with garlic mashed potatoes, braised vegetables, or just a fresh green salad.

Position a rack in the center of the oven and heat the oven to 375°F.

Season the pork tenderloin with the salt and pepper and rub it evenly with the pink peppercorns, if using.

Heat 1 tablespoon of the butter and the oil in a 10-inch ovenproof skillet or straight-sided sauté pan over medium-high heat. Put the pork in the pan and sear it until golden brown on all sides, about 5 minutes total. Transfer the skillet to the oven and roast until an instant-read thermometer inserted in the center of the meat registers 140°F, 10 to 15 minutes. Move the pork to a cutting board and tent loosely with foil.

Pour off and discard most of the fat left in the skillet. Set the skillet over medium-high heat and add the Marsala. Bring to a vigorous simmer, scraping the bottom of the pan with a wooden spoon to loosen any browned bits. Simmer until reduced by half, about 2 minutes. Off the heat, add the remaining 1 tablespoon butter and the chopped sage. Swirl or stir the sauce until the butter melts.

Slice the pork into 12 pieces, arrange them on a platter, and pour the hot pan sauce over the meat. Garnish with the fried sage leaves, if using.
—Ruth Lively

Fried sage: garnish or snack

Fried sage makes an unusual crisp garnish for roasted meats and poultry, mashed potatoes, and even risotto. Or it can be a treat all on its own to enjoy with other nibbles like olives, toasted nuts, and cheese. And it takes only a few minutes to cook.

Always start with clean and dry whole leaves—the bigger the better—with stems left on. Pour enough olive oil in a heavy skillet to cover the bottom by about ⅛ inch and heat over medium heat until the oil shimmers. Add sage leaves in a single layer and fry until brittle but still a bright green color with no browning, 15 to 30 seconds. Transfer to a plate lined with paper towels and sprinkle with salt.

Deviled Pork Chops

Serves four.

¼ cup Dijon mustard

1 tablespoon firmly packed dark
brown sugar

2 teaspoons fresh lemon juice

2 teaspoons Worcestershire
sauce

¼ teaspoon ground cayenne

Four 1-inch-thick, bone-in,
center-cut loin pork chops
(2½ to 3 pounds)

Kosher salt

1 tablespoon coarsely chopped
fresh flat-leaf parsley
(optional)

Pork chops are easy to cook, but can sometimes be bland. This spicy-sweet coating gives pork chops moisture and personality. To make sure you don't overcook them, check the internal temperature with an instant-read thermometer.

Stir together the mustard, brown sugar, lemon juice, Worcestershire, and cayenne in a small bowl.

Position an oven rack 3 to 4 inches from the broiler element and heat the broiler to high. Line the bottom of a broiler pan with foil and replace the perforated top part of the pan. Arrange the pork on the broiler pan and season generously on both sides with salt. Brush about half of the mustard mixture over the top of the chops. Broil until the chops are deeply browned in spots, 6 to 8 minutes. Turn the chops over with tongs, brush with the remaining mustard mixture, and continue to broil until the pork is browned and just cooked through (an instant-read thermometer in the center of a chop should register 145°F), about 5 minutes more. Let rest for a few minutes before serving. Sprinkle the better-looking sides of the chops with the parsley, if using, and transfer to serving plates. *–Lori Longbotham*

Sear-Roasted Pork Chops with Balsamic-Fig Sauce

A sharp balsamic sauce made right in the skillet punches up the mild flavor of the pork chop. Be sure your oven has reached 425°F before starting to sear the pork—most ovens take at least 20 minutes to heat up thoroughly. Serve the chops with some instant polenta and a green salad.

Cook the chops: Heat the oven to 425°F. Turn the exhaust fan on to high. Pat the pork chops dry with paper towels. Season both sides generously with salt and pepper (about 1 teaspoon of each total). Heat a 12-inch heavy-based ovenproof skillet over medium-high heat until a droplet of water vaporizes in 1 or 2 seconds, about 1 minute. (If the water skitters around the pan and doesn't evaporate, the pan is too hot; take it off the heat for about 30 seconds to cool.)

Add the oil, swirl it around the pan, and then space the chops evenly in the pan. Cook without touching for 2 minutes. Using tongs, lift a corner of each chop, check that it is well browned and easily releases from the pan, and flip it over. (If it sticks or isn't well browned, cook for another 1 to 2 minutes before flipping.) Cook the second side for 1 minute and then transfer the skillet to the oven. Roast until the chops are just firm to the touch, 5 to 8 minutes. Using potholders, carefully remove the pan from the oven, transfer the chops to a large plate (don't wash the skillet), tent with foil, and let them rest while you prepare the sauce.

Make the sauce: Pour off any excess fat from the skillet. Return the pan to high heat and add the chicken broth and balsamic vinegar. Cook, scraping the pan with a wooden spoon to incorporate any browned bits, until the broth is reduced to about 1/2 cup, about 5 minutes. Stir in the figs, honey, and thyme and cook until the sauce is reduced by another 1 to 2 tablespoons, about 1 minute. Add the butter and swirl it into the sauce until it's completely melted. Season with salt and pepper to taste and serve immediately, drizzled over the sear-roasted pork chops.

—Tony Rosenfeld

Serves four; yields about 1/2 cup sauce.

For the pork chops:

4 boneless center-cut pork chops, 1 to 1½ inches thick (2 to 2½ pounds)

Kosher salt and freshly ground black pepper

2 tablespoons olive oil, canola oil, or peanut oil

For the balsamic-fig sauce:

1 cup homemade or low-salt chicken broth

3 tablespoons balsamic vinegar

¼ cup finely chopped dried figs

1½ tablespoons honey

1 teaspoon chopped fresh thyme

2 tablespoons unsalted butter, cut into four pieces

Kosher salt and freshly ground black pepper

Coriander-Rubbed Pork Chops with Orange Hoisin Sauce

Serves four.

For the sauce:

¼ cup hoisin sauce

2 tablespoons rice vinegar

1½ teaspoons frozen orange
juice concentrate, thawed

For the pork chops:

4 bone-in center-cut pork chops
(1 to 1½ inches thick)

¼ cup Asian sesame oil

3 tablespoons freshly cracked
coriander seeds

1 tablespoon kosher salt

1 tablespoon coarsely ground
white or black pepper

1 tablespoon olive oil

For the garnish:

6 scallions (white and light
green parts), thinly sliced
lengthwise into julienne strips

1 red bell pepper, cored, seeded,
and thinly sliced lengthwise
into julienne strips

2 tablespoons chopped
fresh ginger

3 tablespoons dry sherry

Kosher salt and freshly ground
white pepper

Thicker pork chops are better at holding their juices during cooking, so it's worth your while to find a market that carries them or that will cut them to order for you. If you can only find 1-inch-thick chops, keep a close eye on them, as they'll cook through more quickly.

Make the sauce: In a small bowl, mix the hoisin sauce, rice vinegar, and orange juice concentrate.

Cook the chops: Pat the chops dry with paper towels and rub both sides with 2 tablespoons of the sesame oil, the coriander, salt, and pepper. Heat the remaining 2 tablespoons sesame oil and the olive oil in a very large sauté pan over medium-high heat until hot but not smoking. (If you don't have a pan large enough to fit the chops without crowding, use two smaller pans, divide the sesame and olive oils between them, and cook two chops in each.) Cook the chops until well browned on one side, 3 to 5 minutes. Turn and cook the other side until the meat is done, 2 to 4 minutes. (If they start to burn, turn down the heat slightly.) To check for doneness, make a small cut near the bone and look inside—the pork should have a hint of pinkness. If it's still red, cook for another minute and check again. Transfer the chops to a plate, tent with foil, and let rest for 3 to 5 minutes before serving.

Make the garnish: Put the scallions, bell pepper, and ginger in the sauté pan over medium-high heat. (If you used two pans for the chops, use just one for the garnish.) Cook, stirring constantly, until crisp-tender, about 2 minutes. Add the sherry; cook for another 30 seconds. Brush each chop generously with the sauce, top with the vegetables, and serve. —*Chris Schlesinger*

Grilled Asian Pork Tenderloin with Peanut Sauce

Butterflying a pork tenderloin is easy and, when you follow with a gentle pounding, allows you to grill the meat to perfect doneness. Serve with steamed jasmine or short-grain rice and stir-fried spinach or snow peas.

In a large bowl, whisk the coconut milk, peanut butter, soy sauce, lime juice, brown sugar, garlic, and coriander to make a smooth sauce.

Trim the pork of excess fat and silverskin. Butterfly the tenderloins by splitting each one lengthwise almost but not quite all the way through, so the halves remain attached.

Open each tenderloin like a book, cover with plastic wrap, and pound to an even ½-inch thickness with a meat mallet or the bottom of a small skillet. Put the pork tenderloins in the bowl with the marinade and turn to coat. Let marinate for 10 to 20 minutes (or up to several hours in the refrigerator).

While the pork marinates, heat a gas grill with all burners on high. Clean and oil the grate. Remove the tenderloins from the marinade, letting excess marinade drip back into the bowl (don't discard the marinade). Grill the tenderloins, covered, turning once, until just cooked through, 5 to 7 minutes total (cut into one to check). Transfer to a carving board and let rest for 5 minutes.

Meanwhile, pour the marinade into a small saucepan and add 2 tablespoons water; bring to a boil, reduce the heat, and simmer for 3 minutes. Remove from the heat. If the sauce seems too thick, thin it with 1 or 2 teaspoons water. Slice the pork and serve with the sauce on the side.
—*Pam Anderson*

Serves four to five.

1 cup light coconut milk

½ cup smooth peanut butter, preferably a natural variety

¼ cup soy sauce

3 tablespoons fresh lime juice

3 tablespoons dark brown sugar

2 large cloves garlic, minced (2½ teaspoons)

2 teaspoons ground coriander

2 small pork tenderloins (about 2 pounds total)

Vegetable oil for the grill

Hoisin Pork with Napa Cabbage

Serves four.

- 1 pound pork tenderloin, cut into ¼-inch-thick strips (about 3 inches long)
- 1 teaspoon kosher salt; more to taste
- 3 tablespoons hoisin sauce
- 2 tablespoons soy sauce
- 1 tablespoon balsamic vinegar
- 3 tablespoons canola or peanut oil
- 2 teaspoons minced garlic
- 6 cups Napa cabbage, cut into 1½-inch pieces (about ¾ pound)
- 1 red bell pepper, cored, thinly sliced, and cut into 2- to 3-inch lengths
- ¼ cup thinly sliced fresh chives

Pork tenderloin is the perfect choice for this quick sauté because it's easy to slice, cooks quickly, and stays so beautifully tender.

In a large bowl, season the pork with ½ teaspoon of the salt. In a small bowl, mix the hoisin sauce, soy sauce, and vinegar.

Heat 2 tablespoons of the oil in a 12-inch nonstick skillet or large stir-fry pan over medium-high heat until shimmering hot. Add the pork and cook, stirring, until it browns and loses most of its raw appearance, about 2 minutes. Transfer to a plate.

Add the remaining 1 tablespoon oil to the skillet. Add the garlic, and once it begins to sizzle, add the cabbage and pepper. Sprinkle with the remaining ½ teaspoon salt and cook, stirring, until the cabbage starts to wilt, about 2 minutes.

Add the hoisin mixture, the pork, and half of the chives and cook, tossing, until heated through, about 1 minute. Let sit for 2 minutes off the heat (the cabbage will exude some liquid and form a rich broth), toss well again, and serve sprinkled with the remaining chives. —*Tony Rosenfeld*

Crown Roast of Pork with Fennel-Apple Stuffing & Cider-Bourbon Sauce

Serves ten to fourteen.

For the sauce:

1 quart apple cider

2 cups bourbon

2 cups low-salt chicken broth

⅓ cup sour cream

1 tablespoon cider vinegar; more to taste

Kosher salt and freshly ground black pepper

For the stuffing:

1 pound Tuscan bread (or similar crusty artisan-style bread), cut into ½-inch cubes (8 to 9 cups)

8 ounces bacon (8 to 10 slices), cut crosswise into ½-inch-wide strips

2½ ounces (5 tablespoons) unsalted butter

2 medium-small yellow onions, cut into small dice (about 2 cups)

1 medium fennel bulb, cut into medium dice (about 3 cups)

1 teaspoon kosher salt; more to taste

½ teaspoon freshly ground black pepper; more to taste

4 medium Granny Smith apples, peeled, cored, and cut into ½-inch pieces (about 4 cups)

2 tablespoons bourbon

2 tablespoons apple cider

2 tablespoons chopped fresh marjoram

1 tablespoon chopped fresh sage

2 teaspoons fennel seeds, lightly chopped or pulsed in a spice grinder

½ teaspoon ground allspice

2 to 2½ cups low-salt chicken broth

This majestic cut of meat is a real show-stopper, and it's super easy to stuff. Since you buy the roast already tied, all you have to do is treat the center like a bowl and fill it up with savory stuffing.

Make the sauce reduction: Put the cider, bourbon, and chicken broth in a 3- to 4-quart (preferably 8-inch-wide) saucepan and bring to a boil over high heat. Reduce the heat to maintain a very brisk simmer and cook until the sauce has reduced to 1¼ cups, about 1 hour. Set aside until the roast is done. (The sauce can be made to this point and refrigerated for up to two days ahead.)

Make the stuffing base: Put the bread on a rimmed baking sheet and let it sit out to dry overnight. Cook the bacon in a 12-inch skillet over medium-high heat, stirring occasionally, until just crisp, 5 to 6 minutes. With a slotted spoon, transfer the bacon to a large mixing bowl. Pour off and discard all but about 1 tablespoon of the bacon fat. Add 3 tablespoons of the butter to the skillet and melt over medium heat. Add the onions, fennel, salt, and pepper and cook, stirring occasionally with a wooden spoon, until just softened and lightly browned, 10 to 12 minutes. Transfer to the bowl with the bacon.

Melt the remaining 2 tablespoons butter in the skillet over medium-high heat. Add the apples and cook, tossing or stirring occasionally, until nicely browned on a few sides but still firm, 4 to 6 minutes. Mix the bourbon with the apple cider and 3 tablespoons water. Carefully add it to the pan, scraping with a wooden spoon to loosen the browned bits stuck to the pan. Cook until the deglazing liquid has reduced and coats the apples, about 1 minute. Add the apples to the bowl. Add the marjoram, sage, fennel seeds, and allspice and stir to combine. (The stuffing base can be prepared to this point and refrigerated for up to 12 hours.)

Stuff and cook the roast: Let the roast sit out at room temperature for 1 hour. If the stuffing base was refrigerated, let it sit at room temperature, too.

Position a rack in the bottom third of the oven and heat the oven to 500°F. Season the roast all over with salt and pepper. Put the roast on an oiled flat rack set in a roasting pan or heavy-duty rimmed baking sheet. Cover the bones tightly with aluminum foil. Roast the pork for 30 minutes.

Meanwhile, stir the dried bread into the stuffing base. Pour 2 cups of the chicken broth over the mixture and stir to combine. If the bread immediately sucks up the liquid, add the remaining ½ cup broth. The bread should be moist but not soggy. Season to taste with salt and pepper.

Take the roast out of the oven and reduce the oven temperature to 325°F. Remove the foil from the bones and loosely fill the center of the roast with stuffing, mounding it half way up to the top of the bones (don't worry if the roast doesn't hold very much stuffing; just put in as much as you can). Cover the bones and stuffing tightly with aluminum foil. Set a timer for 1 hour and return the roast to the oven. Wrap the remaining stuffing in a double layer of aluminum foil and set aside.

When the timer goes off, put the wrapped stuffing seam side up in the oven next to the roast. Set a timer for 30 minutes.

When the timer goes off, remove the foil from the roast and open the package of stuffing so the top can crisp up. Set a timer for 15 minutes. When it goes off, start checking for doneness: Insert an instant-read thermometer into the meat between two bones without hitting the bones. The roast is done when the thermometer reads 155°F. Check the temperature in two or three places. The total roasting time will be 2½ to 3 hours.

Slide a wide spatula under the roast to keep the stuffing in and transfer it to a carving board or serving platter. Tent loosely with foil and let rest for 30 minutes. Meanwhile, continue to bake the package of stuffing until the top is crisp and then turn off the oven. Leave the stuffing in the oven until ready to serve.

Finish the sauce: Shortly before serving, reheat the sauce in a small saucepan over low heat. Remove the sauce from the heat and whisk in the sour cream and vinegar. Season the sauce to taste with salt, pepper, and additional vinegar. Transfer the sauce and the additional stuffing to serving bowls.

Plate and serve: Remove the strings from the roast. At the table, carve the roast into chops by cutting between the ribs into the stuffing. Serve the sauce and additional stuffing on the side. *—Allison Ehri Kreitler*

For the roast:

One 16-rib crown roast of pork (8½ to 9½ pounds), chine bone removed and bones frenched

Kosher salt and freshly ground black pepper

Butchers can cut a crown roast of pork in more than one way, so photos can be helpful.

Do: Ask the butcher to remove the chine bone (part of the backbone) in order to bend the roast into the "crown" but not to cut into the meat of the roast (see photo at left). A roast trimmed like this will stay juicy and look pretty, too, which is important because a crown roast is all about dramatic presentation. (The timing for the recipe here is based on a roast trimmed this way.) Also, instead of weight, some butchers want to know the number of ribs you'd like. Sixteen ribs makes for a nice crown.

Don't: Buy a roast with the chine bone still attached. The chine, which runs perpendicular to the ribs, makes carving the roast difficult, so if the chine is left on, butchers usually cut through it between each rib to facilitate carving. The problem is that these cuts often continue too far into the meat, partially dividing each chop (see photo at left) and making the roast more likely to dry out because more surface area of the meat is exposed.

Oven-Glazed Ham with a Pan Sauce

Serves twelve to fourteen.

1 half-ham, preferably bone-in (7 to 9 pounds)

1 glaze and sauce recipe of your choice (see recipes on pages 260–261)

A supermarket "city ham" is already fully cooked, so heating it isn't essential. But a warm ham tastes better, and baking concentrates the meat's flavor and improves its texture. It also allows you to jazz up the ham with one of my glaze and pan sauce combinations.

Bake the ham: Position a rack in the lower third of the oven and heat the oven to 325°F.

Trim away any skin and external fat to a thickness of about ¼ inch. Set the ham fat side up and score the fat ¼ inch deep with diagonal slices every 2 inches so that it forms a cross-hatched diamond pattern.

Set the ham in a sturdy roasting pan or a baking dish. It should fit fairly snugly with only a couple of inches of space on any side. Add the liquid from the glaze and sauce recipe to reach a ¼-inch depth. Bake, adding water as needed to maintain ¼ inch of liquid, until an instant-read thermometer inserted into the center of the ham registers 105° to 110°F, 1¾ to 2¼ hours (it should take about 15 minutes per pound).

Remove the ham from the oven and raise the temperature to 425°F. Add more water to the pan so the liquid is about ½ inch deep.

Using a large spoon or pastry brush, smear the glaze generously over the top of the ham. Return the pan to the oven (even if it hasn't reached 425°F yet) and bake until the glaze on the ham bubbles and begins to darken, 10 to 15 minutes; the ham should have an internal temperature of 120° to 125°F.

Remove the ham from the oven and transfer to a carving board or large platter. Tent loosely with foil and let rest for 20 to 30 minutes while you make the pan sauce. During this period, the ham's internal temperature should rise to 130° to 140°F.

Make the sauce: Pour the pan juices into a gravy separator or a 4-cup Pyrex measuring cup. Let sit for 10 to 15 minutes to allow any fat to rise and then pour or spoon off the fat and discard (some hams don't exude much fat).

Pour the pan juices into a 2-quart saucepan, whisk in the sauce ingredients (except the cornstarch mixture) from the glaze and sauce recipe and bring to a boil. Taste the sauce, and if the flavor isn't as intense as you'd like, continue to boil to concentrate the flavors as desired.

Stir in about half the cornstarch mixture and whisk until the sauce thickens slightly, about 15 seconds. Add more of the cornstarch mixture for a thicker sauce. Set aside and keep warm while the ham rests.

Carve the ham, arrange on a platter, and serve with the sauce alongside.
—Bruce Aidells

Three Glazes & Sauces for Oven-Glazed Ham

Cherry-Pomegranate Glaze & Sauce

*Yields enough for
1 Oven-Glazed Ham.*

1¼ cups pomegranate juice

½ cup cherry preserves

2 tablespoons Dijon mustard

¼ cup packed light brown sugar

¼ cup kirschwasser or other
cherry liqueur

¼ cup sweetened dried tart
cherries

1 tablespoon cornstarch mixed
with 3 tablespoons water

For baking the ham: Pour 1 cup
of the pomegranate juice into the
roasting pan and add enough water
to reach a ¼-inch depth, as indicated
in the Oven-Glazed Ham recipe. Add
more water during baking as needed.

To make the glaze: Gently warm
¼ cup of the cherry preserves in a
small saucepan. Stir in the mustard
and brown sugar to combine. Smear
over the ham as instructed in the
Oven-Glazed Ham recipe.

To make the sauce: In a small
saucepan combine the kirschwasser,
dried cherries, and the remaining
¼ cup pomegranate juice. Bring to a
boil, cover, and simmer for 5 minutes.

Add this mixture, along with the
remaining ¼ cup cherry preserves, to
the pan juices and boil as instructed
in the Oven-Glazed Ham recipe. Add
the cornstarch mixture as instructed.
—Bruce Aidells

Tangerine Marmalade Glaze & Sauce

*Yields enough for
1 Oven-Glazed Ham.*

1½ cups store-bought orange juice

½ cup tangerine or other citrus
marmalade

¼ cup packed light brown sugar

¼ teaspoon ground ginger

⅛ teaspoon ground cloves

2 tablespoons fresh lemon juice,
more to taste

1 tablespoon cornstarch mixed
with 3 tablespoons water

For baking the ham: Pour the
orange juice into the roasting pan
and add enough water to reach a
¼-inch depth, as indicated in the
Oven-Glazed Ham recipe. Add more
water during baking as needed.

To make the glaze: Gently warm
¼ cup of the marmalade in a small
saucepan set over medium-low heat.
Stir in the brown sugar, ginger, and
cloves to combine. Smear over the
ham as instructed in the Oven-Glazed
Ham recipe.

To make the sauce: Add the
remaining ¼ cup marmalade and
the lemon juice to the pan juices
and boil as instructed in the Oven-
Glazed Ham recipe. Add more lemon
juice to taste. Add the cornstarch
mixture as instructed.
—Bruce Aidells

Maple, Tea & Cardamom Glaze & Sauce

*Yields enough for
1 Oven-Glazed Ham.*

1 cup brewed tea (something basic
like Lipton® is fine)

1 cup apple cider

½ cup pure maple syrup

¼ cup packed light brown sugar

¼ teaspoon ground cardamom

2 tablespoons cider vinegar

1 tablespoon cornstarch mixed
with 3 tablespoons water

For baking the ham: In a medium
bowl, combine the tea, cider, and
¼ cup of the maple syrup. Pour this
mixture into the roasting pan and
add enough water to reach a ¼-inch
depth, as indicated in the Oven-
Glazed Ham recipe. Add more water
during baking as needed.

To make the glaze: In a small
bowl, mix 2 tablespoons of the maple
syrup with the brown sugar and
cardamom to make a thick, wet paste.
Smear over the ham as instructed in
the Oven-Glazed Ham recipe (use a
spatula or your fingers if it's easier).

To make the sauce: Add the
remaining 2 tablespoons maple syrup
and the vinegar to the pan juices and
boil as instructed in the Oven-Glazed
Ham recipe. Add the cornstarch
mixture as instructed.
—Bruce Aidells

tip : The two highest grades of ham are sold as either whole or half hams. For up to 14 people, a half-ham is sufficient.

The butt half is the upper part of the ham. Its meat tends to be very tender and flavorful—and there's more of it—but it often contains part of the hip bone, which makes carving a little awkward.

The shank half is the lower part of the ham. It's easier to carve, but because the muscles in this region get more exercise, this cut is tougher and chewier.

Bone-in ham delivers more flavor

Any meat cooked on the bone generally has better flavor, and in the case of ham, it also has better texture. When producers remove the bone from a ham, they have to then reshape the meat (in a machine called a vacuum tumbler) so it won't fall apart when sliced. This can give boneless ham a bit of a spongy texture. Another bonus to bone-in hams: The leftover bone is great for flavoring soups,

beans, and other dishes. If you can find only boneless ham, try to pick one that has the natural shape of the leg, which indicates that it was minimally tumbled.

And avoid spiral-cut hams, which are partially boned hams that have been sliced before packaging. They tend to dry out when baked, and they often come already coated with a commercial-tasting glaze.

Fried Ham with Redeye Gravy

Serves four.

**2 tablespoons unsalted butter,
softened**

2 teaspoons all-purpose flour

**4 large or 8 small ¼-inch-thick
slices leftover baked ham,
glazed edges trimmed off**

1 cup brewed coffee

1 teaspoon light brown sugar

1 large sprig thyme (optional)

To make this southern classic, you simply fry slices of ham and then deglaze the pan with coffee to make the redeye gravy. Usually it's made with fatty country ham, but leftovers from the Oven-Glazed Ham with a Pan Sauce (see recipe on page 258) tend to be leaner than country ham, so we've tweaked the recipe to make up for the missing fat. It may not be traditional, but it still makes a tasty and quick breakfast or weeknight supper.

In a small bowl, combine 1 tablespoon of the butter with the flour. Stir with a spoon or knead with your fingertips until blended.

Heat the remaining 1 tablespoon butter in a large (preferably cast-iron) skillet over medium heat until melted and hot. Add as much of the ham as will fit without crowding and fry gently until hot and browned in spots, 1 to 2 minutes per side. Move to a platter and repeat with the remaining ham, moving it to the platter as well.

Pour the coffee into the skillet and scrape the bottom of the pan with a wooden spoon to release the drippings. Add ⅓ cup water and the sugar and thyme, if using. Simmer vigorously for about 1 minute. Whisk in the butter and flour mixture until melted, and then continue to simmer until the sauce has thickened to a light gravy consistency and the raw flour flavor has cooked off, 3 to 5 minutes. Serve alongside the ham. —*Jennifer Armentrout*

Roasted Sausages & Grapes

Use a mix of hot and sweet sausages for a more interesting dish, and remember that the quality of the finished dish depends a lot on the quality of the sausages. A side dish of creamy polenta or risotto is just right to balance the sweetness of the roasted grapes and the richness of the sausages.

Position a rack in the center of the oven and heat the oven to 425°F.

Cut the sausages in half on a sharp angle and arrange them on a large rimmed baking sheet or in a shallow roasting pan. Add the grapes to the pan. Sprinkle the vinegar over the sausages and grapes, season with salt and a generous amount of black pepper, and toss so that everything is evenly seasoned.

Roast, turning with a spatula after 15 minutes, until the sausages are browned and cooked through (cut into one to check), 35 to 40 minutes total. Scatter the parsley over the top, stir to mingle all the juices, being careful not to crush the grapes, and serve. —*Molly Stevens*

Serves six.

1¾ to 2 pounds hot or sweet Italian sausage links (or a combination)

2 pounds seedless red grapes, stemmed

2 tablespoons sherry vinegar

Kosher salt and freshly ground black pepper

¼ cup chopped fresh flat-leaf parsley

7 Vegetables

p282

p301

**Stir-Fried Snow Peas
with Shiitakes & Ginger
(recipe on page 270)**

Roasted Asparagus with Lemon & Olive Oil

Serves six.

2 pounds asparagus, preferably thin spears (about 2 bunches)

¼ cup extra-virgin olive oil

Kosher salt

2 to 3 teaspoons fresh lemon juice; more as needed

When asparagus is in season, it's so sweet and nutty that you really don't want to do more to it than this simple preparation. These roast quickly, so just pop them in the oven right before your main dish is ready.

Position a rack in the center of the oven and heat the oven to 450°F. Snap off and discard the fibrous bottom ends of the asparagus spears. Put the asparagus on a large, rimmed baking sheet and drizzle with the olive oil. Gently toss the asparagus with the oil until it's evenly coated. Distribute the asparagus so that it's in an even layer. Sprinkle generously with salt and roast until tender (bite into a spear to check), 10 to 15 minutes. Transfer the asparagus to a platter, toss with lemon juice and salt to taste, and serve.
—*Tasha DeSerio*

Grilled Asparagus & Onions with Balsamic Vinegar & Blue Cheese

This warm salad with its rich ingredients is just the thing for a cool early- or late-summer get-together. The tanginess of the balsamic adds some bounce to the blue cheese and complements the sweetness of the grilled vegetables and figs.

Heat a gas grill to medium or prepare a medium charcoal fire.

Put the asparagus on a rimmed baking sheet, drizzle with 2 tablespoons of the oil, and season with ½ teaspoon of the salt and a few generous grinds of black pepper. Turn to coat. Grill the asparagus (covered on a gas grill) until they have nice grill marks, about 4 minutes. Turn and continue cooking until tender and browned, about 4 more minutes; transfer to a large platter. Reduce the heat on the gas grill to medium low or let the charcoal burn down a bit.

On a rimmed baking sheet, coat the onions with 2 tablespoons of the oil, the remaining ½ teaspoon salt, and several grinds of pepper. Grill, covered, until tender and browned, 8 to 10 minutes per side. Return the onions to the baking sheet.

In a small bowl, whisk together the remaining ¼ cup olive oil, the vinegar, and thyme. Toss the asparagus with about half the vinaigrette and then arrange neatly on the platter. Scatter the onions over the asparagus and drizzle with the remaining vinaigrette. Sprinkle with the blue cheese, figs, and pine nuts, and serve; this can sit for up to 1 hour at room temperature.

—Tony Rosenfeld

Serves ten to twelve as a side dish.

2½ pounds asparagus (about 2 large bunches), trimmed

8 tablespoons extra-virgin olive oil

1 teaspoon kosher salt

Freshly ground black pepper

1 large sweet onion (such as Vidalia), cut into ½-inch disks and threaded onto metal skewers

2 tablespoons balsamic vinegar

2 teaspoons chopped fresh thyme

3 ounces good-quality blue cheese, crumbled (¾ cup)

⅓ cup thinly sliced dried Black Mission figs (preferably small ones)

¼ cup pine nuts, toasted

Pan-Seared Artichokes with Sherry Vinegar & Thyme

Serves four to six.

6 large artichokes

4 tablespoons extra-virgin olive oil

3 tablespoons sherry vinegar

3 medium cloves garlic, peeled and cut in half lengthwise

1 teaspoon finely grated lemon zest (from 1 medium lemon)

½ teaspoon kosher salt; more as needed

⅛ teaspoon freshly ground black pepper; more as needed

1 teaspoon chopped fresh thyme

Once you get the hang of prepping the artichokes, the task goes quickly and the reward is so great—tender, nutty wedges that brown beautifully. Artichokes prepared this way are a versatile side dish for grilled, roasted, or braised chicken, lamb, or beef—or even duck breasts or veal chops.

Prepare the artichoke hearts following the directions on the facing page.

Cut each half into two wedges and toss them with 1 tablespoon olive oil in a large bowl. Combine the vinegar with ¼ cup water in a small dish. Set aside.

Heat the remaining 3 tablespoons olive oil and garlic in a 10-inch straight-sided sauté pan over medium-high heat and cook, stirring, until the garlic just starts to turn golden, 2 to 3 minutes. Remove the garlic with a slotted spoon and discard. Add the artichokes to the pan (they may splatter at first) and arrange them with one cut side down. Cook until nicely browned, 3 to 5 minutes. Turn and cook the other cut side until nicely browned, about 3 minutes more. Turn the artichokes on their curved side. Scatter the lemon zest on the artichokes and season with the salt and pepper.

Reduce the heat to low, add the vinegar and water, cover, and simmer until the liquid has reduced to about 1 tablespoon and the artichokes are tender when pierced with a skewer, about 5 minutes. (If the artichokes are still a bit undercooked after the liquid has reduced, turn off the heat and let them sit, covered, for a few more minutes until they reach the desired doneness.)

Remove the pan from the heat, scatter the thyme on the artichokes and stir well. Season to taste with more salt and pepper. Serve immediately, or let rest, uncovered, and serve slightly warm. *—Ruth Lively*

How to prepare an artichoke heart

Snap off the dark green outer leaves of the artichoke until only the pale, tender inner leaves remain.

Cut off all but 1 inch of the stem, as well as the top third of the artichoke leaves.

Use a paring knife to peel away the tough outer layer of the stem and to remove the base of the leaves, leaving a smooth surface.

Slice the artichoke in half lengthwise; with a melon baller or small spoon, scoop out and discard the hairy choke and thorny inner leaves.

Stir-Fried Snow Peas with Shiitakes and Ginger

See photo on page 265.

Serves four as a side dish.

2 teaspoons soy sauce

½ teaspoon Asian sesame oil

1 tablespoon plus 1 teaspoon canola or other vegetable oil

6 medium fresh shiitake mushrooms, stemmed and cut into ¼-inch slices (about 1 cup)

1 heaping tablespoon finely julienned fresh ginger (from about a 1-inch piece)

¾ pound snow peas (about 4 cups), trimmed

Kosher salt

1 teaspoon sesame seeds, toasted, for garnish (optional)

Snow peas are tender, but do need to be trimmed before use. Simply break off the stem end of each pea and pull the string away from the pod. Serve these alongside steamed fish or sautéed chicken.

In a small bowl, combine the soy sauce and sesame oil with 2 tablespoons water and set aside.

Heat a 10-inch skillet over medium-high heat for about 30 seconds and add 1 tablespoon canola oil, swirling it to coat the pan. When the oil is very hot, add the shiitakes and cook, stirring once, until they begin to brown lightly, about 1 minute. Add the ginger and stir-fry until the mushrooms are golden and the ginger has softened, 1 to 2 minutes more. Add the remaining 1 teaspoon canola oil and then the snow peas and a pinch of salt. Stir-fry for 30 seconds. Add the soy sauce mixture and continue to stir-fry until the peas are crisp-tender and the liquid has reduced to a glaze, 1 to 2 minutes. Season with salt to taste and garnish with the sesame seeds, if using. Serve immediately. —*Andrea Reusing*

The joys of snow peas

Snow peas have more real pea flavor and are often less starchy than sugar snaps. Popular in the 1970s, snow peas should be poised for a revival because of their fresh green crunch, versatility, and fast cooking time.

Shopping and prepping
Choose dark green, dense-looking peas with no signs of drying or cracking. Trim them by breaking off the stem end and pulling the string away from the pod.

Flavor partners
Snow peas partner well with scallions, toasted sesame seeds, ginger, shellfish, and rich nut oils.

Best cooking methods
Snow peas are good eaten raw, blanched, steamed, and stir-fried.

Ideas
• For a quick warm salad, briefly blanch snow peas and toss with a little vegetable oil, sea salt, and toasted sesame seeds.

• Blanch them and toss them with good-quality butter and salt.

• Sauté them quickly along with torn butter lettuce and scallions.

Broccoli with Eggs & Lemony Parmesan Breadcrumbs

This dish is lovely for entertaining, especially because you can get a lot done a day ahead: parcook the broccoli and then combine the eggs with the parsley, the seasoned breadcrumbs with the Parmigiano, and the lemon juice with the zest. Store everything separately in the fridge. Then just before serving, combine the topping ingredients, assemble, and bake.

Position a rack in the center of the oven and heat the oven to 375°F.

Put the eggs in a small saucepan and cover with cold water. Bring to a boil, turn off the heat, and cover the pan. Let sit, covered, for 10 minutes. Immediately pour off the hot water and run the eggs under a steady stream of cold water. Peel the eggs right away. Coarsely chop the eggs and set them aside.

Spread the breadcrumbs on a rimmed baking sheet and toast them in the oven until lightly browned, about 5 minutes.

Melt 8 tablespoons of the butter in a heavy-based 10-inch skillet over medium heat. Add the breadcrumbs, paprika, 1 teaspoon of the salt, and the pepper and cook, stirring, for about 1 minute, just to meld the flavors. Remove from the heat and stir in the chopped eggs, Parmigiano, parsley, lemon zest, and lemon juice.

In a large pot, bring 1 gallon of water and the remaining ½ cup salt to a boil. Trim off the bottom of the broccoli stems, cut each broccoli head lengthwise in half, and then cut each half lengthwise into six spears. Add the broccoli to the boiling water and cook until crisp-tender, about 5 minutes.

Drain the broccoli well and arrange in a snug single layer on a rimmed baking sheet. Melt the remaining 8 tablespoons butter in the microwave or in a small saucepan over medium heat. Top the broccoli with the breadcrumb mixture and then drizzle on the melted butter. Bake until the broccoli is heated through and the topping is crisp, about 20 minutes. Transfer the broccoli to a serving platter and then scatter any topping that fell off back over the broccoli. —Ris Lacoste

Serves twelve.

- 3 large eggs
- 2 cups fresh breadcrumbs
- ½ pound (1 cup) unsalted butter
- ½ tablespoon sweet Hungarian paprika
- 1 teaspoon plus ½ cup kosher salt
- ½ teaspoon freshly ground white pepper
- ½ cup tightly packed, freshly grated Parmigiano-Reggiano
- ½ cup chopped fresh flat-leaf parsley
- 2 tablespoons finely grated lemon zest (from 2 to 3 lemons)
- 1 tablespoon fresh lemon juice
- Two 1-pound heads broccoli

Baby Carrots Pickled in Champagne & Sherry Vinegars

Yields about 20 pickled carrots.

Kosher salt

¾ pound baby carrots with their tops on (18 to 20 carrots, about 6 inches long and ½ inch thick at the wide end)

2 tablespoons whole coriander seeds

1 cup dry white wine

1¼ cups honey

1 cup Champagne vinegar

½ cup sherry vinegar

Serve these zesty little pickles as a starter or cocktail nibble or add them to an antipasto platter.

Bring a medium saucepan of salted water to a boil over high heat. Fill a large bowl with ice water.

Meanwhile, peel the baby carrots and remove all but about ½ inch of the green stems. Boil the carrots until barely tender, about 5 minutes. Immediately drain the carrots and then immerse them in the bowl of ice water.

In a small saucepan, toast the coriander seeds over medium heat just until they become fragrant and lightly browned, 3 to 5 minutes. Add the white wine and boil until reduced to about ¼ cup, 6 to 10 minutes.

In a medium saucepan, heat the honey over medium-high heat until it bubbles, about 3 minutes. Add the Champagne and sherry vinegars, and then the coriander and wine mixture; simmer for 5 minutes—watch carefully and reduce the heat as necessary to prevent a boil-over.

Arrange the carrots upright in a clean 1-quart canning jar or other non-reactive container, and pour the honey mixture over the carrots. Let cool to room temperature. Cover and refrigerate for at least 4 hours but preferably 24 hours before serving. They will keep, refrigerated, for 2 to 3 weeks.
—Dan Barber

tip : To cut a large carrot into 6 baby-carrot-size pieces, slice the carrot in half crosswise; then halve the narrower bottom end and quarter the wider stem end.

Which is the real baby carrot?

Those stubby carrot nubbins on the left in the photo may be called baby carrots, but they're actually mature carrots that have been whittled down to bite-size pieces. The true baby carrot is the immature one on the right. Real baby carrots are tender and juicy; they're usually just 4 to 6 inches long and are generally sold in bunches, with their tops on.

Maple Pan-Roasted Baby Carrots

Serves four.

1 tablespoon extra-virgin
olive oil

1 pound carrots with their tops
on, preferably baby carrots,
peeled and stems trimmed to
about ½ inch

1 tablespoon pure maple syrup

½ teaspoon kosher or sea salt;
more as needed

¼ teaspoon freshly ground
black pepper; more as needed

For this recipe, baby carrots are ideal, but you can also use mature carrots if you cut them down to size. You start cooking the carrots on the stovetop and then move them to the hot oven to roast. The direct heat of the stovetop jump-starts the caramelizing of the carrots.

Position a rack in the middle of the oven and heat the oven to 400°F.

In a large (12-inch) ovenproof skillet or sauté pan, heat the oil over high heat (the oil shouldn't smoke but should crackle when you add the carrots). Add the carrots and cook, stirring frequently, until they blister and turn golden brown in spots, 1 to 2 minutes. Add the maple syrup, salt, and pepper and toss well to coat the carrots. Remove from the heat.

Spread the carrots evenly in the skillet and transfer it to the hot oven. Roast until the carrots are tender, browned in spots, and just a little shriveled, 12 to 15 minutes. Season to taste with salt and pepper before serving.
—Dan Barber

Green Bean Stir-Fry with Shredded Coconut

Serves six.

¼ cup canola oil

1 tablespoon yellow mustard seeds

24 curry leaves, roughly torn (optional)

1¼ teaspoons cumin seeds

2 pounds green beans, trimmed and cut into bite-size pieces (about 7 cups)

¾ cup unsweetened shredded coconut

1½ teaspoons kosher salt; more to taste

Instead of green beans, you could make this with another vegetable cut into bite-size pieces—try zucchini or cabbage. Seasoning with salt at the end of the cooking process may seem unconventional, but it actually works better in these stir-fries. Salt encourages vegetables to release water, and that is not the goal in this dish.

Heat the oil and the mustard seeds in a large wok or skillet over medium-high heat until the mustard seeds start to sizzle and pop, about 1 minute (use a splatter screen, if you have one, so the seeds don't pop out of the pan). Add the curry leaves (if using) and the cumin seeds and cook, stirring often, until the cumin becomes fragrant and browned, 1 to 2 minutes. Add the green beans and cook for 5 minutes, stirring occasionally. Stir in the coconut and 1 cup water and bring to a simmer. Cover the pan, reduce the heat to medium low, and cook until the green beans are tender, 8 to 10 minutes. Uncover, increase the heat to medium, and cook until all of the water has evaporated, stirring often, 2 to 5 minutes. Stir in the salt, taste, and add more salt if needed.
—*Suvir Saran*

Green Beans with Toasted Slivered Almonds

A quick toasting intensifies the flavor of the almonds, which, along with some garlic, power this quick sauté. The extra butter added at the end helps to emulsify the sauce, but you can get away with less, if you like.

Melt 2 tablespoons of the butter in a large sauté pan over medium heat. Add the almonds and cook, stirring frequently, until they're light brown and toasted, 2 to 3 minutes. Transfer them with a slotted spoon to a plate lined with paper towels.

Add the green beans, garlic, and ½ teaspoon salt to the pan. Toss to coat the beans with the residual butter. Add 1 cup water, reduce the heat to medium low, and simmer gently, tossing occasionally, until the beans are fork-tender and fully cooked (taste one to check), about 15 minutes. The liquid should be reduced to about ¼ cup or less; if there's too much liquid, increase the heat to a boil and let it reduce briefly. Add the remaining 2 tablespoons butter and toss to coat the beans and emulsify with the liquid. Add ½ teaspoon pepper, toss, and adjust the seasonings as needed. Scatter the slivered almonds over the beans on a serving platter or over each serving.
—Eve Felder

Serves four.

4 tablespoons unsalted butter

⅓ cup slivered almonds

½ pound fresh green beans, trimmed

2 teaspoons minced garlic (2 to 3 cloves)

Kosher salt and freshly ground black pepper

Browned Cauliflower
with Anchovies, Olives & Capers

Serves four.

1 medium-small head
   cauliflower (about 2 pounds)

1 large clove garlic, peeled

Pinch coarse sea salt or kosher
   salt

6 oil-packed anchovy filets,
   drained

¼ cup extra-virgin olive oil

15 black olives (such as
   Kalamata or niçoise), pitted
   and roughly chopped

1 tablespoon fresh lemon juice;
   more to taste

2 teaspoons capers, roughly
   chopped

1 teaspoon finely grated
   lemon zest

Large pinch of crushed red
   pepper flakes or ⅛ teaspoon
   Aleppo pepper

Anchovies and cauliflower are a sublime pairing. Six fillets may seem too much, but actually you'll simply get a delicious suggestion of anchovy, not an overpowering punch. This is one of those dishes that improves greatly if allowed to sit for several hours before eating. Serve at room temperature or warm it gently on the stove or in the oven.

Trim the leaves and stem from the cauliflower head. Working from the bottom of the head, cut off individual florets until you reach the crown, where the florets are small and fused together. Cut the large florets into quarters, the medium ones into halves, and the crown into four pieces, always trying to keep the top of the florets attached to pieces of stem.

   In a mortar, crush the garlic and the salt with a pestle until you obtain a paste. Add the anchovies and pound them to a paste as well. (If you don't have a mortar, you can mince the garlic, salt, and anchovies very finely and then mash them with the flat side of the knife until they become a paste.) Scrape this mixture into a large shallow bowl. Add 1 tablespoon of the oil, the olives, lemon juice, capers, lemon zest, and red pepper flakes. Stir well.

   Heat 2 tablespoons of the olive oil in a heavy 10-inch skillet over medium-high heat. When the oil is hot, add half the cauliflower pieces in a single layer, flat side down. Cook the cauliflower until well browned on the bottom, 2 to 4 minutes, and then transfer to a plate. Add the remaining 1 tablespoon oil to the pan and repeat with the remaining cauliflower, but don't transfer it to the plate. Return the first batch of cauliflower to the pan, turn the heat down to low and carefully add ⅔ cup water. Cover and let steam until the stems are just tender, 6 to 8 minutes.

   With a slotted spoon, transfer the cooked cauliflower to the bowl with the anchovy mixture. Add 1 tablespoon of the cooking liquid. Let sit 1 minute to warm and loosen the mixture, and then turn gently to coat the cauliflower and evenly distribute the olives and capers. Serve warm or at room temperature. —*Ruth Lively*

**Always start by trimming away
the leaves and the base of the stem.**

Whole florets

Simply cut the florets away from the central stem with a knife. Pay close attention during cooking and remove smaller ones as they're cooked through. Whole florets are great steamed, boiled, or roasted.

Quick idea: Lightly steam florets and serve them with a dip or sauce, such as a pungent anchoiade or bagna cauda (both anchovy-based), a garlic-basil mayonnaise, or a citrus-spiked soy dipping sauce.

Halved or quartered florets

Smaller cut-up florets are wonderful sautéed or roasted. Try to cut them into relatively even sizes so they cook at the same rate. (See the recipe opposite for more cutting details.)

Quick idea: Toss halved or quartered florets with olive oil, salt, and paprika, and roast at 375°F until tender and browned around the edges. Halfway through the cooking, add grated lemon zest and chopped fresh oregano. Squeeze on some lemon juice, toss, and serve warm.

Slices

For something a little different, cut whole florets lengthwise into thin, elegant slices that are perfect for deep frying or baking in gratins. You can also blanch them lightly and add them to salads for crunch.

Quick idea: Dip ¼-inch-thick slices in beaten egg, coat with breadcrumbs, and fry in 365°F peanut oil until golden outside and crisp-tender inside. Season with salt and serve with lemon wedges or a bowl of spicy marinara sauce.

Pickled Cauliflower
with Carrots & Red Bell Pepper

Yields about 3 pints.

1 teaspoon coriander seeds

1 teaspoon black or brown
  mustard seeds (or substitute
  yellow)

½ teaspoon cumin seeds

2 cups cider vinegar

5 medium cloves garlic, lightly
  crushed and peeled

Three ¼-inch-thick slices peeled
  fresh ginger

Half a small yellow onion, thinly
  sliced lengthwise

½ cup sugar

2 tablespoons kosher salt

1 teaspoon black peppercorns

½ teaspoon ground turmeric

¼ teaspoon crushed red pepper
  flakes

Half a head of cauliflower, cut
  into 1½- to 2-inch florets
  (about 4 cups)

5 medium carrots, peeled and
  sliced ½ inch thick on the
  diagonal (about 2 cups)

Half a red bell pepper, cut into
  large dice (about 1 cup)

For the impatient pickle fan, this recipe can be made as quick (refrigerator) pickles—no actual canning required. Serve the pickles as part of an appetizer spread with fresh tomatoes, olives, flatbread, and hummus or baba ghanoush. They're also tasty alongside grilled meats.

Put the coriander, mustard, and cumin seeds in a small saucepan. Toast the spices over medium heat, swirling the pan occasionally, until fragrant and slightly darkened, about 2 minutes. Add the vinegar, garlic, ginger, onion, sugar, salt, peppercorns, turmeric, red pepper flakes, and 1 cup water to the toasted spices. Bring to a boil.

Pack the cauliflower, carrots, and bell pepper in a 2-quart heat-resistant glass bowl or measuring cup. Pour the hot brine over the vegetables. Let cool to room temperature and then cover and refrigerate for at least 2 and up to 14 days. Because they haven't been preserved by a true canning method, the pickles must be stored in the refrigerator both before and after opening.
—*Allison Ehri Kreitler*

A head of a different color

We're all familiar with white cauliflower, but nowadays you can also find a beautiful deep-golden variety and a stunning purple one. Then there's the exotic and weirdly gorgeous lime-green Romanesco, with conical, spiral florets that look like seashells. Despite their different appearances, all types of cauliflower have a similar sweet, assertive flavor that pairs well with both rich, pungent ingredients and more delicate ones.

Slow-Roasted Summer Tomatoes

Yields about 24 tomato halves.

3 tablespoons plus 1 cup extra-
virgin olive oil

4½ to 5 pounds medium-large
ripe beefsteak tomatoes
(about 12), stemmed but
not cored

Kosher salt

Granulated sugar

Scant 1 tablespoon balsamic
vinegar

3 to 4 cloves garlic, very thinly
sliced

2 tablespoons fresh thyme
leaves

For best results, it's important to use a heavy-duty rimmed baking sheet; thin pans could cause burning. Also, pack the sheet full of tomatoes; if it's not full, expect the tomatoes to cook more quickly.

Heat the oven to 350°F. Line a 12x17-inch rimmed baking sheet or two 9x12-inch rimmed baking sheets with foil. (Don't use unrimmed sheets or the oil and juices will spill out; instead, use several shallow gratin dishes.) If you have parchment, put a sheet on top of the foil. Coat the pan or pans with 3 tablespoons of the olive oil.

Cut the tomatoes in half through the equator (not through the stem). Arrange the halves, cut side up, on the baking sheet, turning to coat their bottoms with some of the oil. Sprinkle a pinch each of salt and sugar over each half, and drizzle each with a few drops of balsamic vinegar. Arrange the garlic over the halves and top with a generous sprinkling of thyme. Pour the remaining 1 cup olive oil over and around the tomato halves.

Roast in the center of the oven until the tomatoes are concentrated, dark reddish brown (with deep browning around the edges and in places on the pan), and quite collapsed (at least half their original height; they will collapse more as they cool), about 3 hours for very ripe, fleshy tomatoes, about 4 hours for tomatoes that are less ripe or that have a high water content. (Check on the tomatoes frequently after the first 1½ hours. If they're browning too quickly, reduce the oven temperature.)

Let cool for at least 10 to 15 minutes and then serve warm or at room temperature. Be sure to reserve the tomato oil (keep refrigerated for up to a week) to use on its own or in a vinaigrette.

To store the tomatoes, refrigerate for up to a week or freeze for up to a couple of months. They'll continue to release juice during storage.
—*Susie Middleton*

Lemon-Sherry Vinaigrette with Roasted Tomato Oil

Yields about ²/₃ cups.

This vinaigrette is equally delicious using all olive oil if you don't have roasted tomato oil on hand. Drizzle it on grilled fish or steamed green beans, or toss it with mixed greens, fresh corn, and diced roasted tomatoes for a delicious salad.

¼ cup extra-virgin olive oil

3 tablespoons roasted tomato oil (from the recipe on page 282)

2 tablespoons sherry vinegar

Finely grated zest of 1 small lemon (about 1 teaspoon)

¼ teaspoon Dijon mustard

¼ teaspoon kosher salt

Freshly ground black pepper (about 6 grinds)

Large pinch granulated sugar

3-inch sprig fresh thyme

3-inch sprig fresh rosemary

½ clove garlic

In a jar with a tight-fitting lid, combine the olive oil, tomato oil, sherry vinegar, lemon zest, mustard, salt, pepper, and sugar. Shake vigorously to combine. Add the herb sprigs and garlic clove. Shake well before using. You can use the vinaigrette right away, although the herbs, lemon and garlic will intensify the flavor slightly as they infuse. This vinaigrette keeps in the refrigerator for a week.

Mix up a quick pasta sauce of roasted tomatoes chopped and mixed with their juices. Or make a richly flavored puttanesca sauce by adding capers, olives, and anchovies to the roasted tomato base.

Make a bed for grilled steak by overlapping roasted tomato halves. Top with arugula.

Fill omelets, frittatas, or crépes with finely chopped roasted tomatoes and bold cheeses.

Make a simple crostini or bruschetta by topping grilled bread with a roasted tomato half (or halves) and a little slivered basil.

For antipasto, present the tomatoes on a platter with olives, some prosciutto, a hunk of really good Parmigiano-Reggiano, some greens, and lots of crusty bread.

For an easy hors d'oeuvre, top a crock of warmed goat cheese with chopped roasted tomatoes, a few pine nuts, and a drizzle of pesto. Serve with crackers.

Make a sandwich of aged Cheddar, crisp bacon, roasted tomato halves, and herbed mayonnaise.

As a warm side dish for grilled lamb, reheat roasted tomato halves with a little crumbled feta on top. Garnish with fresh mint. Drizzle the lamb with the tomato oil.

Make a summery salad of spinach or arugula by adding fresh chopped roasted tomatoes, corn kernels, and grilled red onions. Add sliced grilled chicken or grilled shrimp to make it a main dish.

Corn, Sweet Onion & Zucchini Sauté with Fresh Mint

Serves four as a side dish.

2 tablespoons unsalted butter

1 tablespoon extra-virgin olive oil

1½ cups small-diced sweet onion, such as a Vidalia (about 7 ounces or half a large onion)

1 teaspoon kosher salt; more to taste

1¼ cups small-diced zucchini (about 6 ounces or 1 medium-small zucchini)

2 slightly heaping cups fresh corn kernels (from 4 medium ears)

2 teaspoons minced garlic

Scant ½ teaspoon ground cumin

Scant ½ teaspoon ground coriander

2 to 3 tablespoons chopped fresh mint

One-quarter lemon

Freshly ground black pepper

Vidalia, Walla Walla, and Maui are all varieties of sweet onion, which come into season in summer, along with beautiful, sweet corn. Using a sweet onion is ideal for this recipe, but a plain yellow or white onion will work just fine—regular onions are actually quite sweet, as long as you cook them gently to coax out the sugars.

Melt 1 tablespoon of the butter with the olive oil in a 10-inch straight-sided sauté pan or Dutch oven over medium-low heat. Add the onions and ½ teaspoon of the salt, cover and cook, stirring occasionally, until the onions are soft and translucent, about 5 minutes. Uncover, raise the heat to medium, and cook, stirring frequently, until the onions are light golden and shrunken, another 3 to 4 minutes.

Add the remaining 1 tablespoon butter and the zucchini. Cook, stirring occasionally, until the zucchini is slightly shrunken and almost tender, about 3 minutes. Add the corn, garlic, and the remaining ½ teaspoon salt. Cook, stirring frequently and scraping the bottom of the pan with a wooden spoon, until the corn is tender but still slightly toothy to the bite, 3 to 4 minutes. (It will begin to intensify in color, glisten, and be somewhat shrunken in size, and the bottom of the pan may be slightly brown.) Add the cumin and coriander and cook, stirring, until very fragrant, about 30 seconds.

Remove the pan from the heat, add all but about ½ tablespoon of the mint, a good squeeze of lemon, and a few generous grinds of pepper. Stir, let sit for 2 minutes, and stir again, scraping up the browned bits from the bottom of the pan (moisture released from the vegetables as they sit will loosen the bits). Season to taste with more salt, pepper, or lemon. Serve warm, sprinkled with the remaining mint. —*Susie Middleton*

Corn & Mushroom Sauté with Leeks & Pancetta

Serves four as a side dish.

2 tablespoons extra-virgin olive oil

1½ ounces thinly sliced pancetta (4 to 5 slices)

3 tablespoons unsalted butter

1 cup small-diced leeks (white and light-green parts only, from 1 large leek)

1 teaspoon kosher salt; more to taste

2 generous cups medium-diced cremini mushrooms (about 6 ounces)

2 slightly heaping cups fresh corn kernels (from 4 medium ears)

2 tablespoons chopped fresh flat-leaf parsley

1 to 2 teaspoon coarsely chopped fresh thyme or oregano

Freshly ground black pepper

One-quarter lemon

3 tablespoons heavy cream

Pancetta is an unsmoked Italian bacon that adds a sweet pork flavor but no smoke. If you use American bacon (which is smoked and usually lightly sweetened) in this dish, you'll get more of a Southern flavor, which would also be lovely with the sweet corn and earthy mushrooms.

Heat 1 tablespoon of the olive oil in a 10-inch straight-sided sauté pan or Dutch oven over medium-low heat. Add the pancetta and cook, turning occasionally with tongs, until light golden and crisp, 5 to 7 minutes. Transfer the pancetta to a plate lined with paper towels, leaving the fat in the pan.

Increase the heat to medium and carefully add 1 tablespoon of the butter to the fat. When melted, add the leeks and ½ teaspoon of the salt. Cover and cook, stirring occasionally and scraping up any browned bits from the pancetta, until the leeks are softened and slightly shrunken, 3 to 5 minutes. Uncover and cook, stirring frequently, until lightly browned, 1 to 2 minutes.

Add another 1 tablespoon of the butter, the remaining 1 tablespoon olive oil, the mushrooms, and the remaining ½ teaspoon salt. Cover and cook, stirring occasionally, until the mushrooms are softened and a little shrunken (they will have given off a good bit of liquid), 3 to 4 minutes. Uncover and cook, stirring frequently, until the liquid evaporates and the mushrooms are lightly browned, 2 to 3 minutes (the bottom of the pan will be quite brown).

Add the remaining 1 tablespoon butter and the corn. Cook, stirring frequently and scraping the bottom of the pan with a wooden spoon, until the corn is tender but still slightly toothy to the bite, 3 to 4 minutes. (It will begin to intensify in color, glisten, and be somewhat shrunken in size, and the bottom of the pan will be brown.)

Remove the pan from the heat, add the fresh herbs, a few generous grinds of pepper, and a good squeeze of the lemon. Stir in the heavy cream. Let sit for a minute or two and stir again, scraping up the browned bits from the bottom of the pan (moisture released from the vegetables as they sit will loosen the bits). Season to taste with more salt, pepper, or lemon. Crumble the reserved pancetta over top and serve warm. *—Susie Middleton*

A tidy way to cut corn

To prepare corn for sautéing, first shuck the ears and remove all the silks by running your hands up and down the ear. Then break the ears in half cleanly. (Using your hands to do this is easiest and safest, but you can cut the ears in half with a sharp chef's knife, too.) Stand each half cut side down on a large clean dish towel placed over a cutting board.

Cut the kernels off the cob with a sharp chef's knife and a downward sawing motion, cutting around the ear to remove all the kernels. Discard the cobs or save for a soup stock. Gather the towel up and dump the kernels into a bowl.

Grilled Corn on the Cob with Thyme & Roasted Red Pepper Butter

Serves eight.

4 ounce (½ cup) unsalted butter, softened to room temperature

2 jarred roasted red peppers, drained well, patted dry, and finely chopped (½ to ⅔ cup)

1 large shallot, minced (¼ cup)

1½ tablespoons sherry vinegar

1 tablespoon chopped fresh thyme

2 teaspoons kosher salt

½ teaspoon freshly ground black pepper; more as needed

8 ears corn, shucked

2 tablespoons olive oil

The butter in this dish is at once sweet and tangy, a bright addition to simple grilled corn on the cob. There's no need to roast your own peppers either, because ones from a jar will be just fine once blended with the other ingredients.

Put the butter, red peppers, shallot, vinegar, 2 teaspoons of the thyme, 1 teaspoon of the salt, and the black pepper in a food processor and pulse until blended (it's fine if it's still slightly chunky and looks a little separated). Transfer to a large piece of plastic wrap and roll tightly, twisting the ends so the bundle acquires a sausage shape. Store in the refrigerator for up to 1 week. When ready to grill the corn, slice the butter into ⅓-inch-thick rounds.

Heat a gas grill to medium or prepare a low charcoal fire. If desired, cut each ear of corn in half. Toss the corn with the oil, the remaining 1 teaspoon salt, and a few grinds of black pepper. Put the ears on the grill and if using gas, reduce the heat to medium low. Cover and grill the corn, turning every couple of minutes, until browned all over and tender, about 15 minutes. Transfer to a large platter, top with about half of the butter and the remaining 1 teaspoon thyme. Serve, passing the remaining butter on the side.

—Tony Rosenfeld

Don't husk corn until it's time to cook it

Pulling open the husks of corn before you buy it is akin to peeling bananas before buying them. The husks protect the ears of corn within, keeping them fresh and moist, so it's important to use other ways to find good ears without husking:

Choose ears that are snugly wrapped in their husks, which should appear fresh, green, and moist. It's all right if the tassel seems a little dry at its end, but it should feel fresh around the tip of the ear.

Run your fingers along the ear, feeling the formation of the kernels through the husks. They should feel plump and densely packed in even rows. You can feel if the kernels are immature.

Look for worm holes. If you see one, move on to another ear. If you find a worm after husking the corn, it's not a big deal. Just cut it out.

Eat the corn ASAP. As sweet corn ages, its sugar turns to starch—hence the adage to have the pot of water boiling before you pick the corn. Today's varieties have been bred to slow down the sugar-to-starch conversion, but still, the sooner you eat it, the better it'll taste. Refrigeration delays the conversion, so if you must store corn, wrap unhusked ears in damp paper towels and keep them in a plastic bag in your fridge's produce bin for two to three days.

Grilled Eggplant with Roasted Red Pepper Relish, Pine Nuts, Currants & Marjoram

Serves four to six as a side dish.

1 tablespoon dried currants

½ tablespoon red-wine vinegar

½ tablespoon balsamic vinegar

1 small clove garlic

Kosher salt

1 large red bell pepper

2 tablespoons pine nuts, lightly toasted and coarsely chopped

1½ tablespoons extra-virgin olive oil

1 tablespoon chopped fresh marjoram

Pinch of cayenne; more to taste

1 recipe Grilled Eggplant (see recipe on page 294)

3 tablespoons chopped fresh flat-leaf parsley (optional)

This bright and summery relish is delicious on the eggplant, but also is lovely as a bruschetta topping, dolloped with some fresh ricotta cheese. Spoon any leftovers into a sandwich.

Combine the currants and both vinegars in a small bowl.

With a mortar and pestle, pound the garlic and a pinch of salt to a paste, or mince the garlic, sprinkle with salt, and mash into a paste with the side of a chef's knife.

Roast the pepper: Set the pepper directly on a gas burner, under a hot broiler, or on a hot charcoal or gas grill. Keep rotating the pepper until it's evenly charred all over. Transfer to a small bowl, cover tightly with plastic, and let cool.

When cool enough to handle, peel the pepper over the same bowl to catch any juice; discard the skin. Don't rinse the pepper—it's fine if a few charred bits remain. (It's helpful to rinse your fingers occasionally.) Still working over the bowl, split the pepper and remove the stem and as many of the seeds as possible. Set the juice aside. Cut the pepper into very small dice and put in a medium bowl. Strain the pepper juice over the pepper. Add the currants and vinegar, garlic paste, pine nuts, olive oil, marjoram, and cayenne and stir. Season to taste with salt and cayenne.

When ready to serve, stir the relish again and spoon it over the grilled eggplant, or serve it on the side. Garnish with parsley, if using.

—Tasha DeSerio

Grilled Eggplant

*Serves four to six as a
side dish.*

**1 large globe eggplant (about
1 pound), trimmed and cut
into ½-inch-thick rounds**

**3 tablespoons extra-virgin olive
oil; more as needed**

Kosher salt

Prepare a medium-high charcoal or gas grill fire. Brush both sides of the
eggplant slices with olive oil and season with salt. Grill (covered on a gas
grill; uncovered on a charcoal grill) until golden-brown grill marks form, 3 to
4 minutes. Turn the eggplant and grill until tender and well marked on the
second sides, 3 to 4 minutes more. The interior should be grayish and soft
rather than white and hard. Serve warm or at room temperature, by itself, or
dressed with a vinaigrette or other topping. —*Tasha DeSerio*

Grilled Eggplant with Garlic-Cumin Vinaigrette, Feta & Herbs

This dish looks especially nice served on a platter, with the feta and herbs scattered over the eggplant. A sheep's milk feta, such as Valbreso®, will give you the sharp accent you want but the flavor is still quite sweet and creamy.

With a mortar and pestle, pound the garlic and a pinch of salt to a paste, or mince the garlic, sprinkle with salt, and mash into a paste with the side of a chef's knife.

Combine the garlic paste and 1 tablespoon of the lemon juice in a small bowl and let sit for 10 minutes. Combine the shallot with the remaining 1/2 tablespoon lemon juice and a pinch of salt in another small bowl and let sit for 10 minutes. Whisk the olive oil, cumin, and cayenne into the garlic mixture. Season to taste with salt or cayenne, if necessary.

Top the grilled eggplant slices with the shallots, feta, and herbs. Whisk the vinaigrette and drizzle it on top. Serve immediately. —Tasha DeSerio

Serves four to six as a side dish.

1 small clove garlic

Kosher salt

1½ tablespoons fresh lemon juice

1 small shallot, very finely diced

3 tablespoons extra-virgin olive oil

½ teaspoon cumin seeds, lightly toasted and pounded in a mortar or ground in a spice grinder

Pinch cayenne; more to taste

¼ cup crumbled feta

1 recipe Grilled Eggplant (see recipe on the facing page)

2 tablespoons coarsely chopped fresh mint

2 tablespoons coarsely chopped fresh cilantro

Roasted Eggplant with Chiles, Peanuts & Mint

Serves four to six as a side dish.

¼ cup unsalted peanuts

5 tablespoons plus 1 teaspoon peanut oil

Kosher salt

4 skinny Japanese eggplant (about 7 inches long and 1½ inches in diameter)

¼ teaspoon crushed red pepper flakes; more to taste

2 tablespoons fresh lime juice

1 teaspoon honey

12 medium fresh mint leaves, coarsely torn (about 3 tablespoons)

Japanese eggplant are ideal for this dish; they're firm but creamy, less bitter than larger varieties, and will absorb less oil, plus their slender shape makes them attractive on the plate. Other small eggplant varieties will work, but don't use the large, globe eggplant—the dish just won't have the same character. Serve these as an appetizer or as a side dish for roasted lamb or pork.

Position a rack in the center of the oven and heat the oven to 425°F.

Scatter the peanuts in a pie plate or other small baking dish and toss them with 1 teaspoon oil and a generous pinch of salt. Roast, shaking the pan once or twice, until they are golden brown, about 5 minutes. Set aside to cool and then coarsely chop them. Reduce the oven temperature to 375°F.

Rinse the eggplant. Trim off their tops and then cut the eggplant in half lengthwise. In a large, shallow bowl, toss the eggplant with 2 tablespoons of the oil and the red pepper flakes. Put the eggplant cut side up on a rimmed baking sheet and sprinkle generously with salt. Roast until the eggplant is tender when pierced with a fork and the flesh is a light golden brown, 10 to 12 minutes.

Meanwhile, in a small dish, whisk the remaining 3 tablespoons oil with the lime juice, honey, and ¼ teaspoon salt. Season to taste with more salt, if necessary.

With the eggplant still on the center rack, turn the broiler on to high and broil the eggplant until well browned on top, about 5 minutes. Transfer the eggplant to a serving platter. Drizzle with the dressing. Sprinkle with the mint and peanuts and serve. —*Andrea Reusing*

Braised Kale with Pancetta

Serves three to four.

2 tablespoons olive oil

One ¼-inch slice pancetta, diced (about ¼ cup)

1 small onion, chopped

Pinch of crushed red pepper flakes

1½ to 2 pounds kale, stemmed, leaves roughly torn

1½ cups homemade or low-salt chicken broth

1 small clove garlic, minced

Freshly ground black pepper

This recipe is especially good with the tender Red Russian or deep-blue lacinato varieties of kale. A squeeze of lemon makes a good finish.

In a large, heavy saucepan or Dutch oven, heat the oil over medium-high heat. Add the pancetta, onion, and red pepper flakes; sauté until the onion is deep golden, about 5 minutes. Add the kale; toss with tongs to coat the leaves with oil. Add the chicken broth and bring to a boil. Cover, reduce the heat to medium low, and simmer until the leaves are quite tender, about 10 minutes. (Thicker-leaved varieties will need longer, so check the pan, adding water or broth if needed, and taste a leaf.)

Stir in the minced garlic, raise the heat to high, and boil uncovered until the pan is dry. Season with a few grinds of pepper (you probably won't need salt) and serve immediately. *—Amy Albert*

Ham Bone Collards

A ham bone is the perfect flavoring for a big pot of collards, known in the South as a "mess of greens." If you don't have a ham bone, a smoked ham hock (which can be found in most grocery store meat departments) can stand in.

In an 8-quart pot, heat the oil over medium heat. Add the onion and cook, stirring frequently, until it begins to brown, 5 to 7 minutes. Reduce the heat to medium low and continue to cook until it's softened and golden brown, 3 to 5 minutes more. Stir in the cayenne and cook for about 30 seconds.

Add the broth, the ham bone, and ½ cup water. Pile on the collards, cover with the lid ajar, and bring to a simmer over medium-high heat. Reduce the heat to medium low and simmer, stirring occasionally, for 30 minutes. Remove the lid and continue to simmer until the greens are very tender, about 15 minutes more.

Take the pot off the heat. Put the ham bone on a cutting board and cover the pot to keep the greens hot. When the ham bone is cool enough to handle, pull off and shred or dice any meat clinging to the bone. Stir the meat into the greens, along with the vinegar. Season with salt, pepper, and more vinegar to taste. Pass the hot sauce at the table so diners can spice up the greens to their own tastes. *—Jennifer Armentrout*

Serves six.

2 tablespoons vegetable oil

1 medium yellow onion, halved and thinly sliced lengthwise

½ teaspoon cayenne

2½ cups homemade or low-salt chicken broth

1 meaty ham bone (best from a baked ham)

1½ to 2 pounds collard greens (1 large or 2 medium bunches), stemmed, roughly cut into 3-inch pieces, and rinsed (8 packed cups)

2½ teaspoons malt vinegar; more as needed

Kosher salt and freshly ground black pepper

Hot sauce to taste

Brussels Sprouts Braised with Pancetta, Shallot, Thyme & Lemon

Serves six to eight.

¼ pound pancetta, cut into
 ¼-inch dice (about ½ cup)

1 tablespoon olive oil

½ cup small-diced carrot
 (2 small)

⅓ cup minced shallot (2 to
 3 medium)

⅛ teaspoon crushed red
 pepper flakes

2 pounds Brussels sprouts,
 trimmed and cut lengthwise
 through the core into ¼-inch-
 thick slices

Kosher salt and freshly ground
 black pepper

One 14-ounce can low-salt
 chicken broth

1 bushy 3-inch sprig fresh thyme

2 tablespoons chopped oil-
 packed sun-dried tomato

1 tablespoon unsalted butter

1 teaspoon lightly packed finely
 grated lemon zest

Cutting the sprouts into slices is ideal for braising—the liquid surrounds the sprouts and cooks them evenly and relatively quickly, and the flavors of the braising liquid and other ingredients integrate deliciously with the slices.

In a 12-inch skillet over medium heat, cook the pancetta in the olive oil, stirring frequently, until the pancetta has rendered much of its fat and is nicely browned, 4 to 5 minutes. Increase the heat to medium high, stir in the carrot, shallot, and red pepper flakes and cook to soften the vegetables, 1 to 2 minutes. Add the sprouts, season lightly with salt and pepper, stir to coat with the fat, and cook, stirring, until the sprouts wilt slightly and a few brown lightly, 2 to 3 minutes.

Add the broth and thyme, cover with the lid slightly ajar, and adjust the heat to a lively simmer. Cook the sprouts until they're just barely tender, 4 to 6 minutes. Remove the lid, increase the heat to medium high, and cook, stirring frequently, until all the liquid has evaporated and the sprouts are quite tender (but not mushy), about 3 minutes. Off the heat, gently stir in the sun-dried tomato, butter, and lemon zest. Season to taste with salt and pepper.

—Martha Holmberg

Roasted Brussels Sprouts with Dijon, Walnuts & Crisp Crumbs

The mustard-Worcestershire seasoning is a tangy counterpoint to the sprouts, which—despite people's remembrances from childhood—are essentially sweet and nutty. You can fry the crumb topping up to 2 hours before serving.

Serves six to eight.

- ¼ cup plus 1 tablespoon extra-virgin olive oil
- 2 tablespoons Dijon mustard
- 1 teaspoon Worcestershire sauce
- ½ teaspoon caraway seeds, toasted lightly and crushed
- ¾ teaspoon kosher salt; more to taste
- Freshly ground black pepper
- 2 pounds Brussels sprouts, ends trimmed, cut through the core into quarters
- 1 tablespoon unsalted butter
- 1 cup coarse fresh breadcrumbs
- ½ cup chopped walnuts

Position racks in the top and bottom thirds of the oven and heat the oven to 400°F. Line two rimmed baking sheets with parchment.

In a large bowl, whisk ¼ cup of the oil with the mustard, Worcestershire sauce, caraway seeds, ½ teaspoon of the salt, and about 10 grinds of pepper. Add the Brussels sprouts and toss to thoroughly distribute the mustard mixture. Spread the sprouts in an even layer on the two baking sheets.

Roast until the cores of the sprouts are just barely tender and the leaves are browning and crisping a bit, 20 to 25 minutes (if your oven heat is uneven, rotate the pans midway through cooking).

While the sprouts are roasting, make the topping: Line a plate with two layers of paper towel. Heat the remaining 1 tablespoon oil with the butter in a medium (10-inch) skillet over medium-high heat. When the butter has stopped foaming, add the breadcrumbs all at once; toss to coat with the fat. Reduce the heat to medium, add the walnuts and the remaining ¼ teaspoon salt, and cook, stirring constantly, until the crumbs are browned and slightly crisp and the nuts are golden, 4 to 6 minutes. (The crumbs will start to sound "scratchy" as they get crisp.) Dump the breadcrumb mixture onto the paper towels to drain the excess fat.

Transfer the sprouts to a serving bowl and season to taste with salt and pepper if necessary. Sprinkle the crumbs over the sprouts just before serving. *—Martha Holmberg*

Braised Bok Choy with Sherry & Prosciutto

Serves four to six as a side dish.

1 tablespoon vegetable oil

4 medium cloves garlic, thinly sliced

6 heads baby bok choy (about 7 inches long and 2 inches in diameter at their widest), cut in half lengthwise

⅛ teaspoon kosher salt; more as needed

¼ cup dry sherry (or Chinese rice wine)

½ cup homemade or low-salt chicken broth

1 tablespoon soy sauce

¼ teaspoon granulated sugar

1 teaspoon cornstarch mixed with 1 teaspoon cold water to form a slurry

4 thin slices prosciutto, sliced crosswise into ¼-inch strips (⅓ to ½ cup)

Bok choy has a mild, sweet cabbagey flavor and soft crunch. Its gentle bitterness stands up to rich flavors, making it a perfect partner for dishes like braised pork or beef short ribs, or serve it simply, with a pan-seared steak.

Put the oil and garlic in a small wok or a deep, heavy-based, 10-inch, straight-sided sauté pan with a lid. Set over medium-high heat and cook, stirring frequently, until the garlic begins to sizzle steadily, about 1 minute. Add the bok choy (the pan will be crowded) and, using tongs, turn it in the oil and garlic, and then season it with the salt. When the tender tops begin to wilt, in about 1 minute, add the sherry (or rice wine) and toss again for about 15 seconds before adding the chicken broth, soy sauce, and sugar. Reduce the heat to medium, cover, and simmer until the bok choy tops are completely wilted and the stalks are crisp-tender, about 5 minutes. Transfer the bok choy to a plate.

Give the cornstarch slurry a stir to recombine and then whisk it into the cooking liquid. Simmer vigorously until the liquid has thickened, about 30 seconds. Remove from the heat and return the bok choy to the pan. Add the prosciutto and toss quickly to coat the bok choy with the broth and to mix in the prosciutto. Season to taste with salt and serve. *—Andrea Reusing*

How to enjoy bok choy

Shopping and prepping

Look for tight, unwilted heads ranging from bright green to dark green, with no signs of yellowing or drying. Wash bok choy well. You can leave baby bok choy whole or cut it in half, but cut larger bok choy into pieces for stir-frying.

Flavor partners

Bok choy harmonizes with assertive flavors like sesame, soy sauce, garlic, ginger, oyster sauce, chiles, and mushrooms.

Best cooking methods

Bok choy is excellent steamed, quick-braised, and stir-fried. Its chubby, spoon-shaped stalks capture sauces, making it a great last-minute addition to rich stews.

Ideas

- Quickly sauté bok choy in hot oil flavored with a little garlic or ginger and then briefly braise it in broth until just tender.

- Add bok choy to pork shoulder that's been slow-braised with soy sauce, a little sugar, and star anise.

Roasted Parsnips with Cinnamon & Coriander

Serves four.

1½ pounds parsnips (about 10 medium)

¼ cup extra-virgin olive oil

½ teaspoon ground cumin

½ teaspoon ground coriander

½ teaspoon sweet paprika (or a mix of mostly sweet and some hot)

½ teaspoon kosher salt; more to taste

¼ teaspoon ground cinnamon

2 tablespoons chopped fresh cilantro

2 teaspoons fresh lemon juice

The cooking method and the spices play up parsnips' sweetness, counter-balanced by last-minute additions of lemon juice and chopped fresh cilantro, which add brightness. If cilantro isn't to your liking, use parsley.

Position a rack in the center of the oven and heat the oven to 375°F. Peel the parsnips and cut each into 1-inch pieces crosswise, then cut the thicker pieces into halves or quarters to get chunks of roughly equal size. (Don't try to match the skinny tail-end pieces.) If the core seems tough or pithy, cut it out. You'll have about 4 cups.

Arrange the parsnips in a single layer in a 9x13-inch baking dish. Drizzle with the olive oil and toss to coat evenly. Combine the cumin, coriander, paprika, salt, and cinnamon in a small bowl and stir to mix. Sprinkle the spices evenly over the parsnips and toss until the parsnips are well coated.

Roast until completely tender and lightly browned on the edges, 35 to 45 minutes, stirring once or twice during cooking. Sprinkle with the cilantro and lemon juice and toss well. Taste and adjust the seasoning if necessary before serving. *—Ruth Lively*

Parsnips are so versatile they can be cooked almost any way you want. Here are some quick ideas for mashing, roasting, and braising.

Mashed or puréed

- Mash boiled parsnips with cream, milk, and butter. Season with salt and pepper and a spoonful or two of sherry or Madeira. Transfer to a shallow baking dish, scatter chopped walnuts or pecans over the top, if you like, and bake until lightly browned on top.

- Purée boiled parsnips and carrots with a bit of cream, season with salt and a little white pepper, and stir in some finely chopped crystallized ginger.

- For a twist on applesauce, boil and mash together parsnips and tart apples. Add butter, freshly grated nutmeg, and a little lemon juice and zest. Serve with roast chicken, turkey, duck, or goose.

Roasted

- Toss a blend of parsnips and carrots in olive oil, salt, and pepper and roast until tender and lightly caramelized. Stir in some cilantro pesto.

- For a colorful mélange, toss parsnips, turnips, beets, and sweet potatoes with oil and season with salt, pepper, and a little cayenne. Roast until almost tender. Stir in lots of chopped parsley, some minced garlic, and lemon zest and finish roasting.

- Toss the parsnips in oil, salt, and pepper and roast them with whole shallots until almost tender. Drizzle with a blend of maple syrup and fresh orange juice, toss with some chopped rosemary, and finish roasting.

Braised

Cut parsnips crosswise into 1-inch pieces, then cut the thicker pieces in halves or quarters to get chunks of roughly equal size. Brown the pieces in butter, olive, or vegetable oil.

- As the parsnips brown, season with a healthy sprinkle of chopped fresh sage. Then simmer in apple cider until the parsnips are tender and the cider boils away to a brown glaze.

- Brown the parsnips, season with salt and pepper, toss in a few thyme sprigs, and braise in chicken broth until tender.

- Combine parsnips with 2-inch chunks of leek and brown. Add salt and pepper, deglaze the pan with white wine or dry vermouth, and let it boil away. Add a little water, cover, and cook until tender.

Crispy Smashed Roasted Potatoes

Serves four as a side dish.

12 to 15 baby red or yellow potatoes (about 1½ ounces each; 1½ to 2 inches in diameter)

2¾ teaspoons kosher salt

½ cup extra-virgin olive oil

A simple ingredient list and a mostly make-ahead technique make these delicious potatoes perfect for parties. Do the busy work—boiling and flattening the potatoes—up to 8 hours ahead. Let the potatoes cool completely and store them on the pan, lightly covered, in the fridge. Then all you have to do at the last minute is coat with oil and salt and roast.

Put the potatoes in a large saucepan (preferably in one layer) and cover with at least an inch of water. Add 2 teaspoons of the salt to the water. Bring the water to a boil over high heat, reduce to a simmer, and cook the potatoes until they are completely tender and can be easily pierced with a metal or wood skewer. Make sure they are cooked through but don't overcook. The total cooking time will be 30 to 35 minutes.

While the potatoes are cooking, set up a double layer of clean dishtowels on your countertop. As the potatoes finish cooking, remove them individually from the water, and let them drain and sit for just a minute or two on the dishtowels.

Fold another dishtowel into quarters, and using it as a cover, gently press down on one potato with the palm of your hand to flatten it to a thickness of about ½ inch. Repeat with all the potatoes. Don't worry if some break apart a bit; you can still use them.

Cover a large rimmed baking sheet with aluminum foil; put a sheet of parchment on top of the foil. Transfer the flattened potatoes carefully to the baking sheet and let them cool completely at room temperature. (If making ahead, cover loosely with plastic wrap and refrigerate.)

Heat the oven to 450°F. Alternatively, if you have a convection function, turn it on and set the temperature at 400°F. Sprinkle the potatoes with about ¾ teaspoon salt and pour the olive oil over them. Lift the potatoes gently to make sure some of the oil goes underneath them and that they are well coated on both sides. Roast the potatoes until they're crispy and deep brown around the edges, about 30 minutes if using a convection oven, 30 to 40 minutes if roasting conventionally, turning over once gently with a spatula or tongs halfway through cooking. Serve hot. *—Susie Middleton*

Potato Stir-Fry with Mint & Cilantro

Serves six.

2 pounds red potatoes (about 6 medium), peeled and cut into ¾-inch cubes (about 5 cups)

3 tablespoons canola oil

1 tablespoon yellow mustard seeds

24 curry leaves (optional)

1 small whole dried red chile

2 teaspoons ground coriander

2 teaspoons cumin seeds

½ teaspoon ground turmeric

2 medium cloves garlic, minced

1 jalapeño (seeds and ribs removed if you prefer a milder flavor), finely chopped

1 medium red onion, finely chopped

2 teaspoons kosher salt; more to taste

½ teaspoon cayenne (optional)

⅔ cup fresh mint leaves, finely chopped

½ cup loosely packed fresh cilantro sprigs, finely chopped

Juice of ½ lemon (1 to 2 tablespoons)

Mint and cilantro are amazing partners for creamy potatoes; all the flavors in this stir-fry are like the best samosa filling. It's delicious with a roasted chicken or even scrambled eggs.

Put the potatoes in a medium bowl, cover with cool water, and set aside.

Heat the canola oil and the mustard seeds in a large wok or 12-inch skillet over medium-high heat until the mustard seeds start to sizzle and pop, 1 to 2 minutes (use a splatter screen, if you have one, so the seeds don't pop out of the pan). Add the curry leaves (if using), chile, coriander, cumin seeds, and turmeric and cook, stirring occasionally, until the cumin browns and the curry leaves are crisp, 1 to 1½ minutes. Stir in the garlic and jalapeño and cook until the garlic is fragrant, about 30 seconds.

Drain the potatoes and add them to the pan, along with the onions. Cook, stirring occasionally, until the potatoes are translucent around the edges, 2 to 3 minutes. Cover, reduce the heat to medium low, and cook, stirring and scraping the bottom of the pan every 5 minutes, until the potatoes are just tender, 12 to 15 minutes. (Reduce the heat to low if the potatoes seem to be burning.)

Add the salt and cayenne (if using) and cook for 30 seconds. Stir in the mint, cilantro, and lemon juice, cover the pan, and let the potatoes sit off the heat for 10 minutes. Scrape up the browned bits and stir them into the potatoes. Taste, add more salt if needed, and serve. —*Suvir Saran*

New Potatoes with Butter, Shallots & Chervil

This simple preparation is appropriate for any variety of new potato, so in spring, check out the offerings at your farmers' market. Whatever type of potato you use, be sure to choose ones of similar size, or else cut them uniformly, so that they cook evenly.

Put the potatoes in a medium pot, add water to cover by 1 inch, and season generously with about 2 tablespoons salt (the water should taste almost as salty as sea water). Bring to a boil, reduce the heat to a simmer, and gently cook the potatoes until tender when pierced with a fork, 10 to 12 minutes. (You want them to maintain their shape, so be careful not to overcook them.)

Meanwhile, combine the shallot, lemon juice, and a pinch of salt in a small bowl, and let sit for at least 10 minutes and up to 2 hours.

Drain the potatoes and return them to the warm pot. Immediately add the shallot mixture, butter, and chervil or parsley and gently stir to combine. Season with salt and pepper to taste and serve. —*Tasha DeSerio*

Serves six.

2¼ pounds small (2-inch) new potatoes, such as Yukon Gold or Yellow Finn, peeled and halved lengthwise (about 14 potatoes)

Kosher salt

1 large shallot, minced (about ¼ cup)

2 teaspoons fresh lemon juice

6 tablespoons unsalted butter, cut into 8 pieces, softened to room temperature

2 tablespoons chopped fresh chervil or flat-leaf parsley

Freshly ground black pepper

Classic Potato Pancakes (Latkes)

Yields eighteen to twenty pancakes.

2½ pounds russet (Idaho) potatoes (4 medium), peeled, cut in quarters lengthwise, and reserved in cold water

2½ teaspoons kosher salt; more to taste

About ¾ cup corn oil

1 medium yellow onion, diced (about 1¼ cups)

1 large egg

2 tablespoons all-purpose flour

1 teaspoon baking powder

⅛ teaspoon freshly ground black pepper

Sour cream and applesauce, for serving (optional)

Latkes are a wonderful celebration food, whether you're Jewish or not, but they can be a challenge to cook for a crowd. To prepare several batches for a party, fry the pancakes, let them cool, and freeze them on baking sheets. Once they're frozen, transfer them to freezer bags. You can reheat the pancakes on rimmed baking sheets in a 350°F oven for 10 to 15 minutes.

Heat the oven to 250°F.

Set a colander in the sink. Grate the potatoes in a food processor fitted with a medium (4 mm) grating disk. Transfer them to the colander and sprinkle with 2 teaspoons of the salt. Toss and let drain for 10 minutes, tossing occasionally.

Meanwhile, replace the processor's grating disk with the chopping blade. Add 1 tablespoon of the oil and the onion, egg, flour, baking powder, pepper, and the remaining ½ teaspoon salt to the food processor bowl.

In batches, squeeze the liquid from the shredded potatoes with your hands. Put the potatoes in the food processor with the other ingredients and process for 10 seconds. Stop the machine, scrape the bowl with a rubber spatula, and process until the mixture is finely chopped, 10 to 15 seconds more. Transfer the mixture to a large bowl.

Have ready a large plate lined with paper towels. In a 10-inch skillet, heat ⅛ inch of the remaining oil over medium heat until the surface of the oil shimmers very slightly. With a soup spoon, carefully ladle four mounds of the potato mixture into the oil and spread them slightly with the back of the spoon until they are about 3½ inches in diameter. (The oil should be bubbling gently around the pancakes.) Cook until the pancakes are a deep golden color, 2 to 3 minutes. Lift the pancakes with a slotted metal spatula and carefully turn them over. Continue to cook until the second side is a deep golden color, about 2 minutes more. Using the spatula, transfer the pancakes to the paper-towel-lined plate and blot well with more paper towels. Sprinkle lightly with salt. Use the spatula to transfer the pancakes to a baking sheet; keep them warm in the oven while you finish the rest. Continue to add oil between batches as needed to maintain the ⅛-inch level of oil. Serve with the sour cream and applesauce on the side, if using. *—Arlene Jacobs*

Frying right

Pan-frying these pancakes is a snap, but a few helpful tips can ensure the best—and crispiest—results.

For an even, golden color, add enough oil to maintain a ⅛-inch depth before cooking each new batch, and wait a minute for it to come up to temperature.

Don't crowd the pancakes in the pan, or they'll run together. Also, too much batter in the pan will drop the oil's temperature.

For extra-crisp pancakes, press on them with a spatula several times during cooking. You'll get thinner pancakes with less-chewy insides.

After a few batches, you'll see bits of potato batter accumulating in the oil. If they look like they're burning, clean the oil by passing it through a strainer into a clean bowl. Wipe out the skillet with a paper towel and return the clean oil to the skillet.

8 Desserts

p354

p319

Pecan Pineapple Upside-Down Cake
(recipe on page 344)

Balsamic-Macerated Strawberries with Basil

Serves four as a dessert; six to eight as a filling or topping.

2 pounds fresh strawberries, rinsed, hulled, and sliced 1/8 to 1/4 inch thick (about 4 cups)

1 tablespoon granulated sugar

2 teaspoons balsamic vinegar

8 to 10 medium fresh basil leaves

There's no need for an expensive balsamic vinegar for this recipe. Just use whatever you have on hand. Serve the berries in a shortcake, fold into whipped cream for a fool, or simply spoon on top of vanilla ice cream.

In a large bowl, gently toss the strawberries with the sugar and vinegar. Let sit at room temperature until the strawberries have released their juices but are not yet mushy, about 30 minutes. (Don't let the berries sit for more than 90 minutes, or they'll start to collapse.)

Just before serving, stack the basil leaves on a cutting board and roll them vertically into a loose cigar shape. Using a sharp chef's knife, very thinly slice across the roll to make a fine chiffonade of basil.

Portion the strawberries and their juices among four small bowls and scatter with the basil to garnish, or choose one of the serving suggestions below. —*Sarah Breckenridge*

Sweet ways to serve

- **Serve the strawberries** over grilled or toasted pound cake (see photo on the facing page).

- **Put the berries on split biscuits** for shortcakes; top with whipped cream and scatter with the basil.

- **Layer the berries** with ice cream or yogurt for a parfait. Garnish with the basil.

- **Spoon the strawberries** over a poached or roasted peach half.

- **Use the berries as a filling** for crêpes or a topping for waffles.

- **Mash the berries slightly** and fold into whipped cream for a quick fool. Garnish with the basil.

Phyllo Chips with Vanilla Ice Cream & Strawberry Mash "Dip"

Serves eight.

Three 9x14-inch sheets frozen phyllo dough, thawed overnight in the refrigerator

2 ounces (4 tablespoons) unsalted butter, melted

6½ tablespoons granulated sugar; more as needed

1 pint strawberries, rinsed and hulled

1 pint good-quality vanilla ice cream, slightly softened

tip: To make it easier to cut the phyllo chip triangles, slightly separate each strip before you begin.

Forget about nachos and salsa—for dessert lovers, this is the ultimate take on chips and dip. The chips are best served the same day but will stay crisp for 2 days if stored in an airtight container.

Position a rack in the center of the oven and heat the oven to 375°F. Line a 13x17-inch baking sheet with parchment. Put one sheet of phyllo on the pan and brush with some of the melted butter. Sprinkle evenly with 1½ tablespoons sugar and lay another sheet of phyllo on top. Brush with the melted butter and sprinkle with 1½ tablespoons sugar. Lay the last sheet of phyllo on top, brush with more melted butter, and sprinkle with 1½ tablespoons sugar.

With the tip of a sharp knife, cut the phyllo lengthwise into 4 even strips. Then cut each strip on the diagonal, alternating the direction of the knife to form little triangles. Cover with parchment and set another baking sheet on top. This will keep the phyllo from buckling during baking.

Bake until the phyllo is golden brown (lift the pan and top piece of parchment to check the color), about 15 minutes. To keep the phyllo chips extra flat, let them cool before unstacking the pans and removing the chips.

While the chips are baking, make the strawberry mash. With a pastry cutter or a potato masher, smash the strawberries in a medium bowl with the remaining 2 tablespoons sugar until pulverized but still a bit chunky. Taste; try to keep it on the tart side since the phyllo chips and ice cream are quite sweet. Cover with plastic wrap and keep chilled.

Put two scoops of vanilla ice cream in eight individual dessert bowls and spoon about an eighth of the strawberry mash over each portion. Tuck some phyllo chips in the ice cream or serve the chips on the side. If the ice cream is soft enough, you can use the chips to scoop it like a dip. —*Gale Gand*

Twin pack phyllo is best

We used phyllo from a 1-pound twin pack to test this recipe. Twin-pack sheets are 9x14 inches, smaller than those from a single pack. If you can find only larger, single-pack phyllo, either cut the sheets to size or use the larger sheets as they are, sprinkling 2 tablespoons sugar instead of 1½ tablespoons between each layer. Frozen phyllo dough is available in grocery stores. For this recipe you'll need only three phyllo sheets. Thaw one entire roll and refreeze what you don't need.

Triple Berry Cobbler with Pecans and Cinnamon

Yields one 9x13-inch cobbler; serves eight to ten.

For the cobbler dough:

7½ ounces (1⅔ cups) all-purpose flour

⅓ cup granulated sugar or packed light brown sugar

¾ teaspoon cinnamon

1 tablespoon baking powder

¼ teaspoon table salt

3 ounces (6 tablespoons) cold unsalted butter, cut into 10 pieces

½ cup chopped toasted pecans

¾ cup sour cream, chilled

For the filling:

8 cups mixed blueberries, raspberries, and medium strawberries, halved

1 teaspoon pure vanilla extract

½ to ¾ cup granulated sugar

2 tablespoons all-purpose flour, for tossing

Pinch table salt

2 teaspoons minced fresh ginger

Stone fruits and berries go with so many different flavors—from spices to nuts—that you can mix and match them into dozens of different cobblers all summer long. Feel free to experiment, just make sure the fruit (which you can prepare 8 hours ahead) equals 8 cups.

Position a rack in the center of the oven and heat the oven to 350°F. Have ready a 9x13-inch Pyrex® dish or a similar dish.

Make the dough: In a food processor, combine the flour, sugar, cinnamon, baking powder and salt. Pulse briefly to blend the ingredients, about 10 seconds. Add the butter pieces and pulse until they are the size of small peas, 5 to 7 one-second pulses.

Dump the mixture into a large mixing bowl. Add the pecans and stir until evenly dispersed. Add the sour cream. Using a rubber spatula, gently smear the ingredients together until the flour is evenly moistened and the dough begins to form large, soft, moist clumps. Bring the dough together into an 8-inch-long log. Divide the log into 10 roughly equal round pieces. Refrigerate the pieces in the bowl while preparing the fruit.

Make the filling: Put the berries in a large bowl and toss with the vanilla extract. In a small bowl, mix the granulated sugar (start with only ½ cup and taste the fruit to see if you need the whole amount), the flour, salt, and ginger. Gently toss the mixture with the fruit, making sure to mix evenly.

Assemble the cobbler: Pile the fruit into the baking dish, scraping in any remaining juices or sugar from the bowl, and spread evenly. Remove the pieces of dough from the refrigerator and arrange them randomly on top of the filling, leaving spaces between the pieces. Don't be tempted to flatten the dough—the large pieces are important for proper and even baking of the filling and topping.

Bake until the filling is bubbling and the topping is browned, 50 to 60 minutes. Let sit for about 20 minutes to allow the juices to settle. You can serve this cobbler hot or warm (it will stay warm at room temperature for 1 to 1½ hours). Serve with lightly sweetened whipped cream or vanilla ice cream, if you like.

—Abigail Johnson Dodge

Rhubarb Brown Sugar Crumble

When shopping for rhubarb, look for firm, crisp, unblemished stalks with bright, intense color. Thinner stalks tend to be less stringy and tough. Serve this homey dessert slightly warm with vanilla ice cream.

Position a rack in the center of the oven and heat the oven to 350°F. Grease an 8x8-inch Pyrex baking dish with the softened butter.

Make the topping: In a food processor, combine the flour, brown sugar, oats, cinnamon, and salt and pulse several times to combine. Add the cold butter and pulse until the mixture has the texture of coarse meal and clumps together when squeezed lightly, about 1 minute.

Make the filling: Combine the rhubarb, brown sugar, cornstarch, lemon juice, lemon zest, and salt in a large bowl and stir with a spatula until evenly mixed. Transfer the rhubarb mixture to the baking pan and sprinkle the topping evenly over the fruit; the pan will be very full, but the crumble will settle as it bakes.

Bake until the topping is lightly browned, the rhubarb is tender (probe in the center with a skewer to check), and the juices are bubbling thickly around the edges, 45 to 60 minutes. Transfer to a rack to cool to warm or room temperature and to allow the juices to thicken, at least 1 hour. *–Karen Barker*

Serves six to eight.

1 tablespoon unsalted butter, softened at room temperature

For the topping:

4½ ounces (1 cup) all-purpose flour

1 cup lightly packed light brown sugar

½ cup old-fashioned oats

½ teaspoon ground cinnamon

¼ teaspoon kosher salt

4 ounces (8 tablespoons) cold unsalted butter, cut into small pieces

For the filling:

7 cups ⅓-inch-thick sliced rhubarb (about 2 pounds)

1 cup lightly packed light brown sugar

¼ cup cornstarch

1 tablespoon fresh lemon juice

2 teaspoons finely grated lemon zest (from 1 medium lemon, using a rasp-style grater)

¼ teaspoon kosher salt

Raspberry-Peach Cobbler with Cornmeal Biscuits

Yields one 9x13-inch cobbler; serves eight to ten.

For the cobbler dough:

7½ ounces (1⅔ cups) all-purpose flour

¼ cup finely ground cornmeal

⅓ cup granulated sugar or packed light brown sugar

1 tablespoon baking powder

¼ teaspoon table salt

3 ounces (6 tablespoons) cold unsalted butter, cut into 10 pieces

¾ cup sour cream, chilled

For the filling:

5 cups peaches, cut into 1-inch-thick wedges

3 cups raspberries

1¼ teaspoons finely grated lemon zest

½ to ¾ cup granulated sugar

2 tablespoons all-purpose flour, for tossing

Pinch table salt

1½ tablespoons granulated sugar (optional)

Cornmeal adds a pleasing crunch to this cobbler's Melba-inspired filling. You can make the dough up to 8 hours ahead.

Position a rack in the center of the oven and heat the oven to 350°F. Have ready a 9x13-inch Pyrex dish or a similar dish.

Make the dough: In a food processor, combine the flour, cornmeal, sugar, baking powder, and salt. Pulse briefly to blend the ingredients, about 10 seconds. Add the butter pieces and pulse until they are the size of small peas, 5 to 7 one-second pulses.

Dump the mixture into a large mixing bowl. Add the sour cream. Using a rubber spatula, gently smear the ingredients together until the flour is evenly moistened and the dough begins to form large, soft, moist clumps. Bring the dough together into an 8-inch-long log. Divide the log into 10 roughly equal round pieces. Refrigerate the pieces in the bowl while preparing the fruit.

Make the filling: Put the peaches, raspberries, and lemon zest in a large bowl. In a small bowl, mix ½ to ¾ cup granulated sugar (use less for very ripe, sweet fruit and more for fruit that's not perfectly ripe and sweet), flour, and salt. Gently toss the mixture with the fruit, making sure to mix it in evenly.

Assemble the cobbler: Pile the fruit into the baking dish, scraping in any remaining juices or sugar from the bowl, and spread evenly. Remove the pieces of dough from the refrigerator and arrange them randomly on top of the filling, leaving spaces between the pieces. Don't be tempted to flatten the dough—the large pieces are important for proper and even baking of the filling and topping. If desired, sprinkle a little sugar evenly over the cobbler.

Bake until the filling is bubbling and the topping is browned, 50 to 60 minutes. Let sit about 20 minutes to allow the juices to settle. You can serve this cobbler hot or warm (it will stay warm at room temperature for 1 to 1½ hours). Serve with lightly sweetened whipped cream or vanilla ice cream, if you like. *—Abigail Johnson Dodge*

Apple Crisp with Pecans & Orange

Serves eight.

About 1 teaspoon softened butter for the baking dish

For the topping:

4½ ounces (1 cup) unbleached all-purpose flour

⅓ cup old-fashioned rolled oats

¼ cup plus 2 tablespoons lightly packed light brown sugar

¼ cup plus 2 tablespoons granulated sugar

½ teaspoon ground cinnamon

¼ teaspoon kosher salt

4 ounces (½ cup) cold unsalted butter, cut into 8 pieces

1 cup lightly toasted, coarsely chopped pecans

For the filling:

3 pounds Granny Smith apples (6 large or 8 medium), peeled, cored, and sliced ¼ inch thick

½ cup granulated sugar

2 tablespoons fresh orange juice (from 1 orange)

1 tablespoon finely grated orange zest (from 1 orange)

1½ teaspoons unbleached all-purpose flour

¾ teaspoon ground cinnamon

⅛ teaspoon kosher salt

This crisp topping is so versatile, try doubling it and freezing half for another day. It will go just as deliciously with summer's stone fruits, such as peaches and plums, as it does with autumn's apples and pears.

Position a rack in the center of the oven and heat the oven to 350°F. Lightly butter a 9x9x2-inch pan or other 10-cup ovenproof baking dish.

Make the topping: In a food processor, pulse the flour and the oats until the oats are finely ground. Add the brown sugar, granulated sugar, cinnamon, and salt and pulse until just combined. Add the butter and pulse in short bursts until the mixture just starts to form crumbs and has a streusel-like consistency. When squeezed together with light pressure, the mixture should just clump. Add the pecans and pulse just to blend; you don't want to chop the nuts further. (You can make and refrigerate this topping up to 2 days ahead, or freeze for up to 2 months. Bring to room temperature before using.)

Assemble and bake the crisp: In a large bowl, combine all of the filling ingredients and gently toss until well combined. Transfer the mixture to the prepared baking dish. Press down to compact slightly into an even layer. Sprinkle the topping in a thick, even layer all over the filling.

Bake until the topping is golden brown, the juices are bubbling around the edges, and the apples are soft when pierced with the tip of a knife, 55 to 60 minutes. Transfer to a rack to cool for 20 to 30 minutes before serving. The crisp can be served warm or at room temperature, but it's best served the day it's made. *—Karen Barker*

Gingerbread-Pear Cobbler

Yields one 10x15-inch cobbler; serves twelve to sixteen.

1 tablespoon softened unsalted butter for the pan

For the pear layer:

5¼ pounds ripe pears (about 12 medium), peeled, cored, and cut into ⅛- to ¼-inch-thick slices (Bosc or Anjou pears work well)

¾ cup granulated sugar

2 tablespoons fresh lemon juice (from 1 lemon)

1½ teaspoons minced lemon zest (from 1 lemon)

2 tablespoons minced crystallized ginger (about 1 ounce)

1½ tablespoons unbleached all-purpose flour

1 ounce (2 tablespoons) unsalted butter, at room temperature, cut into small pieces

For the gingerbread biscuit layer:

9 ounces (2 cups) unbleached all-purpose flour

5½ tablespoons granulated sugar

1 tablespoon ground ginger

2½ teaspoons baking powder

2 teaspoons ground cinnamon

¾ teaspoon ground cloves

½ teaspoon table salt

¼ teaspoon baking soda

3 ounces (6 tablespoons) vegetable shortening

1¼ ounces (2½ tablespoons) unsalted butter, at room temperature

2 large eggs

6 tablespoons whole milk

⅓ cup molasses

¾ teaspoon pure vanilla extract

For the topping:

½ cup sliced almonds

2 tablespoons granulated sugar

Though best eaten warm from the oven—and even better with whipped cream or ice cream—this cobbler can be made ahead. Once completely cool, wrap the cobbler in plastic and store it at room temperature for up to 24 hours. For longer storage, refrigerate for up to one week. To reheat, remove the plastic, cover loosely with foil, and set in a 300°F oven until warmed through, 20 to 25 minutes.

Position a rack in the center of the oven and heat the oven to 400°F. Lightly butter a 10x15x2-inch baking dish.

Make the pear layer: In a large bowl, gently toss the sliced pears with the sugar, lemon juice, and lemon zest. Make sure the lemon juice completely coats the pears to keep them from browning. Sprinkle the crystallized ginger and flour over the top. Stir until evenly incorporated, breaking apart any ginger pieces that may be stuck together. Spread the pear mixture evenly in the bottom of the prepared pan and dot with the softened butter pieces.

Make the biscuit layer: In a medium bowl, stir the flour, sugar, ginger, baking powder, cinnamon, cloves, salt, and baking soda with a fork. With the fork, work in the shortening and the softened butter until they're the size of small peas.

In a small bowl, whisk the eggs, milk, molasses, and vanilla extract. Make a well in the center of the dry ingredients and pour the egg mixture into the well. Stir just until the dry ingredients are completely blended. Dollop the batter by heaping tablespoonfuls onto the pears to create a cobbled effect, taking care to space the dollops about 1 inch apart. (Though the batter will cover only about half of the pear layer, don't spread it out. It will rise and spread to cover most of the pears as it bakes. If you run out of space to dollop the batter before it's all used, distribute what remains among the existing dollops.)

Apply the topping and bake: Sprinkle the nuts and sugar evenly over the cobbler. Bake until the pears are tender and the topping is golden brown, 35 to 40 minutes. If needed, rotate the pan midway through the baking to allow the top to brown evenly. Let rest for at least 20 minutes before serving. Serve warm.

—Julia M. Usher

Earl Grey Crème Brûlée

Yields four 5-ounce custards; serves four.

1¾ cups heavy cream

5 Earl Grey tea bags

4 large egg yolks (ideally cool or cold)

¼ cup plus 2 to 4 teaspoons granulated sugar

Pinch of kosher salt

tip: Homemade crème brûlée is just as good as and probably better than any you've had in a restaurant. But to get great results, you need the right tool: a mini blow torch. It really makes the difference between professional and pitiable results. A mini blowtorch isn't expensive, and it's fun to fire it up and finish off the crème brûlée while your guests look on.

The best thing about this impressive dessert is that you can make the custards—minus the burnt-sugar topping—a couple of days ahead. Of course, you can eat them on the day you make them, too; just be sure to chill the custards for at least 3 hours before topping them with sugar.

Position a rack in the center of the oven and heat the oven to 300°F. Fill a teakettle with water and bring to a boil. Put four 5- or 6-ounce ramekins (about 3 inches in diameter and 1¾ inches deep) in a baking dish that's at least as deep as the ramekins.

Pour the cream into a small saucepan and bring just to a simmer over medium heat. Remove the pan from the heat. Add the tea bags, cover, and let sit for about 10 minutes.

Meanwhile, in a medium mixing bowl, lightly whisk the egg yolks, ¼ cup of the sugar, and a pinch of salt just to combine. Set aside.

With an instant-read or candy thermometer, check the temperature of the cream; it should be no higher than 165°F. (If it is, let cool to 165°F before proceeding.)

Remove the tea bags. Lightly whisk about ½ cup of the cream into the yolk mixture and stir for about 30 seconds; this tempers the yolks. Then gently whisk in the remaining cream, stirring for about 15 seconds to blend. Use a light hand—you don't want to make the mixture frothy or the baked custards will have a foamy-looking surface. If using vanilla extract (for the orange variation, facing page), stir it in now.

Set a fine sieve over a large Pyrex measuring cup or a heatproof bowl with a spout. Pour the custard base through the sieve to strain out any solids.

Divide the custard base evenly among the four ramekins in the baking pan. There should be a little more than an inch of custard in each ramekin; it should not come all the way to the rim.

Carefully transfer the baking pan to the center of the oven. Slowly pour hot water from the teakettle into the baking pan (don't get any water in the ramekins) until the water comes about two-thirds of the way up the sides of the ramekins.

Lay a sheet of aluminum foil over the pan. Bake the custards until the edges are set about ⅓ inch in from the sides of the ramekins and the center is slightly jiggly (like Jell-O®), 40 to 55 minutes. To test for doneness, reach into the oven with tongs and give one of the ramekins a gentle shake or nudge. If the custard responds with a wavelike motion rather than a slight jiggle, it's not firm enough; bake for another 5 minutes and check again. (If you're not sure about the doneness, stick an instant-read thermometer into the center of a custard—don't worry about making a hole; you'll cover it with sugar later—it should register 150° to 155°F.) The custards should not brown or rise.

Carefully remove the baking pan from the oven and take the ramekins out of the water bath using rubber-band-wrapped tongs or a slotted spatula. Let the ramekins cool on a rack at room temperature for 30 minutes and then transfer, uncovered, to the refrigerator to cool completely. Once the custards are refrigerator-cold, wrap each ramekin with plastic wrap. Refrigerate for at least 3 hours or up to 2 days before proceeding.

Just before serving, remove the ramekins from the fridge and set them on a work surface. Working with one custard at a time, sprinkle ½ to 1 teaspoon of the remaining sugar over each one—the more sugar, the thicker the crust. You may need to tilt and tap the ramekin to even out the layer of sugar. Wipe any sugar off the rim of the ramekin. Hold the torch flame 2 to 3 inches from the top of the custard and slowly glide it back and forth over the surface until the sugar melts and turns a deep golden brown. Allow the sugar to cool and harden for a few minutes, and then serve immediately, before the sugar softens and gets sticky.

—Kimberly Y. Masibay

It's easy to vary the flavors

Orange

Omit the tea bags and after the cream comes to a simmer, remove from the heat and immediately add 1 tablespoon Grand Marnier® or Triple Sec, 2 teaspoons (firmly packed) finely grated orange zest, and ½ teaspoon pure vanilla extract. Cover and let sit for 10 minutes.

Ginger

Omit the tea bags and instead add ½ tablespoon (firmly packed) finely grated fresh ginger to the cold cream before bringing it to a simmer.

Café au lait

Omit the tea bags and right after the cream comes to a simmer, remove it from the heat and whisk in 1½ teaspoons instant espresso powder until dissolved. Cover and let sit for 10 minutes.

Bourbon-Chocolate Mousse

Yields 3 cups; serves four.

½ cup heavy cream

3 tablespoons confectioners' sugar

2 tablespoons bourbon

1 teaspoon pure vanilla extract

4 ounces bittersweet chocolate, finely chopped (¾ cup)

4 large egg whites (see note), preferably at room temperature

Pinch table salt

Chocolate mousse can turn any meal into a special occasion. This simple version comes together so quickly it can elevate even a weeknight dinner. Top the mousse with a dollop of whipped cream or crème fraîche and sprinkle with cocoa powder, and to make it look even prettier, garnish with fresh raspberries or strawberries. Note that the egg whites in this recipe are not cooked; we don't recommend using pasteurized egg whites, because they tend to separate after they're folded into the ganache.

Put 4 small (at least ¾ cup) individual serving bowls in the refrigerator.

Bring the heavy cream and sugar to a boil in a small saucepan and remove the pan from the heat (don't just turn off the burner). Stir in the bourbon and vanilla. Add the chocolate and let it sit for 5 minutes without stirring. Whisk the chocolate and cream until smooth and then transfer the ganache to a large bowl. Don't refrigerate.

In a medium bowl, beat the egg whites and the salt with a hand mixer on high speed just until they form stiff peaks when you lift the beaters.

With a rubber spatula, fold about one-quarter of the beaten whites into the ganache to lighten it. Then gently fold in the remaining whites, taking care not to deflate them. Divide the mousse among the chilled bowls and refrigerate for at least 30 minutes but preferably 1 hour and up to 24 hours.

—Allison Ehri Kreitler

Fried Chocolate-Hazelnut Wontons with Orange Dipping Sauce

Look for wonton wrappers in the produce section of the supermarket. If not frying immediately, you can stuff the wontons and refrigerate them for up to 2 days. Just cover tightly with plastic wrap to prevent them from drying out. The sauce can also be made ahead and refrigerated for one day.

Set out a bowl of water and a pastry brush. If necessary, trim the wonton wrappers into squares. Lay the wrappers on a work surface, orienting them so they look diamond shaped instead of square. Working quickly, put 1 heaping teaspoon of chilled Nutella in the lower half of each diamond. Brush the edges of one wonton with a little water and fold the top point of the diamond down to meet the bottom, forming a triangle. Gently press around the filling to force out any air and pinch the edges to seal. Repeat with the remaining wontons. Set the wontons on a baking sheet, cover, and keep chilled.

In a small bowl, combine the heavy cream with the orange juice concentrate, Grand Marnier, and vanilla. Refrigerate the sauce until ready to serve.

Heat the oil to 365°F in a heavy 3-quart saucepan over medium heat. Set a baking sheet lined with a thick layer of paper towels next to the pot. Slip 6 to 8 wontons into the oil and fry, turning occasionally, until golden brown, 2 to 3 minutes. Scoop them out with a slotted spoon and drain on the paper towels while you fry the rest.

Arrange 4 wontons on individual serving plates and sprinkle with confectioners' sugar. Serve with small individual dishes (I like tea bowls or sake cups) filled with the orange sauce for dipping. –*Gale Gand*

Serves six.

24 wonton wrappers, preferably square

One 13-ounce jar Nutella® (or other chocolate-hazelnut spread), chilled

¾ cup heavy cream

½ cup thawed orange juice concentrate

2 teaspoons Grand Marnier

¼ teaspoon pure vanilla extract

3 cups vegetable oil for frying

Confectioners' sugar for serving

Vanilla Ice Cream with Espresso-Caramel Sauce

Serves six; yields about 1½ cups sauce.

¾ cup heavy cream

1 cup granulated sugar

3 tablespoons brewed espresso

1 tablespoon Kahlúa® (optional)

3 pints vanilla ice cream

About ½ cup chocolate-covered espresso beans, roughly chopped, for sprinkling (optional)

You can make the caramel sauce up to a week in advance and refrigerate; it may separate, so stir to combine as you gently reheat the sauce before serving. If you don't have an espresso machine, just pick up a cup at your local café.

Measure the heavy cream into a liquid measuring cup. Put ½ cup water in a small, heavy saucepan with steep (at least 4-inch) sides. Add the sugar and swirl the pan to moisten it. Cover and bring to a boil over medium heat, swirling the pan occasionally, until the sugar dissolves, about 1 minute. Increase the heat to high and cook, still covered but checking frequently, until the sugar starts to turn light brown, 3 to 7 minutes. Remove the lid and continue to cook, swirling the pan occasionally, until the sugar turns dark amber, 2 to 4 minutes. Immediately remove the pan from the heat and slowly and very carefully stir in the heavy cream; it will bubble and splatter. Continue to stir until the sauce is smooth.

Pour the caramel into a small, heatproof bowl and let it cool slightly. Stir in the espresso and the Kahlúa, if using.

To serve: If the caramel is cold or has thickened from sitting, reheat it gently over low heat. Put a scoop or two of ice cream into six individual cups or dishes. Drizzle some caramel on top and sprinkle with a spoonful of the espresso beans, if using. *—Tasha DeSerio*

Ginger-Spice Ice Cream

Yields a generous 1 quart; serves eight.

4 large egg yolks

¾ cup plus 1 tablespoon granulated sugar

1½ cups heavy cream

1½ cups whole milk

1½ teaspoons ground ginger

1 teaspoon ground cinnamon

¼ teaspoon ground cloves

2 tablespoons molasses

1 teaspoon pure vanilla extract

Pinch table salt

Use mild molasses—not blackstrap—for desserts. The intense and somewhat bitter flavor of blackstrap molasses makes it a better match for savory dishes.

Set a medium metal bowl in a large bowl of ice water and have a fine sieve at the ready.

Whisk the egg yolks with ¼ cup of the sugar in a medium heatproof bowl. Combine the remaining ½ cup plus 1 tablespoon sugar with the heavy cream and milk in a 3-quart saucepan. Set over medium heat and stir occasionally until the milk is hot but not simmering. Whisk about ½ cup of the hot milk into the yolks and then whisk the yolk mixture back into the milk.

Reduce the heat to medium low and cook, stirring constantly with a clean wooden spoon or rubber spatula, until you see wisps of steam and the custard thickens slightly, 3 to 4 minutes. An instant-read thermometer should register 170° to 175°F. Don't let the custard overheat or boil, or it will curdle. Immediately strain the custard through the sieve into the bowl set in the ice-water bath to halt the cooking process.

Sprinkle the ginger, cinnamon, and cloves over the custard while it's still warm and whisk well to distribute evenly. Wait 10 minutes and then whisk in the molasses, vanilla, and salt. Cover the surface of the custard with plastic to prevent a skin from forming and let it cool to room temperature. Take the bowl out of the water bath and cool thoroughly in the refrigerator (ideally overnight) before freezing.

Stir the chilled custard to evenly distribute any molasses or spices that may have settled to the bottom. Freeze in an ice cream maker according to the manufacturer's instructions. With most ice cream makers, the custard will reach its thickest consistency after churning 30 to 35 minutes. However, the ice cream can still be somewhat soft at this point. If you prefer a firmer consistency, transfer it to a covered storage container and freeze until it reaches the desired consistency.

Tightly covered, this ice cream will keep fresh and freezer burn–free for about a week. *–Julia M. Usher*

A twist on tuiles

To make the twisty tuile garnish shown with the Ginger-Spice Ice Cream above, make the batter for Maple-Walnut Tuiles on page 360, but omit the nuts.

First make a stencil from a moisture-resistant paper plate by cutting off its border with scissors so that it can lie flat and then cutting out a 5x½-inch rectangle from the center of the plate with scissors or a utility knife.

Next, line a baking sheet with parchment or a nonstick baking liner. Have ready a few wooden spoons to shape the tuiles after they're baked.

Lay the stencil on the baking sheet and thinly spread some of the batter over the top of the stencil with a small offset spatula. Lift the stencil and repeat until you've made two tuiles per spoon (depending on handle length, a wooden spoon can usually shape two tuiles, so bake only as many tuiles in a batch as you have spoons to shape them). Bake at 350°F until golden brown, 3 to 5 minutes.

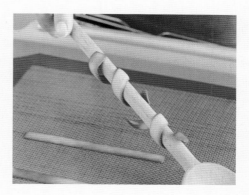

Remove the pan from the oven and, working very quickly, drape the tuiles over the spoon handles and loosely twist them around the handles like candy-cane stripes. Let them sit for 1 minute to set the shape and then slide them off onto a rack to cool completely. If you find that they harden before you can get them twisted, make fewer per batch or try shaping them in the oven (but remember, they'll be hot). Use twisty tuiles not just on ice cream but as a cute garnish for mousses and puddings, too.

Free-Form Pear Tarts with Almond & Cinnamon

Yields four tarts.

¼ cup granulated sugar

¼ teaspoon ground cinnamon

1 sheet frozen puff pastry (9x14-inch square), thawed overnight in the refrigerator

Flour for dusting

2 tablespoons almond paste (from a can or tube)

4 teaspoons sour cream

2 small firm-ripe pears (preferably Bartlett), peeled, cored, and cut into 12 wedges each

Puff pastry, pears, and almond paste combine in an elegant yet surprisingly easy dessert. During baking, the corners of the pastry unfurl like petals. Serve topped with a quenelle of vanilla ice cream, if you like.

Position a rack in the center of the oven and heat the oven to 425°F.

Line a baking sheet with parchment. Combine the sugar and cinnamon in a small bowl. Unroll or unfold the puff pastry on a lightly floured surface. Pinch any creases together and then smooth them out with your fingertips. Cut the pastry sheet into four equal squares and transfer them to the lined baking sheet.

Roll 1½ teaspoons of the almond paste into a small ball, flatten it slightly with the palm of your hand, and put it in the center of one puff pastry square. Drop 1 teaspoon of the sour cream on top. Sprinkle about ½ tablespoon of the cinnamon sugar over the sour cream. Arrange four pear wedges in the center of the puff pastry, two leaning away from the center one way and two leaning the other way. Sprinkle with another ½ tablespoon of the cinnamon sugar. Repeat with the remaining three puff pastry squares and filling ingredients—you won't need all of the sliced pears.

Fold the corners of the puff pastry over the pears until the tips are just touching but not overlapping and press the dough against the pears. (The tarts won't look pretty now, but they'll be beautiful once they bake and puff up.) Bake until puffed and golden brown on the edges, 22 to 27 minutes. Let cool. Any juices that leak onto the baking sheet will harden to a candy-like consistency, so break off and discard these bits before serving. *–Gale Gand*

Almond paste isn't marzipan

Made with finely ground blanched almonds and sugar, almond paste is commonly used in cake batters and pastry fillings. It's also the base ingredient in marzipan (which is made by adding hot sugar syrup and light corn syrup to almond paste). In this recipe, almond paste provides a subtle, perfumy almond flavor that marries perfectly with the sweetness of the pears. You'll find cans or tubes of almond paste in most grocery stores.

Shaping the tarts

Arrange four pear slices in the center of a puff pastry square, sprinkle with cinnamon sugar, and then bring the pastry edges together so they touch but don't overlap. This allows the puff pastry tips to "blossom" while baking.

Strawberry-Rhubarb Pie

Serves eight.

For the crust:

12 ounces (2⅔ cups)
unbleached all-purpose
flour; more for rolling

2½ teaspoons granulated sugar

¾ teaspoon kosher salt

4 ounces (8 tablespoons) cold
unsalted butter, cut into small
pieces

4 ounces (½ cup plus 1 tablespoon) cold vegetable
shortening, cut into small
pieces

For the filling:

4 cups ½-inch-thick sliced
rhubarb (about 1¼ pounds)

1 pound strawberries, hulled
and sliced ½ inch thick (about
2½ cups)

1½ cups plus 2 tablespoons
granulated sugar

¼ cup plus 1½ tablespoons
quick-cooking tapioca

2 tablespoons fresh
orange juice

1 teaspoon finely grated
orange zest

½ teaspoon ground cinnamon

¼ teaspoon ground cloves

¼ teaspoon ground allspice

¼ teaspoon kosher salt

2 tablespoons cold unsalted
butter, cut into small pieces

For the glaze:

1 large egg yolk

Rhubarb releases a surprising amount of liquid when cooked. Quick-cooking tapioca does a great job at soaking up all the juice. Don't worry if the crust cracks slightly during baking; it only adds to the homemade look of the pie.

Make the crust: In a food processor, combine the flour, sugar, and salt, and pulse to combine. Add the butter and shortening and pulse until the mixture resembles coarse meal, about 1 minute. Transfer the mixture to a large bowl.

Fill a measuring cup with ½ cup very cold water. While tossing and stirring the flour mixture with a fork, add the water 1 tablespoon at a time until the dough just begins to come together in small clumps and holds together when you pinch a little between your fingers (you may need only ¼ cup of the water).

Transfer the dough to a clean work surface and gather it together with your hands. Lightly knead the dough once or twice, divide it in half, and shape the halves into disks. Wrap the disks separately in plastic and refrigerate for at least 1 hour or up to 2 days.

Prepare the filling: Position a rack in the center of the oven and heat the oven to 375°F. In a large mixing bowl, combine the rhubarb, strawberries, sugar, tapioca, orange juice, zest, cinnamon, cloves, allspice, and salt. Toss gently to mix well, and then let sit for at least 10 minutes and up to 30 minutes (while you roll out the bottom crust).

Assemble the pie: If the dough was refrigerated for several hours or overnight, let it sit at room temperature until pliable, about 20 minutes. On a lightly floured surface, roll out one of the dough disks into a ⅛-inch-thick circle, 12 to 13 inches in diameter, and transfer it to a 9-inch Pyrex pie plate. Pour the filling into the pie shell and dot the top with the cold butter. In a small bowl, beat the egg yolk with 1 teaspoon water. Brush the edges of the pie shell with some of the egg glaze.

Roll out the second dough disk as above and set it over the fruit filling to form a top crust. Press the edges of the dough together to seal the crust, trim the overhang to ½ inch, and fold it under. Flute or crimp the dough all around. Brush the top crust with the remaining egg glaze (you won't need all of it). Cut four 1- to 1½-inch-long steam vents in the top crust.

Set the pie on a foil-lined rimmed baking sheet and bake until the pastry is golden brown and the fruit juices bubble thickly out of the pie, 70 to 80 minutes. Transfer to a rack and let cool completely before serving, about 4 hours.

—Karen Barker

What pairs well with rhubarb?

Spring strawberries and rhubarb are a classic combination, but other sweet fruits such as peaches, apples, and pears make wonderful partners, too. Accent flavors like vanilla, caramel, cinnamon, ginger, orange juice, and orange zest as well as brown sugar make a nice complement, showing off rhubarb's bright personality. Nuts provide great textural contrast.

Piecrusts are one of the hardest things for a home cook to master. When it comes to rolling them out, experience counts for a lot, but good techniques are crucial, too. Here are some of our best pointers for rolling out lovely, even rounds of dough.

- **Start with dough at the right temperature.** If it's too warm and soft, it'll stick like crazy to the rolling pin and the work surface, forcing you to add too much flour as you work it. Dough that's too cold and hard resists rolling and cracks if you try to force it. Press the dough lightly to check its rolling readiness—your fingertips should leave an imprint but shouldn't easily sink into the dough.

- **Go easy on the flour.** Even dough that's at the perfect temperature needs a little extra flour to keep it from sticking, but try not to use more than you really need—the more extra flour you work into the dough as you roll it, the drier and tougher the crust will be.

- **Try an alternative rolling surface.** Beyond the usual lightly floured countertop, other options for rolling surfaces include a pastry cloth, a silicone rolling mat, and sheets of parchment, waxed paper, or plastic wrap. Choose whichever one you like best.

- **Use the fewest possible passes of the rolling pin.** Overworked dough equals tough crust, so the less you have to work it during rolling, the better.

Roll around the clock

Start with the rolling pin in the center of your dough disk. Roll toward 12 o'clock, easing up on the pressure as you near the edge (this keeps the edge from getting too thin). Pick up the pin and return it to center. Roll toward 6 o'clock, as shown below. Repeat this motion toward 3 and then 9 o'clock, always easing up the pressure near the edges and then picking up the pin rather than rolling it back to center. Continue to roll around the clock, aiming for different "times" (like 1, 7, 4, 10) on each round until the dough is the right width and thickness, as shown at bottom right.

Turn the dough and check often for sticking. After each round of the clock, run a bench knife underneath the dough, as shown at top right, to make sure it's not sticking, and reflour the surface if necessary. When you do this, give the dough a quarter turn—most people inevitably use uneven pressure when rolling in one direction versus another, so the occasional turn helps average it out for a more even thickness.

Desserts **339**

Chocolate Espresso Pecan Pie

Serves eight to ten.

For the crust:

6 ounces (1⅓ cups) unbleached all-purpose flour; more for rolling out the crust

1 teaspoon granulated sugar

¼ teaspoon plus ⅛ teaspoon kosher salt

2 ounces (4 tablespoons) chilled unsalted butter, cut into ½-inch pieces

2 ounces (4 tablespoons) vegetable shortening, chilled and cut into ½-inch pieces (put it in the freezer for 15 minutes before cutting)

For the filling:

3 ounces unsweetened chocolate, coarsely chopped

2 ounces (4 tablespoons) unsalted butter

4 large eggs

1 cup light corn syrup

1 cup granulated sugar

¼ teaspoon kosher salt

2 tablespoons instant espresso powder (or instant coffee)

2 tablespoons coffee liqueur (Kahlúa or Caffé Lolita®)

2 cups lightly toasted, coarsely chopped pecans

About ½ cup perfect pecan halves

The deep flavors of chocolate and espresso keep this pie from being tooth-numbingly sweet. Pouring the filling over the pecans allows them to develop a delicious glaze as they rise to the surface during baking. This pie tastes best if chilled for several hours or overnight.

Make the crust: Pulse the flour, sugar, and salt in a food processor just to blend. Add the butter and shortening and pulse several times until the mixture resembles coarse cornmeal, 8 to 10 pulses. Transfer the mixture to a medium bowl. Tossing and stirring quickly with a fork, gradually add enough cold water (2 to 4 tablespoons) that the dough just begins to come together. It should clump together easily if lightly squeezed but not feel wet or sticky. With your hands, gather the dough and form it into a ball. Flatten the ball into a disk and wrap it in plastic. Chill the dough for 2 hours or up to 2 days before rolling. The dough can also be frozen for up to 2 months; thaw it overnight in the refrigerator before using.

Remove the dough from the refrigerator and let it sit at room temperature until pliable, 10 to 15 minutes. On a lightly floured surface with a lightly floured rolling pin, roll the dough into a ⅛-inch-thick, 13-inch-diameter round. Be sure to pick up the dough several times and rotate it, reflouring the surface lightly to prevent sticking. Use a bench scraper, a giant spatula, or the bottom of a removable-bottom tart pan to move the dough around. Transfer the dough to a 9-inch Pyrex pie pan and trim the edges so there's a ½-inch overhang. Fold the overhang underneath itself to create a raised edge and then decoratively crimp or flute the edge. (Save the scraps for patching the shell later, if necessary.) Chill until the dough firms up, at least 45 minutes in the refrigerator or 20 minutes in the freezer.

Position a rack in the center of the oven and heat the oven to 350°F. Line the pie shell with parchment and fill with dried beans or pie weights. Bake until the edges of the crust are light golden brown, 25 to 30 minutes. Carefully remove the parchment and beans or weights. If necessary, gently repair any cracks with a smear of the excess dough. Transfer the shell to a rack to cool.

Make the filling: Melt the chocolate and butter in the microwave or in a small metal bowl set in a skillet of barely simmering water, stirring with a rubber spatula until smooth.

In a medium mixing bowl, whisk the eggs, corn syrup, sugar, and salt. Dissolve the instant espresso in 1 tablespoon hot water and add to the egg mixture, along with the coffee liqueur and the melted chocolate and butter. Whisk to blend.

Evenly spread the toasted pecan pieces in the pie shell. To form a decorative border, arrange the pecan halves around the perimeter of the pie shell, on top

of the pecan pieces, keeping the points of the pecans facing in and the backs just touching the crust (see photo below left). Carefully pour the filling over the pecans until the shell is three-quarters full. Pour the remaining filling into a liquid measuring cup or small pitcher. Transfer the pie to the oven and pour in the remaining filling. (The pecans will rise to the top as the pie bakes.)

Bake the pie until the filling puffs up, just starts to crack, and appears fairly set, 45 to 55 minutes. Transfer it to a rack and allow it to cool completely (at least 4 hours) before serving. Serve it lightly chilled with a dollop of very lightly sweetened whipped cream. —*Karen Barker*

Pecan halves make a decorative border

Arrange the pecan halves in a ring around the perimeter of the pie shell interior, keeping the points of the pecans facing in and the backs just touching the pie shell.

Carefully pour the filling over the pecans until the shell is three-quarters full. The pecans will rise to the top as the pie bakes.

Ginger-Molasses Cheesecake

Yields one 10-inch cheesecake; serves eight to ten.

For the crust:

2 cups finely crushed gingersnap cookies (about 8½ ounces; crush in a food processor or in a zip-top bag with a rolling pin)

2 tablespoons granulated sugar

2½ ounces (5 tablespoons) unsalted butter, melted; plus 1 teaspoon melted butter for the pan

For the ginger-molasses filling:

Five 8-ounce packages cream cheese, at room temperature

1¾ cups granulated sugar

1 tablespoon unbleached all-purpose flour

1 tablespoon ground ginger

1½ teaspoons ground cinnamon

½ teaspoon ground cloves

¼ teaspoon table salt

4 large eggs, at room temperature

3 large egg yolks, at room temperature

¼ cup molasses

2 tablespoons heavy cream, at room temperature

1 teaspoon pure vanilla extract

Crunchy, store-bought gingersnaps grind up perfectly for this crust. Serve the cheesecake with a sprinkle of candied pecans. To store, cover the cake loosely with plastic and refrigerate. It's best if eaten within a day or two, as the crust will soften.

Position one rack in the center of the oven and another directly beneath it. Heat the oven to 350°F.

Make the crust: Mix the crushed gingersnaps and sugar in a small bowl. Using a fork or your hands, gradually work in the melted butter, mixing until all the crumbs are moistened. Use your fingers and the bottom of a straight-sided, flat-bottomed metal measuring cup or drinking glass to press the mixture firmly into a 10x3-inch springform pan to create a uniform ⅛- to ¼-inch-thick crust that covers the bottom and goes 1 to 1½ inches up the sides. Bake the crust on the middle oven rack until it's fragrant and warm to the touch, 5 to 7 minutes. Let the pan cool on a rack while you prepare the filling.

Make the filling: Put the softened cream cheese in the bowl of a stand mixer fitted with a paddle attachment. Beat on medium speed until very smooth and entirely free of lumps. Gradually add the sugar. Scrape down the sides of the bowl and continue mixing until the sugar has dissolved, 1 to 2 minutes. (Smear a small amount of the mixture between your fingertips; there should be no grittiness if the sugar has dissolved.)

In a small bowl, mix the flour, ginger, cinnamon, cloves, and salt. Sprinkle the mixture evenly over the cream cheese and mix on low speed until blended.

Add the eggs and yolks, one at a time, beating on medium speed until just combined. Scrape down the sides of the bowl after every other addition. (Beat no more than necessary to mix in each egg or you'll incorporate too much air, making the cheesecake dry and porous as opposed to dense and creamy.) Add the molasses, cream, and vanilla and mix until well combined.

Assemble and bake the cheesecake: Brush the inside rim of the pan above the crust with the remaining 1 teaspoon melted butter, without disturbing the crust. Pour the batter into the pan—it should fill the pan to a little above the crust. Put the pan on the middle oven rack and position a foil-lined baking sheet directly beneath it to catch any butter drips. Bake until the top of the cake is golden brown and the center just barely jiggles when the side of the pan is gently tapped, 1 hour and 10 to 20 minutes. It's fine if the cake develops a few cracks on the surface. Turn off the oven, open the door, and let the cheesecake cool in the oven for 15 minutes.

Set the cake on a rack until completely cool, at least 4 hours. Cover the cake loosely with plastic, cut a few air vents in the plastic, and refrigerate it

overnight in the pan. When ready to serve, slowly release the pan sides. If any of the cake edge appears stuck, gently loosen it with a sharp paring knife before continuing to release the pan.

For the cleanest servings, use a sharp chef's knife and wipe it clean with a warm, damp cloth between slices. —*Julia M. Usher*

Molasses: What it all boils down to

Gingerbread and many other old-fashioned desserts owe much of their deep, complex sweetness to molasses. True molasses is a byproduct of sugar cane processing. Sugar cane juice is boiled, crystallized, and then centrifuged to separate the crystallized cane sugar from the liquid. That leftover liquid is molasses; it can be refined and processed as is, or it may be boiled up to two more times to produce different grades of sweetness and intensity. The preservative sulphur dioxide is often added to molasses. It alters the flavor somewhat, so use unsulphured molasses when you can. Three basic grades exist, but producers use several different terms to refer to them.

Light, mild, Barbados, or robust molasses has been boiled only once. It has a high sugar content and a mild flavor, and it can be used directly on foods as a syrup. Some brands of single-boil molasses haven't even had any sugar removed from them—they're simply refined sugar cane juice that's been reduced to a syrup. A widely distributed brand of this type is Grandma's Original®, and it's what we used to test this recipe.

Dark, full, or cooking molasses has been boiled twice. It's slightly bitter and less sweet than single-boil molasses. It's typically used for baking and cooking.

Blackstrap molasses has been boiled three or more times. It has the deepest, most intense flavor of the three. It is generally used for animal feed, although some people prize it for its nutritional value.

Pecan Pineapple Upside-Down Cake

Serves ten to twelve.

7 ounces (14 tablespoons) unsalted butter at room temperature; more for the pan

½ cup plus 2 tablespoons light or dark brown sugar

Six to eight ¼-inch-thick fresh pineapple rings

¼ to ⅓ cup pecan halves

½ cup lightly toasted pecan pieces

5½ ounces (1¼ cups) cake flour

1 teaspoon baking powder

½ teaspoon freshly grated nutmeg

¼ teaspoon baking soda

¼ teaspoon kosher salt

1 cup granulated sugar

2 large eggs, at room temperature

1 teaspoon pure vanilla extract

½ cup plus 2 tablespoons buttermilk

Baking finely chopped, toasted pecans into the cake provides an earthy counterpoint to the bright flavor of the pineapple.

Position a rack in the center of the oven and heat the oven to 350°F. Butter a 10x2-inch round cake pan or 10-inch cast-iron skillet.

Combine 6 tablespoons of the butter with the brown sugar in a small saucepan and cook over medium heat, whisking until the butter is melted, the sugar is dissolved, and the mixture is smooth, 1 to 2 minutes. Remove from the heat and immediately pour the mixture in the bottom of the prepared pan, tilting to evenly cover the surface.

Set one pineapple ring in the center of the pan. Surround it with several other rings, packing them tightly or even overlapping them slightly. Cut the remaining rings in quarters or sixths and fill in the spaces around the perimeter of the pan. Set a pecan half, curved side down, in the center of each pineapple ring. If you like, fill in any additional spaces with pecan halves, curved sides down. (You may not need all the pecans.)

Finely grind the toasted pecan pieces in a food processor but don't overprocess or you'll make pecan butter. In a small bowl, sift together the cake flour, baking powder, nutmeg, and baking soda. Add the salt and ground pecans, mix well, and reserve.

In a stand mixer fitted with the paddle attachment, beat the remaining 8 tablespoons butter with the granulated sugar on medium speed until fluffy, 2 to 3 minutes. Beat in the eggs one at a time, pausing to scrape the bowl. Mix in the vanilla. On low speed, alternate adding the dry ingredients and the buttermilk in five additions, beginning and ending with the dry ingredients, scraping the bowl once or twice, and mixing until the batter is smooth. Pour the batter over the fruit and spread it evenly with a spatula.

Bake until the cake is golden brown and springs back when pressed lightly in the center with a fingertip, 40 to 45 minutes. Transfer the cake to a rack and cool in the pan for 15 minutes. Run the tip of a paring knife around the edge of the cake. Cover with a serving plate, and gripping both the cake and the plate, invert the two. Carefully lift off the cake pan, rearranging the fruit if necessary. Allow the cake to cool completely before serving. *–Karen Barker*

Pineapple rings: 1, 2, 3

The easiest way to prepare the glistening, caramelized fresh pineapple rings that top our Pecan Pineapple Upside-Down Cake is to buy a peeled and cored fresh pineapple from the grocery store and just slice it into rings. But if your market carries only whole fresh pineapples, here's how to trim one down into picture-perfect rings.

1 **Cut off the top** and bottom and stand it on a cut end. Slice off the skin, cutting deeply enough into the pine-apple to remove the eyes, too. You'll lose some edible flesh this way, but it's the best way to get nice round rings.

2 **Cut the pineapple** into ¼-inch-thick slices and then trim any pointy edges off each slice to round it off.

3 **Remove the core** from each slice with a small round cutter or a paring knife.

Steamed Coriander-Gingerbread Cake with Eggnog Crème Anglaise

Yields two 9-inch cakes; each serves eight to ten.

Cooking spray for the cake pans

1 pound 1 ounce (3¾ cups) unbleached all-purpose flour

1 tablespoon baking soda

1 tablespoon ground ginger

1½ teaspoons ground cinnamon

1½ teaspoons ground cloves

1¼ teaspoons table salt

6 ounces (generous 1 cup) pitted dates, chopped into ¼-inch pieces

2 tablespoons plus 1 teaspoon whole coriander seeds

6 ounces (12 tablespoons) unsalted butter, at room temperature

¾ cup granulated sugar

1½ cups molasses

3 large eggs, at room temperature

3 ounces (¾ cup) walnut halves, toasted and coarsely chopped

1 recipe Eggnog Crème Anglaise (facing page)

Though the steaming process leaves it deliciously moist straight from the oven, this cake is even better one or two days later, after the spices have had a chance to meld. You can even bake the cake ahead and freeze for 2 months. To bake ahead, wrap the cakes tightly in plastic while still slightly warm to the touch. (Any trapped steam will condense, adding moisture to the cakes.) Store up to a week at room temperature. To reheat, remove the plastic, put the cakes on a cookie sheet, and cover loosely with foil. Heat in a 300°F oven until warmed through, 15 to 20 minutes. You can freeze the cakes, wrapped in plastic and then foil, for up to 2 months.

Bring a large kettle of water to a boil—you'll need 1½ cups for the cake batter and about 2 quarts for the steaming pan.

Position one rack in the center of the oven and another beneath it in the lowest slot. Set a 10x15x2-inch baking pan or Pyrex dish on the lower rack and fill the pan halfway with boiling water. Heat the oven to 350°F. Lightly coat two 9x2-inch round cake pans with cooking spray and line the bottoms with parchment. Apply another light coat of cooking spray to the parchment.

Prep the ingredients: Sift the flour, baking soda, ginger, cinnamon, cloves, and salt into a large bowl. Stir to combine. Put the chopped dates in a small bowl with 3 tablespoons of the flour mixture. Pull apart any date pieces that may be stuck together and toss to evenly coat with the flour.

Crush the coriander seeds with a mortar and pestle or in a spice grinder. Alternatively, seal the seeds in a zip-top plastic bag and use a rolling pin to crush them finely.

Mix the batter: Put the softened butter in the bowl of a stand mixer fitted with a paddle attachment. Cream the butter on medium speed until very soft and smooth. Gradually add the sugar and continue to beat on medium speed until light and fluffy, about 2 minutes. Stop the mixer and scrape down the sides of the bowl with a spatula. Add the molasses and beat again on medium speed just until evenly incorporated. Add the eggs one at a time, mixing for about 10 seconds after each addition and scraping down the bowl as needed between additions. The batter will look broken.

Measure out 1½ cups boiling water. Turn the mixer to very low speed or, if you prefer, do all remaining mixing by hand. Alternate adding the flour mixture and the boiling water in five additions, beginning and ending with the flour. Mix just until each addition is incorporated, as overmixing will lead to a tougher cake—it's fine if the batter looks slightly lumpy. Stir in the reserved date-flour mixture, crushed coriander seeds, and chopped walnuts. The batter will be quite loose.

Bake the cakes: Divide the batter equally between the two prepared cake pans. Set both pans on the center rack and bake until a toothpick inserted in the center of each cake comes out clean, 40 to 55 minutes. Let the cakes cool in their pans for about 10 minutes and then invert them onto cooling racks and peel off the parchment paper. (Allow the water-filled baking pan to cool in the oven until it can be safely moved without spilling hot water.)

Serve the cakes warm or at room temperature. Cut each cake into 8 to 10 slices and serve each piece with 2 to 3 tablespoons of Eggnog Crème Anglaise. *—Julia M. Usher*

tip: Crème anglaise is prone to curdling if over-heated, so as soon as it begins to thicken, you'll need to stop the cooking by putting the bowl in an ice-water bath. Be sure to set up the water bath before you start cooking the crème anglaise, so you won't have to scramble at the last minute and take the risk of scrambling your sauce, too.

Eggnog Crème Anglaise

Yields about 2¹⁄₄ cups, enough sauce for two 9-inch cakes.

Spiked with bourbon, rum, and grated nutmeg, this holiday-inspired cream sauce will quickly get you in the spirit. It thickens to a rich, velvety consistency as it chills, so for the most luxurious texture, make it a day ahead.

2 cups heavy cream

¹⁄₂ cup granulated sugar

4 large egg yolks

¹⁄₈ teaspoon table salt

1 tablespoon dark rum

1 tablespoon bourbon

1 teaspoon freshly grated nutmeg

1 teaspoon pure vanilla extract

Set a medium metal bowl in a large bowl of ice water and have a fine sieve at the ready.

Combine the cream and sugar in a 3-quart saucepan. Set the pan over medium heat, stirring occasionally to encourage the sugar to dissolve. Heat the mixture through but do not allow it to boil. Remove from the heat.

Put the egg yolks and salt in a small heatproof bowl and gently whisk to break up the yolks. Gradually whisk in ¹⁄₂ cup of the warm cream mixture. Pour the yolk mixture into the cream remaining in the saucepan and whisk to combine.

Cook over medium-low heat, stirring constantly with a clean wooden or heatproof plastic spoon until the custard thickens slightly, enough to coat the back of the spoon and hold a line drawn through it with a finger, 4 to 8 minutes. An instant-read thermometer should register 170° to 175°F. Do not let the sauce overheat or boil, or it will curdle. Immediately strain the sauce through the sieve into the bowl set in the ice-water bath.

Gently whisk in the rum, bourbon, nutmeg, and vanilla extract. Stir the sauce occasionally until cool, 20 to 30 minutes. Transfer it to another container, if you like, and cover the surface of the sauce with plastic to prevent a skin from forming. Wrap the container tightly with more plastic and refrigerate for a minimum of 2 hours, until velvety and slightly thick.

The sauce can be stored in the refrigerator in a tightly sealed container for 2 to 3 days. Cover the surface of the sauce with plastic wrap to prevent a skin from forming. *—Julia M. Usher*

Bourbon-Glazed Brown Sugar Pecan Pound Cake

Serves twelve to sixteen.

For the cake:

12 ounces (1½ cups) unsalted butter, at room temperature; more for the pan

½ cup fine, dry, plain breadcrumbs (store-bought are fine)

15¾ ounces (3½ cups) unbleached all-purpose flour

1 teaspoon baking powder

¼ teaspoon baking soda

¼ teaspoon kosher salt

3 cups lightly packed light brown sugar

5 large eggs, at room temperature

2 teaspoons pure vanilla extract

¾ cup buttermilk

¼ cup bourbon

2¼ cups toasted, coarsely chopped pecans

For the glaze:

⅓ cup granulated sugar

⅓ cup bourbon

Taste your pecans to make sure they're fresh because even slightly rancid nuts will ruin such a simple cake. To store pecans for the long-haul, keep them in an airtight container in the freezer for up to a year. If freezing turns them flabby, lightly toast them for 5 to 8 minutes at 350°F to bring back their crunch and enhance their flavor.

Make the cake: Position a rack in the center of the oven and heat the oven to 350°F. Butter a 10-inch (12-cup) Bundt® pan and dust it with the breadcrumbs, shaking out and discarding the excess crumbs.

Sift together the flour, baking powder, and baking soda into a medium bowl. Add the salt and mix with a rubber spatula.

In a stand mixer fitted with the paddle attachment, beat the butter on medium speed, gradually adding the brown sugar until the mixture is light and fluffy, about 3 minutes. Add the eggs one at a time, mixing just enough to incorporate and pausing to scrape the bowl once or twice. Add the vanilla and mix until just combined.

In a measuring cup, combine the buttermilk with the bourbon. With the mixer running on low speed, alternate adding the flour mixture and the buttermilk mixture in five additions, beginning and ending with the dry ingredients, stopping occasionally to scrape the bowl. Mix until just combined. Add the toasted pecan pieces and mix until the nuts are just incorporated.

Pour the batter into the prepared pan and smooth the top with a spatula. Bake until the cake is golden brown and a cake tester or skewer comes out clean, 65 to 70 minutes. Transfer the cake to a rack and cool in the pan for 15 minutes.

Meanwhile, make the glaze: Combine the sugar and bourbon in a small saucepan or skillet. Cook over medium-low heat until the mixture comes to a simmer and the sugar dissolves, 3 to 5 minutes. Turn the cake out of the pan onto a cooling rack. With a pastry brush, brush the warm glaze over the entire surface of the cake. Allow to cool completely. This cake can be made up to 2 days ahead. —*Karen Barker*

Cooking with bourbon

When it comes to cooking and baking with liquor, bourbon is one of our favorites. Its smoky caramel and vanilla flavor adds a special nuance to savory and sweet dishes alike. It pairs particularly well with brown sugar, pecans, vanilla, chocolate, mint, apples, pears, peaches, ham, and pork. It's great in sauces, marinades, brines, glazes, cakes, pies, truffles, and cookies.

Bourbon whiskey, which gets its name from Bourbon County, Kentucky, is distilled from a grain mash that's at least 51% corn (but usually 65% to 80%) and may also contain barley, rye, and sometimes wheat (as in Maker's Mark® brand). The distilled liquor is then aged in new charred-oak barrels, from which the spirit gets its color and smoky, caramelly undertones.

Save expensive single-barrel bourbons like Blanton's® or Eagle Rare® and small-batch bourbons like Knob Creek® or Basil Hayden's® for sipping. For cooking, a regular bourbon such as Jim Beam®, Wild Turkey®, Old Crow®, or Heaven Hill® is fine.

Lemon-Coconut Pound Cake

Yields one 12-cup Bundt cake; serves twelve to sixteen.

For the cake:

10 ounces (1¼ cups) unsalted butter, softened at room temperature; more for the pan

10¼ ounces (2½ cups) cake flour or 11 ounces (2⅓ cups) unbleached all-purpose flour; more for the pan

1½ teaspoons baking powder

½ teaspoon table salt

1¾ cups granulated sugar

2 large egg yolks, at room temperature

3 large eggs, at room temperature

½ cup whole milk, at room temperature

¼ cup fresh lemon juice

1½ teaspoons pure vanilla extract

1 tablespoon finely grated lemon zest

1 cup loosely packed sweetened flaked coconut

For the glaze:

1¼ cups confectioners' sugar

6 tablespoons fresh lemon juice

What do you get when you mix a pound of butter, a pound of sugar, a pound of eggs, and a pound of flour? Pound cake, of course. Although early recipes were easy to remember, the results weren't exactly moist and tender. More sugar, fewer eggs, and a touch of milk solves that problem. If you don't have cake flour, you can use all-purpose, but the cake will be slighter denser, though still moist.

Make the cake: Position a rack in the center of the oven and heat the oven to 350°F. Butter a 12-cup Bundt pan, dust the pan with flour, and tap out the excess. In a small bowl, whisk together the flour, baking powder, and salt until evenly combined.

In the bowl of a stand mixer fitted with the paddle attachment, beat the butter and the sugar at medium speed until light and fluffy, about 2 minutes.

On low speed, beat in the yolks until smooth. Stop the mixer and scrape the bowl and the paddle. With the mixer running on medium-low speed, add the whole eggs, one at a time, mixing for at least 20 seconds after each addition. Stop the mixer and scrape the bowl and paddle again.

With the mixer running on the lowest speed, add half of the flour mixture and mix just to combine, add the milk and lemon juice and mix until combined, and then add the remaining flour mixture and mix just until combined.

Scrape the bowl one last time, add vanilla extract, and mix at medium speed until the batter is smooth and fluffy, 20 to 30 seconds. Stir in the lemon zest and coconut.

Scrape the batter into the prepared pan and spread it evenly. Run a knife through the batter and tap the pan against the counter to dislodge trapped air. Bake until golden brown and a toothpick inserted in the center comes out with only moist crumbs clinging to it, 45 to 55 minutes.

Make the glaze and glaze the cake: Mix the confectioner's sugar and lemon juice together until smooth.

Cool the cake in the pan for 10 to 15 minutes and then invert onto a wire rack to cool completely. Place the cake on a serving plate. Using a skewer, poke holes all over the cake. Brush the cake—every visible inch of it—with the glaze, until the glaze is gone. When the cake is completely cool, the glaze will form a protective crust over the cake, keeping it moist for 5 to 7 days.

—Nicole Rees

What a difference the flour makes

The flour you use can noticeably affect the appearance and texture of a finished cake. To see for yourself, try this tasty little experiment: Make this pound cake with cake flour and then again with all-purpose and compare them side by side. The cake-flour version rises higher in its pan as it bakes, so it's a taller cake with a fluffier texture. The cake made with all-purpose flour, on the other hand, is denser, moister, and closer to a quick bread in texture.

Cake flour really is different from other flours. It's specially milled and processed to have finer granules, lower protein, and higher starch. The flour is bleached, which weakens its gluten and makes baked goods more tender.

If you use cake flour, check the cake on the early side of the doneness window to prevent overbaking—cake flour has a lower pH, which can help the batter set faster.

Dark Chocolate Crackles

Yields about 5 dozen cookies.

11¼ ounces (2½ cups) unbleached all-purpose flour

1 teaspoon baking soda

¼ teaspoon table salt

8 ounces (1 cup) unsalted butter, at room temperature

2 cups firmly packed light brown sugar

2 ounces (⅔ cup) natural, unsweetened cocoa, sifted if lumpy

2 teaspoons finely grated orange zest

1 teaspoon pure vanilla extract

3 large eggs

8 ounces bittersweet chocolate, melted and cooled until barely warm

¾ cup (4 ounces) chopped chocolate (white, bittersweet, or semisweet)

⅓ cup granulated sugar; more as needed

These decadent cookies sparkle from a hint of orange zest and a dip in granulated sugar. Add chunks of white chocolate for a contrast in color and flavor, or stick with bittersweet or semisweet for added intensity.

Position a rack in the center of the oven and heat the oven to 350°F. Line three large cookie sheets with parchment or nonstick baking liners.

In a medium mixing bowl, whisk together the flour, baking soda, and salt. In the bowl of a stand mixer fitted with the paddle attachment (or in a large mixing bowl with a hand mixer), beat the butter, brown sugar, cocoa, orange zest, and vanilla on medium speed until well combined, about 4 minutes. Add the eggs one at a time, beating briefly between additions. Add the cooled chocolate and mix until blended, about 1 minute. Add the dry ingredients and mix on low speed until almost completely blended, about 1 minute. Add the chopped chocolate and mix until blended, about 15 seconds.

Shape the dough into 1¼-inch balls with a small ice-cream scoop or 2 tablespoons. (The balls of dough may be frozen for 1 month. Thaw them overnight in the refrigerator before proceeding with the recipe.)

Pour the granulated sugar into a shallow dish. Dip the top of each ball in the sugar and set the balls sugar side up about 1½ inches apart on the prepared cookie sheets. Bake one sheet at a time until the cookies are puffed and cracked on top, 11 to 12 minutes. Let the cookies cool on the sheet for 5 minutes before transferring them to a rack to cool completely.

—Abigail Johnson Dodge

Macadamia Double-Decker Brownie Bars

Yields forty-eight bars.

For the brownie layer:

Cooking spray

6 ounces (12 tablespoons) unsalted butter, cut into large chunks

1½ cups granulated sugar

2¼ ounces (¾ cup) unsweetened cocoa powder (natural or Dutch processed)

¼ teaspoon table salt

2 large eggs

1 teaspoon pure vanilla extract

3½ ounces (¾ cup) unbleached all-purpose flour

For the macadamia layer:

½ cup firmly packed light brown sugar

1½ ounces (⅓ cup) unbleached all-purpose flour

⅔ cup light corn syrup

1½ ounces (3 tablespoons) unsalted butter, melted

1½ teaspoons pure vanilla extract

2 large eggs

1½ cups roughly chopped salted macadamia nuts

⅓ cup sweetened coconut flakes

These gorgeous two-layer bars have a brownie base topped with a gooey nut-and-coconut-studded topping. Dipping a knife in warm water and wiping it dry between cuts will keep the gooey topping from sticking to it.

Position a rack in the center of the oven and heat the oven to 325°F. Line the bottom and sides of a 9x13-inch baking pan with foil, leaving some overhang on the sides, and spray with cooking spray.

Make the brownie layer: In a medium saucepan over medium heat, whisk the butter until it is melted. Remove the pan from the heat and add the sugar, cocoa powder, and salt. Whisk until well blended, about 1 minute. Add the eggs and vanilla and whisk until smooth. Add the flour and stir with a rubber spatula until blended. Scrape into the prepared pan and spread evenly. Bake until the top is shiny and dry-looking and the brownie springs back very slightly when pressed with a fingertip, about 20 minutes. (The brownie should not be completely baked.) Remove from the oven and put on a rack.

While the brownie layer is baking, make the macadamia topping: In a large mixing bowl, combine the brown sugar and flour. Whisk until well blended, breaking up any large clumps. Add the corn syrup, melted butter, and vanilla. Whisk until blended, about 1 minute. Add the eggs and whisk just until combined, about 30 seconds. (Don't overmix or the batter will be foamy.) Add the nuts and coconut and stir with a rubber spatula until evenly blended.

Pour the macadamia topping over the warm, partially baked brownie layer. Using a spatula, carefully spread the mixture into an even layer. Return the pan to the oven and bake until the top is golden brown, 37 to 40 minutes. Transfer the pan to a rack to cool completely. (At this point, the entire pan can be wrapped in plastic wrap, then foil, and frozen for up to 1 month.)

Using the foil as handles, lift the rectangle from the pan and invert onto a work surface. Carefully peel away the foil. Flip right side up. Using a sharp knife, cut into 2x2-inch squares and then cut each square into triangles.

—Abigail Johnson Dodge

Peanut Butter & Chocolate Sandwiches

Yields about thirty sandwich cookies (or sixty single cookies).

For the peanut butter cookies:

2½ cups smooth peanut butter, at room temperature

1½ cups firmly packed light brown sugar

1 teaspoon baking soda

2 large eggs

2 teaspoons pure vanilla extract

For the chocolate filling:

10 ounces bittersweet chocolate, coarsely chopped (about 2 cups)

4 ounces (8 tablespoons) unsalted butter, cut into 4 pieces

These flourless cookies gain sophistication from their soft texture and bittersweet flavor. If you like your chocolate a little sweeter, use semisweet instead.

Make the cookies: Position a rack in the center of the oven and heat the oven to 350°F. Line four cookie sheets with parchment or nonstick baking liners.

In the bowl of a stand mixer fitted with the paddle attachment (or in a large mixing bowl with a hand mixer), beat the peanut butter, brown sugar, and baking soda on medium speed until well blended, about 1 minute. Add the eggs and vanilla and mix on low speed until just blended, about 25 seconds.

Shape level tablespoonfuls of the dough into balls about 1 inch in diameter. (The balls of dough may be frozen for 1 month. Thaw them overnight in the refrigerator before proceeding with the recipe.) Arrange the balls 1½ inches apart on the prepared baking sheets. Do not press down. Bake one sheet at a time until the cookies are puffed and crackled but still moist-looking, about 11 minutes. Transfer the cookie sheet to a rack to cool for about 10 minutes. Using a spatula, move the cookies to the rack and let cool completely. Repeat with the remaining cookies.

Make the filling: Melt the chocolate and the butter in the microwave or in a medium heatproof bowl set in a skillet with 1 inch of barely simmering water, stirring with a rubber spatula until smooth. Remove from the heat and set aside until cool and slightly thickened, 20 to 30 minutes.

Assemble the sandwiches: Turn half of the cooled cookies over so they are flat side up. Spoon 2 teaspoons of the chocolate filling onto the center of each cookie. Top with the remaining cookies, flat side down. Press gently on each cookie to spread the filling almost to the edge. Set on the rack until the filling is firm, 20 to 30 minutes.

—Abigail Johnson Dodge

Vanilla Slice & Bake Cookies

Slice and bake cookies are generally convenient as well as yummy, but it can be hard to preserve that round shape as you slice the dough. For perfectly round cookies, shape the dough into logs, wrap in plastic, and insert into empty paper towel tubes.

In a medium mixing bowl, combine the flour, baking powder, and salt. Whisk until well blended.

In the bowl of a stand mixer fitted with the paddle attachment (or in a large mixing bowl with a hand mixer), beat the butter and sugar on medium speed until fluffy and well blended, about 3 minutes. Scrape down the bowl and the beater. Add the egg, egg yolk, and vanilla. Continue mixing on medium until well blended, about 1 minute. Add the flour mixture and mix on low speed until the dough is well blended and forms moist clumps, about 1 minute.

Gently knead the dough by hand in the bowl until smooth. Shape it into two square or round logs, each about 10 inches long, and wrap in plastic wrap. Refrigerate until chilled and very firm, about 4 hours. (The dough may be refrigerated for up to 3 days or frozen for 1 month. Thaw overnight in the refrigerator before proceeding with the recipe.)

Position a rack in the center of the oven and heat the oven to 350°F. Line two or three cookie sheets with parchment or nonstick baking liners.

Using a thin-bladed, sharp knife and a ruler, mark off ³⁄₁₆-inch-wide slices on the top of the log. Using the same knife, cut straight down to form cookies. Arrange the cookies about 1 inch apart on the lined cookie sheets. Bake one sheet at a time until the cookies' edges are golden brown, 11 to 13 minutes (for even browning, rotate the sheet after about 5 minutes). Let the cookies cool on the sheet for about 10 minutes and then transfer them to a rack to cool completely.

—*Abigail Johnson Dodge*

Yields about 8 dozen cookies.

15 ounces (3⅓ cups) unbleached all-purpose flour

¾ teaspoon baking powder

½ teaspoon table salt

9 ounces (18 tablespoons) unsalted butter, at room temperature

1½ cups granulated sugar

1 large egg

1 large egg yolk

1½ teaspoons pure vanilla extract

Raspberry-Pistachio Rugelach

Yields about forty cookies.

For the dough:

10½ ounces (2⅓ cups) unbleached all-purpose flour

¼ cup granulated sugar

½ teaspoon table salt

8 ounces (1 cup) cold unsalted butter, cut into 10 pieces

8 ounces cold cream cheese, cut into 10 pieces

For the filling:

6 tablespoons raspberry or apricot jam

For the topping:

1 large egg

1 tablespoon water

¼ cup finely chopped salted pistachios (1¼ ounces)

These buttery, flaky cookies feature a jewel-like filling of jam and a dusting of chopped pistachios. If your food processor is small, make a half batch of dough.

Make the dough: Put the flour, sugar, and salt in a large (11-cup or larger) food processor. Pulse briefly to blend the ingredients. Scatter the butter and cream cheese pieces over the dry ingredients. Pulse until the dough begins to come together in large (about 1-inch) clumps.

Divide the dough into four pieces and on a lightly floured surface, knead each until smooth. Shape each into a flat 6x3-inch rectangle and wrap in plastic wrap. Refrigerate until well chilled, about 1½ hours. (The dough may be refrigerated for up to 3 days or frozen for 1 month before proceeding with the recipe.)

Shape and fill the cookies: Working with one piece of dough at a time, roll the dough on a piece of lightly floured plastic wrap into a rectangle slightly larger than 5x13 inches (if refrigerated overnight, let sit at room temperature until pliable enough to roll). Dust with additional flour as needed. Using a sharp knife, trim off the ragged edges to make a 5x13-inch rectangle. Position the dough with one long edge facing you. Using a metal spatula (offset is best), spread evenly with 1½ tablespoons of the jam. Using the plastic wrap as an aid, roll up the dough jelly roll-style, beginning with one long side. Wrap in plastic and refrigerate until firm, at least 1 hour. Repeat with remaining dough and jam. (The logs can be wrapped well and frozen for up to 1 month. Thaw overnight in the refrigerator before proceeding with the recipe.)

Top and bake the cookies: Position racks in the top and bottom thirds of the oven and heat the oven to 350°F. Line two cookie sheets with parchment or nonstick baking liners. In a small bowl, mix the egg and water with a fork until blended.

Unwrap one roll and set on a cutting board. Using a serrated knife and a ruler, cut the roll into 1¼-inch-wide pieces. Arrange the cookies seam side down 1 inch apart on the cookie sheets. Repeat with the remaining rolls. Lightly brush the tops with the egg mixture (you won't need it all) and sprinkle with the chopped pistachios. Bake until the rugelach are golden brown, 28 to 30 minutes, swapping the cookie sheets' positions about halfway through. Let cool on the sheets for about 20 minutes. Transfer to a rack to cool completely.

—Abigail Johnson Dodge

Maple-Walnut Tuiles

Yields about twenty cookies.

Cooking spray (if baking
    on parchment)

2 large egg whites

¼ cup granulated maple
    sugar or firmly packed light
    brown sugar

Pinch table salt

¼ cup pure maple syrup
    (preferably Grade B)

1½ ounces (3 tablespoons)
    unsalted butter, melted and
    cooled slightly

½ teaspoon pure vanilla extract

3 ounces (⅔ cup) unbleached
    all-purpose flour

2 tablespoons finely chopped
    walnuts

To give them their curved form, the tuiles are draped over a rolling pin when they're hot from the oven. Measure your rolling pin to figure out how many 4-inch cookies you'll be able to drape over it at once, so you'll know how big your batch of cookies should be. If you don't want to shape them, don't bother—they're just as delicious flat. It's worth seeking out the granulated maple sugar, as it elevates these cookies into something truly special.

Position a rack in the center of the oven and heat the oven to 350°F. Line four cookie sheets with nonstick baking liners or parchment paper sprayed with cooking spray. If shaping the tuiles, have a rolling pin at the ready.

In a medium mixing bowl, combine the egg whites, sugar, and salt. Whisk until blended and a bit foamy, about 1 minute. Add the maple syrup, melted butter, and vanilla and whisk until blended. Add the flour and continue to whisk until smooth and blended.

Drop the batter by scant tablespoonfuls onto the prepared cookie sheets, positioning them about 4 inches apart (you should be able to fit 4 to 5 to a cookie sheet, but bake only as many as you can drape over your rolling pin, if you plan to shape them). Spread each round of batter into a 4-inch circle with the back of a spoon (use a circular motion to spread the batter outward from the center).

Sprinkle about ¼ teaspoon of the walnuts over each cookie. Bake until the cookies are browned around the edges and in spots toward the center, 7 to 9 minutes. The cookies will inevitably be slightly uneven and, therefore, will have a few darker-brown spots. Not to worry—they'll still taste good. Don't underbake or the cookies won't be crisp.

Working quickly, move the cookie sheet to a rack. Using a metal spatula, lift off the hot cookies one by one and, if shaping, immediately drape them over the rolling pin. Let cool until set, about 1 minute. Carefully remove the tuiles from the rolling pin and set them on a rack to cool completely. If not shaping, immediately transfer them to a rack. *—Abigail Johnson Dodge*

Cardamom-Honey Cutouts

Yields six dozen 2½-inch cookies.

13½ ounces (3 cups) unbleached all-purpose flour; more for rolling

1 teaspoon ground cardamom

½ teaspoon table salt

¼ teaspoon baking soda

8 ounces (1 cup) unsalted butter, at room temperature

¾ cup granulated sugar

¼ cup honey

1 large egg

1 teaspoon pure vanilla extract

Too often, sugar cookies and butter cookies are just forgettable vehicles for fancy piping, but in this case, cardamom elevates holiday cookies to standout status. If you make larger or smaller cookies, adjust the baking time—only the edges should turn light brown.

In a medium mixing bowl, combine the flour, cardamom, salt, and baking soda. Whisk until well blended.

In the bowl of a stand mixer fitted with the paddle attachment (or in a large mixing bowl with a hand mixer), beat the butter and sugar on medium speed until well blended and slightly fluffy, about 3 minutes. Scrape down the bowl and the beater. Add the honey, egg, and vanilla. Continue mixing on medium speed until well blended, about 1 minute. Add the flour mixture and mix on low speed until the dough is well blended and comes together in moist clumps, 30 to 60 seconds.

Divide the dough roughly in half. On a piece of plastic wrap, shape each dough half into a smooth 5-inch disk. Wrap well in the plastic. Refrigerate until chilled and firm enough to roll out, 1 to 1½ hours. (The dough may be refrigerated for up to 3 days or frozen for 1 month. Thaw overnight in the refrigerator before proceeding with the recipe.)

Bake the cookies: Position a rack in the center of the oven and heat the oven to 350°F. Line two or more cookie sheets with parchment or nonstick baking liners. Working with one disk at a time, roll the dough on a floured work surface to about ³⁄₁₆ inch thick. Dust with additional flour as needed. Choose one or more cookie cutters of any shape that are about 2½ inches wide and cut out shapes. Arrange the cookies about 1 inch apart on the lined cookie sheets. Gather the scraps and gently press together. Re-roll and cut. Repeat with the remaining dough.

Bake one sheet at a time until the cookies' edges develop a ¼-inch-wide light-brown rim, 11 to 13 minutes (rotate the sheet halfway through baking for even browning). Let the cookies cool on the sheet for about 10 minutes and then transfer them to a rack to cool completely. —*Abigail Johnson Dodge*

Start by making a batch of icing and then coloring it however you like. You can split the batch up and make lots of colors, or you can leave it white.

To outline a cookie

Spoon some of the icing into a pastry bag fitted with a very small plain tip and outline the rim of a cookie with the icing. (Practice first on a piece of cardboard or waxed paper. If the icing is too thick to pipe evenly, put it back in the bowl and stir in water, a drop or two at a time, until it pipes easily but still retains its shape.) Scatter sprinkles or sparkling sugar over the icing, if you like. Set the iced cookies aside to dry.

To coat an entire cookie with icing

Have ready a small clean artist's brush (one that you use only for food). If you want to use colors, set out a bowl for each color, portion the icing into the bowls, and stir drops of food coloring into each until the desired shade is reached. Outline the rim of a cookie with the icing as described above and let harden slightly. Dampen the brush in water and spread a small amount of additional icing in an even layer within the cookie's border. Decorate the cookie with sprinkles, sparkling sugar, or edible dragées, if you like. Set the cookie aside to dry.

Once the icing is completely dry and hard, store the cookies in airtight containers at room temperature for 2 to 3 days or in the freezer for longer storage.

Royal Icing

Yields about 3 cups.

A blend of egg whites and confectioners' sugar, royal icing hardens to a durable, rock-hard consistency when dry.

2 tablespoons powdered egg whites or meringue powder plus 6 tablespoons warm water OR 3 large egg whites

1 pound (4 cups) confectioners' sugar

Food coloring (optional)

If using the powdered egg whites or meringue powder and warm water, combine them in the bowl of a stand mixer or in a large mixing bowl. Let stand, whisking frequently, until the powder is dissolved, about 5 minutes. If using fresh egg whites, just put them in the bowl.

With the whisk attachment on a stand mixer or with a hand mixer, begin mixing on medium speed until frothy. Add the confectioners' sugar and continue beating until blended. Increase the speed to high and beat until the mixture is thick and shiny, about 3 minutes for fresh eggs and 5 minutes for powdered. Stir in food coloring (if using). Put a damp paper towel directly on the icing to keep a skin from forming. If not using within 2 hours, cover the bowl with plastic and refrigerate.

—Abigail Johnson Dodge

Risk-free royal icing

Royal icing carries a very slight risk of salmonella infection from the raw egg whites used to make it. If you want to eliminate that risk completely, use pasteurized whites, which are available either dried or fresh. Look for dried egg white powder or meringue powder (dried egg white powder plus sugar and stabilizers) in the baking section of the market. You'll need to reconstitute the powder before making the icing.

Fresh pasteurized egg whites are kept in the dairy case near the other eggs and egg products. Depending on your store, you may find cartons of whole in-shell pasteurized eggs (look closely at all the cartons because they're packaged just like regular eggs and are sometimes hard to notice), or you may find containers of liquid egg whites. Use fresh pasteurized egg whites just as you would use regular egg whites.

Contributors

Fine Cooking would like to thank all the talented and generous contributors who have shared their recipes with our readers.

Bruce Aidells is the author of *Bruce Aidells's Complete Book of Pork* and *The Complete Meat Cookbook*. He also founded Aidells Sausage Company.

Amy Albert was a senior editor for *Fine Cooking*. She is now a senior associate editor at *Bon Appetit* magazine.

Pam Anderson is a contributing editor to *Fine Cooking* and the author of several books, including *Perfect Recipes for Having People Over.*

Jennifer Armentrout is a graduate of The Culinary Institute of America. She is *Fine Cooking's* Test Kitchen Manager and senior food editor.

Dan Barber is the chef and co-owner of two restaurants: Blue Hill in New York City and Blue Hill at Stone Barns in Pocantico Hills, New York.

Karen Barker is the pastry chef and co-owner of the award-winning Magnolia Grill restaurant in Durham, North Carolina and the author of *Sweet Stuff: Karen Barker's American Desserts.*

David Bonom is a freelance food writer and recipe developer.

Sarah Breckenridge is *Fine Cooking's* managing web editor.

Biba Caggiano is the author of eight cookbooks and the chef and owner of Biba Restaurant in Sacramento, California; she is also the host of the syndicated show *Biba's Italian Kitchen.*

Scott Conant is the chef and owner of the award-winning L'Impero and Alto restaurants in New York City and the author of *Scott Conant's New Italian Cooking* and *Bold Italian.*

Erica DeMane is a food writer specializing in Italian cooking, whose books include *Pasta Improvvisata* and *The Flavors of Southern Italy.*

Tasha DeSerio is a former cook at Chez Panisse restaurant and café and is now the co-owner of Olive Green Catering in Berkeley, California. She also teaches cooking and writes about food.

Abigail Johnson Dodge is the author of *The Weekend Baker* and a contributing editor to *Fine Cooking*. She was the founding director of the *Fine Cooking* test kitchen.

Tom Douglas is the award-winning owner of several restaurants in Seattle, including The Dahlia Lounge.

Maryellen Driscoll is one of *Fine Cooking's* contributing editors.

Rebecca Fasten is a sous-chef at the Liberty Café in San Francisco.

Eve Felder is an associate dean and instructor at The Culinary Institute of America.

Gale Gand is the executive pastry chef and partner at four restaurants in Chicago, including Tru and Gale's Coffee Bar. She is also the host of the Food Network's *Sweet Dreams* and has written six cookbooks.

Joyce Goldstein is the former chef-owner of the famed Square One restaurant in San Francisco; she currently teaches and writes about cooking.

Martha Holmberg is the former editor in chief of *Fine Cooking*. She is currently the food editor at *The Oregonian* newspaper in Portland, Oregon, and a freelance food writer.

Arlene Jacobs is a New York City-based restaurant consultant, freelance recipe developer, cooking instructor, and food writer.

Elizabeth Karmel is the author of *Pizza on the Grill* (published by Taunton) and *Taming the Flame: Secrets for Hot-and-Quick Grilling and Low-and-Slow BBQ.*

Allison Ehri Keitler is a graduate of the French Culinary Institute in New York City and works as *Fine Cooking's* Test Kitchen Associate and food stylist.

Evan Kleiman is the owner and chef of Angeli Caffè in Los Angeles. She is also the author of numerous cookbooks, including *Pasta Fresca.*

Ris Lacoste has been a professional award-winning chef for nearly 25 years, including 10 years as the executive chef at 1789 Restaurant in Washington, D.C.

Barbara Lauterbach is a cooking instructor and cookbook author of *Chicken Salad: 50 Favorite Recipes.* She teaches at King Arthur Flour Baking Education Center in Norwich, Vermont, and at La Combe, in southwest France.

Ruth Lively is a food and garden writer; she is the former editor of *Fine Gardening* magazine.

Lori Longbotham is a New York City-based food writer, cookbook author, and recipe developer.

Kimberly Y. Masibay trained as a pastry chef in Germany and studied journalism at Columbia University before becoming a senior editor at *Fine Cooking*. She is now a freelance food writer.

Nancie McDermott is a cooking teacher and cookbook author specializing in the cuisines of Southeast Asia.

Perla Meyers teaches cooking at workshops around the country and has cooked in restaurants throughout Italy, France, and Spain.

Susie Middleton was *Fine Cooking's* editor; she is now *Fine Cooking's* editor at large as well as a food writer and cookbook author.

James Peyton is a food writer and expert in Mexican cooking.

Mary Pult is a chef at the Liberty Café in San Francisco.

Nicole Rees is a food scientist, cookbook author, and baker based in Portland, Oregon. She co-wrote the revised edition of *Understanding Baking*, as well as its companion recipe book, *The Baker's Manual*.

Peter Reinhart is the author of seven books on bread and food, including *The Bread Baker's Apprentice*. Peter is also a baking instructor at Johnson & Wales University in Charlotte, North Carolina.

Andrea Reusing is the chef and owner of Lantern, a pan-Asian restaurant in Chapel Hill, North Carolina.

Tony Rosenfeld is a contributing editor to *Fine Cooking* and the author of Taunton's *150 Things to Make with Roast Chicken*.

Lynne Sampson is a food writer, chef, and baking expert based in Joseph, Oregon.

Suvir Saran owns the New York restaurant Dévi and is the author of *Indian Home Cooking and America Masala*.

Chris Schlesinger is a chef and cookbook author, whose books include *The Thrill of the Grill*.

Maria Helm Sinskey is the culinary director and executive chef at Robert Sinskey Vineyards and the author of *The Vineyard Kitchen: Menus Inspired by the Seasons*.

Molly Stevens is a contributing editor to *Fine Cooking*. She won the IACP Cooking Teacher of the Year award in 2006; her book *All About Braising* won the James Beard and International Association of Culinary Professionals awards.

Meg Suzuki is a cooking instructor and freelance writer based in San Jose, California. Meg was an assistant test kitchen director for *Cook's Illustrated* magazine.

Julia M. Usher is a pastry chef based in St. Louis, Missouri.

Annie Wayte is the chef at fashion designer Nicole Farhi's Nicole's in New York City. Her first cookbook is *Keep It Seasonal: Soups, Salads, and Sandwiches*.

Kathy Wazana, a native Moroccan, is a writer and a cooking teacher in Toronto.

Joanne Weir is a cooking teacher, cookbook author, and star of the PBS show *Joanne Weir's Cooking Class*.

Index

P

Equivalent Charts

LIQUID/DRY MEASURES	
U.S.	**METRIC**
¼ teaspoon	1.25 milliliters
½ teaspoon	2.5 milliliters
1 teaspoon	5 milliliters
1 tablespoon (3 teaspoons)	15 milliliters
1 fluid ounce (2 tablespoons)	30 milliliters
¼ cup	60 milliliters
⅓ cup	80 milliliters
½ cup	120 milliliters
1 cup	240 milliliters
1 pint (2 cups)	480 milliliters
1 quart (4 cups; 32 ounces)	960 milliliters
1 gallon (4 quarts)	3.84 liters
1 ounce (by weight)	28 grams
1 pound	454 grams
2.2 pounds	1 kilogram

OVEN TEMPERATURES		
°F	**GAS MARK**	**°C**
250	½	120
275	1	140
300	2	150
325	3	165
350	4	180
375	5	190
400	6	200
425	7	220
450	8	230
475	9	240
500	10	260
550	Broil	290